Normative Discourse and Persuasion

Normative Discourse and Persuasion

An Analysis of Ga'dang Informal Litigation

Michael R. Walrod

Summer Institute of Linguistics

Linguistic Society of the Philippines

Manila, 1988

Linguistic Society of the Philippines
Special Monograph Issue, Number 26

The *Philippine Journal of Linguistics* is the official publication of the Linguistic
Society of the Philippines. It publishes studies in decriptive, comparative, historical,
and areal linguistics. Although its primary interest is in linguistic theory, it also
publishes papers on the application of theory to language teaching, sociolinguistics,
etc. Papers on applied linguistics should, however, be chiefly concerned with the principles which underlie specific techniques. Articles are published in English, although
papers written in Pilipino, an official language of the Philippines, will occasionally appear. Since the Linguistic Society of the Philippines is composed of members whose
paramount interests are the Philippine languages, papers on these and related languages are given priority in publication. This does not mean, however, that the journal will limit its scope to the Austronesian language family. Studies on any aspect of
language structure are welcome.

Manuscripts for publication, exchange journals, and books for review or listing
should be sent to the Editor, Brother Andrew B. Gonzalez, FSC, De La Salle University, 2401 Taft Avenue, Manila, Philippines. Manuscripts from the United States and
Europe should be sent to Dr. Lawrence A. Reid, Pacific and Asia Linguistics Institute, University of Hawaii, 1980 East-West Road, Honolulu, Hawaii 96822, U.S.A.

Editorial Board

ISBN: 971-1059-12-6
488 3.0c

Cover Motif: Bud Speck

Table of Contents

viii

Figures

Abbreviations

accus	accusative
caus	causative
cl	clause
cmp	comparative aspect
cond.cl	conditional clause
emph	emphatic
expos.	expository
fut	future
imper.	imperative
inc	inclusive
n-p	non-past
obj	object marker
p	particle
pl	plural
pm	personal marker
prs	person
recipr	reciprocally
rl	relative clause marker
rhet.Q	rhetorical question
s.	sentence number
sg	singular
UT	utterance number
vb	verb
2	in gloss line signifies dual
.	in gloss line signifies a compound gloss
-	in gloss line and in vernacular signifies morpheme boundary

Preface

More than a decade ago, Kenneth Pike impressed on me the need to study and describe modes of argumentation and persuasion that differ from those of Western culture. Since then, I have spent several years with my family residing among the Ga'dang people of Paracelis municipality of Mountain Province in the Philippines. In 1980, with the cooperation of all people involved, I was able to record a substantial corpus of data from actual dispute settlements in the Ga'dang community of Bananao. I am grateful for the kindness of those who participated in these discussions and who allowed me to record them. Mr. Juan (Siddayaw) Domingo of Bananao assisted me with the transcriptions of the recordings. These Ga'dang texts provided ample evidence of the integrity and oratorical skills of the participants, and of the admirable fabric of their society. This work, based on those texts, describes normative discourse and persuasion in Ga'dang and proposes tentative generalizations concerning the differences between normative discourse in oral versus literate societies.

I offer sincere thanks to Donald Burquest, Ray Gordon, George Huttar, Lenore Langsdorf, Robert E. Longacre, Kenneth L. Pike, and Ilah Fleming, all of whom have had an influence on me and my work; I feel very privileged to have known and associated with each one. Kenneth Pike and Ilah Fleming, in particular, are two scholars from whom I have learned important insights in linguistic theory.

There are many others to whom I owe thanks, far too many to mention individually. I thank all of my family and close friends who have made special efforts to give encouragement and tangible help.

I dedicate this work to Robert E. Longacre. To call him simply "a scholar and a gentleman" is an understatement. He was able to point out the shortcomings in my work and still leave me feeling encouraged to press on. I also dedicate it to my wife, Verna, and my sons, Marty and Toby—the most important people in my life and my support team in this project.

Introduction

This work is a study in textlinguistics (i.e., discourse analysis), focusing on the area of normative discourse and persuasion, and how the former is used to accomplish the latter. The theoretical framework of this study is the subject of the first five chapters. Then the focus shifts to the structure and function of normative discourse in Ga'dang.

Textlinguistics has become an interdisciplinary science. Perhaps it would be more accurate to say that the discipline of textlinguistics is still in its formative phase, that the boundaries are still being defined, and that some of the boundaries necessarily overlap with those of other disciplines. Thus the first four chapters are taken up with explicating the relationships that this study has with other disciplines.

Chapters 1 and 2 place textlinguistics and normative discourse in a philosophical context. Textlinguistics is shown to be a phenomenological endeavor (ideally). The nature of the data is that of cultural objects (phenomena), and the researcher's approach to the data should be to suspend preconceptions and refrain from premature categorizations or reductions. Hasty gestalt formation can only result in imputing structure to the data other than what it really has.

Normative discourse is that which is primarily intended to influence the opinions, beliefs, or behavior of other people. This is done by uttering evaluations and prescriptions, supporting them with valid reasons or justifications. The unique feature of normative discourse is that the reasons given in support of the statements are the cultural values or norms of the community. Therefore chapter 2 is a discussion of normative discourse in the context of axiology, that is, the philosophy of value.

Chapter 3 brings together concepts from cognitive science (knowledge structures), neuropsychology (brain hemisphere specialization), and the study of the consequences of literacy (analytic thought) to provide an explanation for the substantial differences between Ga'dang normative discourse and that of Western society, especially in written normative texts.

The conciliatory nature of dispute settlement in Ga'dang is the essence of chapter 4. This relates to the sociology or ethnology of law and social control. The normative discourse of dispute settlement aims to produce group harmony and consensus.

The first four chapters are highly interdisciplinary, their purpose being to present factors essential to the study of normative discourse, factors which contributed to my understanding of Ga'dang persuasive discourse. These chapters also present something more substantial than an annotated bibliography for those who might wish to work on some of the topics to which I have been able to give only brief attention.

In chapter 5 the focus begins to narrow to those aspects of the theory of normative discourse that are central to the domain of textlinguistics. Normative monologue and dialogue texts are considered, and normative discourse is placed within a taxonomy of text types. Four subtypes of normative discourse are identified.

Chapters 6-9 narrow the focus still further to a particular type of normative discourse in Ga'dang, the informal litigation. A large part of one litigation is presented in the Appendix; this text provides most of the examples throughout this work. Any example cited from the Appendix is given with the sentence number, so the reader may refer to it in its context in the Appendix.

The notional constituents of the text are identified in chapter 6, as well as the backbone and peak of the discourse, features of the social setting, and the mechanics of interaction. Chapter 7 focuses on the surface structure of the text, describing the features of cohesion, paragraph, sentence, verb, pronominal reference, and particles in normative discourse.

Strategies of persuasion are presented in chapter 8 and related to some of the categories presented in Aristotle's Rhetoric. Not all strategies of persuasion in Ga'dang are rhetorical strategies, even though this would seem contradictory if the broadest definition of rhetoric were employed.

A scale of normativity is presented in chapter 9, and the various grammatical features of Ga'dang normative discourse are ranked on this scale. Certain features have more normative or persuasive force than others, and at the peak of a normative discourse, there is a clustering of high ranking features. This is a part of the grammar of normative discourse, and a speaker must control this as well as the other features in order to produce a persuasive discourse in Ga'dang.

The treatment of each consideration is far from exhaustive. Nevertheless, it is my hope that it is credible and accurate as far as it goes, and that I will not have misinterpreted the authors cited from other disciplines.

1 Philosophy of Textlinguistics

1.1 Phenomenology and textlinguistics

To the things themselves is an expression of the primary aim of phenomenology. Thus phenomenology is an empiricist theory, but not in the traditional sense. The "things" that phenomenology focuses on may be actual phenomena that appear to us in the here and now, or they may be aspects of our previous experience that we reflect upon. In textlinguistics, the object of study is actual linguistic texts as they occur in actual human communicative experience. This is in contrast to a point of view in linguistics that focuses primarily on the sentence level and is satisfied with contrived or hypothetical sentences as objects for analysis apart from a context of actual communicative experience.

Phenomenology not only points us to the things; it tells us how we should look at the things. We should attend to the phenomena as they appear, not imposing a preconceived notion of how they are structured. We should suspend preconceptions about the object of attention or investigation.

At this point we are faced with a paradox, one that phenomenologists are not unaware of. "The paradox consists in the fact that without some—at least general—idea of what and how one is to look at a thing, how can anything be seen? Yet, if what is to be seen is to be seen without prejudice or preconception, how can it be circumscribed by definition?" (Ihde 1977:31). This is one way of describing the hermeneutic circle, which Ihde calls the "dialectic of interpretation." It is understood that it is not possible to approach any inquiry totally without preconceptions. Even the inclination to perform the inquiry is a sort of preconception. But the emphasis of phenomenology is to suspend bias as much as possible, giving primary emphasis to observation initially. "Careful looking precedes classification and systematization, and systematization and classification are made to follow what the phenomenon shows" (Ihde 1977:32).

The approach of textlinguistics is (or should be) compatible with this philosophy. This is especially true when the inquiry involves analysis of a language radically different from one's own. As linguists, we do approach any language with some preconceptions of what we are likely to find. But these preconceptions should be suspended as much as possible in the initial investigation, to allow for the phenomena of the target language to be experienced as they are, rather than be forced into the mold of the linguist's preconceptions or the structure of his own native language.

The emphasis in phenomenology on actual lived experience is another tenet to which textlinguists adhere. Not only do textlinguists aim to pay scrupulous attention to the linguistic context of an utterance, but also to its situational or behavioral context (Longacre 1983:337). The *whole* situational milieu enters into the experiencing of any text utterance or text reception. Naturally, the whole of a text cannot be adequately described apart from a description of its parts and their relationships to each other and the whole text and its whole context. Finite limitations prevent us from doing this exhaustively (otherwise we would probably not finish the description of one text in one lifetime), but the point here is the emphasis on the *whole*. Pike and Pike, who see texts as the most natural unit of linguistic behavior and therefore the appropriate initial focus in linguistics, point out that "no unit of purposive behavior can be identified or recognized in complete abstraction from other units; it exists only in reference to them" (1977:2). Phenomenology also recognizes that there are no things-by-themselves, but that "all items that appear do so in relation to a background and in strict relation with that background" (Ihde 1977:58); that is, they are situated within a field. The initial experiencing of a phenomenon cannot be isolated from the experiencing of the field or situational milieu within which it appears.

However, although our initial direct experiencing of a phenomenon cannot be isolated from its contextual milieu, subsequent considerations can be. This is done by means of various reductions, especially in the analysis of oral texts. The very act of transcribing a text that the linguist has already had an immediate firsthand experience of is a reduction. The text is reduced from the infinite detail and variability of its original form and situational context to a finite and manageable written form. Even if the textlinguist graphically encodes prosodic features of the text in its transcription, it is still a quantum reduction from the actual experience of the text. Various charting procedures may effect still more substantial reductions if abbreviations are used in representing the text (e.g., NP for noun phrase) rather than the actual alphabetic characters or phonetic symbols representing the morphemes. Even a chart on which all the morphemes are written may constitute a reduction, if discourse level constituents are identified and somehow demarcated.

Reductions such as these are analytical methods of textlinguistics, not ultimate aims of the theory. A subsidiary aim would be to identify the macrostructure of a text and its constituent units, but this would be only a part of a larger accounting or description of a text. A full description of a text would include description of as many features of the situational milieu (at the initial experiencing of the text) as practical and analytically productive. There may have been 80% atmospheric humidity at the time of text reception, but this is a part of the milieu that is not significant if it has no effect on text production or reception, so it would not be included in the description. But the full description would include mention of background noise (e.g., strong wind, radio) if it had an effect on speaker or hearer (or reader). Thus the description, no matter how nearly exhaustive, is a reduction. But this reduction is still not the ultimate aim of textlinguistics, but a step in the procedure.

Before defining the aim of textlinguistics, it would be helpful to compare the types of reduction practiced by the textlinguist to *phenomenological reduction*, a term used by philosophers. If there is not identity between the two, there are at least some important similarities. Performing a phenomenological reduction requires a reflective move, "characterized as a move outside or above or distanced from straightforward experience" (Ihde 1977:45). In ordinary firsthand experiencing of a text (oral or written), the object of our experience is the content of the text, along with the total communicative experience, infinitely complex in light of the fact that we are simultaneously experiencing features of the situational milieu. To perform textlinguistic analysis, this complexity must be reduced. So by a reflective move we distance ourselves from straightforward experiencing of the text. In the straightforward experience, we (as text receptors) are in a hermeneutic relationship to the text; that is, we are constantly construing meanings and anticipating what is likely to follow (see chap. 3). By the reflective move, we distance ourselves from this function and allow the text to appear to us in a form other than as immediate communication of meaning intended by the speaker or author. Having done so, we have done the first two steps of the phenomenological reduction, namely, *retention* and *bracketing* (Reeder 1983).

Retention is described as the presence in *this* moment of a living trace of the moment just past (ibid.). This is not identical to memory; it is more immediate and vivid. (It may be indistinguishable from short-term memory in psychology—cf. Neisser 1976:141.) It is impossible to retain a living trace of the entirety of any substantial text, so the textlinguist must assist his memory or imagination with tape recordings and transcriptions. It could be said of these tools that they recreate the experience so that we can hold some parts of it in retention again. But in fact they do not recreate the original experience just as it was; nothing could do so. Rather, these tools phase us into the bracketing step of the phenomenological reduction; that is, they enable us to distance or detach ourselves from the experiencing of the text and attend to it apart from our preconceptions or knowledge structures. This could not be done at our initial experiencing of the text (unless we deliberately attempted not to understand it), because the knowledge structures we have are our means of construing meaning (Minsky 1980:12).

The third and final step in the phenomenological reduction is the *eidetic reduction*, which is the determination of the essential or "universal" features of the phenomenon, that is, its *essence*.

In light of the definition of phenomenological reduction, consider the aim of textlinguistics—to reduce texts to their phenomenological *essences*, that is, to the structural features or invariants within the text phenomena (Ihde 1977:38). This involves the identification and description of all emic units and their tactics or combinatorial possibilities. Texts with identical essences (at the text or discourse level of the grammatical hierarchy) constitute a single text type (see chap. 5), and the set of essences of all text types, as well as all the lower levels of structure in a language, is the grammar of the language. Textlinguistics aims to discover and describe this grammar, beginning with text-level grammar and continuing through all lower levels. A text grammar is the product of phenomenological reduction.

Textlinguistics as currently practiced (e.g., by Pike, Longacre, and Fleming) departs from traditional phenomenology by explaining as well as describing. In discussions of such concepts as role, function, purpose, speaker's intention, and speech acts, we attempt to determine why things are the way we have described them to be. The primary reason for the interdisciplinary nature of textlinguistics is not just to describe the larger context in which a text is uttered, but to determine what it is about that context that affects the surface structure of the text itself, and why. Current practice of phenomenology also departs from the "describe only" restriction, allowing the reintroduction of explanatory concepts such as motive and purpose (Ricoeur 1978:86) after preliminary phenomenological investigation has been done.

1.2 Cultural objects and reference in language

Phenomenology and textlinguistics are compatible because cultural objects (some of which are the objects of study in textlinguistics) may *appear* to us as surely as physical objects may. Cassirer (1961:157-58) observed that the "object of nature appears to lie immediately before our eyes," whereas the cultural object "lies in back of us, so to speak." Cultural objects "lie in back of us" in that we cannot apprehend them with the physical senses. We can physically observe the objects of nature which are the "ground" of some of the cultural objects, and we can observe behavior resulting from other cultural objects, but we do not directly observe the cultural objects. We know them through construal or abstraction; that is, we apprehend them cognitively.

The objects of study in textlinguistics are cultural objects. Cultural objects are the cognitive objects or units shared to a great extent by the members of a given speech/cultural community. The units may be somewhat generic or comprehensive, such as knowledge of different types of text or discourse (e.g., narrative, expository) and knowledge of the conditions of appropriateness for the use of each. The units may also be lower level, such as the words of the language. A word-level cognitive unit includes knowledge of how to produce and recognize the sound or graphic representation, a sign used by that cultural community, and the range of meaning or significance conventionally associated with that sign.

In the case of words that refer to physical objects, that is, words that are conventionally associated with a class of phenomena perceived with the physical senses, the cultural unit also includes the knowledge of the criteria for identifying any particular phenomenon as belonging to that class. (In a sense it is redundant to say that the cultural unit includes knowledge of the criteria for determining membership in the class; the concept of a cognitive class includes this by definition.) Notice, however, that this explication of the function of reference in language could serve equally well for the relationship between words with no physical referents and the meanings conventionally associated with them. These words are also associated with a class of phenomena. The difference is that the phenomena referred to by these words are apprehended cognitively, rather than by the senses. These phenomena may be cognitive events such as thinking and knowing, or they may be abstract relationships such as ownership or attribution, agent or patient.

Some very early theories of reference in language viewed words as names of actual objects. This simple view fails to give any basis for the study of cultural objects in linguistics. A more accurate understanding of reference needs to include the distinctions between the actual world, the phenomenal world, the cognitive grid or "native paradigm," and an explication of how language relates to these.

The "actual world" is the real, existing universe in its totality. We do not have direct, exhaustive access to it, either actually or in principle. Due to human limitations we cannot apprehend it as it really is, either cognitively or by the physical senses. Therefore even to posit its existence is, admittedly, a step of faith.

The "phenomenal world" is that which appears to us, or that which we can in principle perceive or apprehend, including physical objects and cultural objects. All phenomena are included in the actual world, since the actual world is all inclusive. But only a subset of the actual world is included in the phenomenal world. The phenomenal world, then, is real and actual, not deceptive or illusory. But it differs from the actual world in that it is not exhaustive; it is not all that there is.

Our "cognitive grid" or "native paradigm" is our whole corpus of knowledge about the phenomenal world. But it is not identical to the phenomenal world. The phenomenal world does not contradict the actual world at any point, but our cognitive grid might. In other words, our cognitive grid is a less perfect reflection of the actual world than the limits of our perceptual abilities would require due to further limitations imposed on our perception and cognition by the conventions of our culture.

Cultural conventions stored in one's cognitive grid make up a set of expectations that can be referred to as one's native paradigm. To a great extent, this paradigm governs the focus of our attention when something appears to us; it also governs our interpretation of what we attend to. Kuhn (1970:52) speaks of "paradigm-induced expectations," and although his discussion is referring to scientific observation, the concept also holds true for ordinary nonscientific observation. It is not true that we cannot see anything that our paradigm has not led us to expect, but it is true that we have a strong tendency to see what we expect to see. To see things in other ways requires that we be confronted with obvious anomaly, or that we make a conscious effort to see more clearly or objectively by reflective analysis (Langsdorf and Reeder 1983:20).

The relation of language to the cognitive grid is the most difficult relationship to explicate. For on the one hand our cognitive grid includes knowledge that we have about our language, and on the other hand the surface structure units of language refer to cognitive concepts. Moreover, the conventional relationship between the surface structure unit and the cognitive content it refers to is also a cognitive unit. It is the conventional relationship that supports the view of a form-meaning composite in language. If we examine the physical phenomena of speech sounds or ink marks apart from their function in a language system, they are not a part of any linguistic form-meaning composite. It is only as they function within a system of meaningful relationships that must be perpetuated in the cognitive grids of language users that they can be considered as form-meaning composites.

The physical phenomena of linguistic expressions are themselves a part of the actual world. The sounds or marks that we physically perceive are of the phenomenal world. And the conventional associations that we attach to certain sounds or marks are a part of the cognitive grid.

Notice that I use language to talk about all of these worlds or categories. In fact, language is interdependent with all of the concepts.

The purpose of this discussion is to show that meaning in language is directly linked to cultural objects. One's *knowledge* or set of expectations about what segment of the phenomenal world may conventionally be referred to by a given term is a cultural object. Meaning is not restricted to what can be empirically verified, as some extreme empiricist theories have suggested. In fact, empirical verifiability does not even enter into the role of meaning in language. The notion of verifiability is just a remnant of our scientific tradition (the Western or Greek paradigm; cf. Van Doren

1981:205), which allowed for the possibility of an ideal observer, that is, one who was not predisposed to see things according to paradigmatic expectations.

The meaning of units of language is what is communicated by the units, and that is a function of cultural conventions. These conventions are in a constant state of flux. "The contextual associations of meaning are continuously being sheared off as the units are being re-used in different contexts" (Bloch 1975:18). But the flux or semantic shift is generally so gradual that all the members of the speech community are kept up to date concerning the current relationships or referential conventions.

The meaning of words is not tied to sense data in a direct way. Thus language dealing with events, behavior, attitudes, emotions, and social interaction has conventional referents, circumscribed intersubjectively by the members of the cultural community, in the same way that language dealing with physical objects has.

1.3 Norms as cultural objects

The cultural objects or units within the cognitive grid of each member of a speech community are arranged or organized in a variety of ways. A system of organizing knowledge makes it possible to cope with the quantity and complexity of knowledge that a member of a society is expected to control. The analysis of knowledge structures, which is a current frontier in cognitive science and artificial intelligence, will be discussed in chapter 3. The point to be made here is that knowledge structures are also cultural objects.

Each knowledge structure includes awareness of the attitudes shared by the society toward the things or events to which that knowledge structure pertains. Thus each member of the community knows how to evaluate things and events according to standards and rules. The conventional standards and rules comprise the norms of the cultural community. These are cultural objects, known by community members, which may be expressed in the form of a proposition (e.g., running is good). Norms are the operating rules of a society without which it would disintegrate. "The values expressed by a given set of rules are thus the *operating values* of those who abide by them; and they are the *public values* of any social group whose members regard observing these rules as a condition of membership in the group" (Goodenough 1981:77). Norms or public values are invoked repeatedly in Ga'dang normative discourse, and they become discourse themes.

A phenomenological approach to the study of societal norms is warranted just as in any other type of inquiry. It is especially warranted in the case of a cross-cultural study. The textlinguist must suspend his own point of view as much as possible and detach himself from his own value system in order to be able to understand the value systems that are emic to the target speech community. If he fails to do so, he will impose his own values and normative logic on the text data and fail to see the inherent structure.

Normative or emotive language does not present a problem in this approach to discourse. It is not less referential or less meaningful than other uses of language. On the contrary, I contend that normative discourse is the primary function of language.

2   Axiology and Normative Discourse

Axiology is the philosophy of value. Normative discourse has to do with the application of public values or norms within a society. The two are integrally related and may be subsumed under the heading of normative ethics, which defines how people ought to act according to the values or norms of a particular cultural community. Normative ethics has a more restricted focus than ethics or moral philosophy, which defines how people ought to act in general. This work will be confined to the area of normative ethics. (For treatments of the more comprehensive subject, see Frankena 1963 and Toulmin 1970.)

2.1 Normative discourse: evaluation and prescription

Longacre (1983:3-6) has proposed four broad types of discourse: narrative, procedural, expository, and behavioral. Behavioral discourse includes eulogy, promissory speeches, and any type of hortatory discourse such as sermons, pep talks, advice, or any discourse intended to bring about a change of conduct. Behavioral discourse is the primary linguistic component in social control.

In this work, I will refer to any discourse of the behavioral type as normative discourse. *Normative* is not a more specific term than *behavioral*. If anything, it is more generic. It includes all prescriptive discourse (commands, exhortations, etc.), evaluative discourse, and any discourse that aims to persuade. Thus normative discourse is not only that which is intended to bring about a change in behavior, but also that which is intended to influence or modify cognitive choices or beliefs. Normative discourse therefore includes argumentation, the primary function of which is to prove (illocution) in order to persuade (perlocution) (Walker 1983:12).

"We carry on normative discourse when we use language for the purposes of evaluating and prescribing and when we give reasons for or against our evaluations and prescriptions" (Taylor 1961:191). Taylor makes a clear distinction between evaluation and prescription:

> 1. An act of prescribing is a linguistic act, whereas a value judgment is a mental disposition. 2. All prescribing is done for the purpose of guiding conduct, but most evaluating is not done for that purpose. 3. Prescribing an act is not giving a reason for doing it, while on the contrary evaluating an act is giving a reason for (or against) doing it. [Ibid.:223]

Taylor is discussing two kinds of things in this passage. One is the linguistic act of prescribing; the other is the psychological act of formulating an evaluation. By mixing the two kinds of things, Taylor obscures the logical and psychological relationship between the two, namely, that an evaluation frequently leads to the uttering of a prescription, and a prescription always presupposes an evaluation.

Furthermore, in the study of normative discourse, our focus is on expressions of evaluations and prescriptions. The act of uttering a prescription versus the act of uttering an evaluation cannot be distinguished in the same way that prescribing and evaluating are distinguished. Both types of utterances are linguistic acts.

In psychological sequence, prescription may occur as a result of evaluation. But in normative discourse the distinction loses significance. Expressions of prescriptions or evaluations have a common purpose or function underlying them, a social-control or normative purpose. Thus we are not analyzing the intention in evaluating versus the intention in prescribing (a psychological consideration), but rather the intention in *uttering* evaluations and prescriptions (a discourse consideration).

In the context of discourse, Taylor (1961:191) holds that the basic concepts of evaluative discourse are "good" and "right," whereas the basic concept of prescriptive discourse is "ought." I contend that the concept "ought" is a part of the connotative meaning of "good" and "right." Thus the distinction between uttering prescriptions versus evaluations in normative discourse is not a difference in kind, but a difference in degree. The two have different ranks on a scale of normativity; they differ in the degree to which they are likely to influence or alter the beliefs or behavior of others (see chaps. 7 and 9).

Notice that all of the distinctions Taylor posited between evaluating and prescribing break down in the context of normative discourse. First, in discourse, there is not the distinction between a linguistic act versus a psychological act; uttering evaluations and uttering prescriptions are both linguistic acts. Second, while most evaluating is not done for the purpose of guiding conduct, the *uttering* of evaluations *is* done for the purpose of guiding conduct; it does have that purpose, if to a lesser degree than the uttering of prescriptions. Third, in Ga'dang normative discourse, prescriptions are routinely accompanied by reasons for doing the prescribed act. It is true that the prescription per se is not the reason for doing it, but reasons are provided in Ga'dang evaluative and prescriptive discourse.

Moreover, the similarity between evaluation and prescription in normative discourse should be emphasized (or the difference de-emphasized) because the same logic holds for both. This is the subject of the following section.

2.2 The logic of normative discourse

Normative discourse consists of evaluations, prescriptions, and the justification of evaluations and prescriptions. They are all done on the basis of norms.

2.2.1 Norms, standards, and rules

Norms may be either standards or rules (Taylor 1961, chap. 1). If we evaluate something according to standards, we grade it as good or bad, clever or obtuse, pleasing or disgusting, etc. If we evaluate according to rules, we grade the evaluatum as right or wrong, correct or incorrect. Behavior or thought is likely to be evaluated according to rules. That which is obligatory or permissible is right behavior, and that which is prohibited is wrong behavior.

An evaluatum may be ranked rather than graded, that is, determined to be better or worse than some other thing in the class of comparison. But this can be done only in the case of evaluating according to standards. The evaluatum is then determined to have more or less of the good-making or bad-making characteristics than the other object has, according to the particular standard used. If the norms being applied to the evaluation are rules, the evaluatum may not be ranked. It can only be graded as right or wrong, that is, whether it fulfills or does not fulfill the rule.

Figure 1 displays the two types of norms and the types of evaluations that may be performed using each type.

Types of norms	Types of evaluation	Evaluation positive	negative
rules	grading	right/correct	wrong/incorrect
standards	grading	good/pleasing, etc.	bad/disgusting
standards	ranking	better	worse

Fig. 1. The role of norms in evaluation

2.2.2 Points of view or value systems

Taylor (1961:7) correctly points out that in evaluation a class of comparison may remain constant while a point of view changes and two different evaluations of the same object could result. For example, if our class of comparison were meat, a sirloin steak could be evaluated as good or bad depending on the point of view adopted. From an aesthetic point of view (taste), it might be evaluated as good, better than hamburger. But from an economic point of view (price), it might be evaluated as bad, worse than hamburger.

In discussing the notion of points of view, Taylor (1961, chap. 4) makes more philosophical and psychological distinctions than are warranted, resulting in a proliferation of metalanguage. He distinguishes between points of view, value systems, canons of reasoning, rules of relevance, and rules of valid inference. The definition of each depends much on the definitions of the others, and there is some circularity in this section of his work. I will try to explicate Taylor's schemata and show why fewer categories are needed.

First, adopting a point of view is defined as "nothing but adopting certain canons of reasoning as the framework within which value judgments are to be justified" (Taylor 1961:109). Canons of reason are defined as being constituted of the two sets of rules, those of relevance and those of valid inference. The rules of relevance are defined as the criteria for determining relevance of a reason given. The rules of valid inference are defined as the criteria for determining whether a relevant reason is also a good, warranted, or valid reason.

Taylor desires to maintain a distinction between "value system" and "point of view." Point of view is a cross-cultural (universal) concept, while value system is culture bound. This distinction is not tenable. Taylor suggests that points of view such as moral, aesthetic, and political are universal. There is a potential error in this (though probably not what Taylor intends). It is like saying that the categories of fruit and grain are universal and assuming that the membership of these categories is identical across cultures. It may be true that in the case of very generic categories every culture in the world has an approximate equivalent. But the Ga'dang people include coconuts in their category *bunga* 'fruit' and yams in their category *baggat* 'grain'. Clearly their categories are not identical with the categories of English.

Just so with points of view. Behavior that is considered morally offensive in one culture might be considered aesthetically offensive in another, and what is inoffensive in one culture may be offensive in another. For example, eating with the left hand is offensive among Muslim groups of Mindanao where the left hand is used for dirty tasks according to the norms of their culture and must not be used for eating.

If it were true that every possible point of view had an approximate equivalent in every culture of the world, there would be nothing more to say about the concept of point of view. However, although the existence of points of view is a cultural universal, the set of points of view is not. For example, a small, close-knit, egalitarian society might not have a political point of view.

Points of view are not identical across cultures. Rather, a point of view is an emic cultural cognitive gestalt. To assume a particular point of view is to employ the whole value system of the point of view as defined by the conventions of the cultural community. Thus to adopt a point of view is tantamount to adopting a value system, and the value system is simply the culture-specific knowledge frame that defines the relative values assigned to the members of a particular set of cultural objects. For the purpose of the analysis of normative discourse within a particular cultural community, no conceptual distinction is required between point of view and value system.

The notion of canons of reason would be needed only to have a category in which both rules of relevance and rules of valid inference are included. However, the two sets of rules, if they need to be distinguished at all, are simply some of the cultural objects or bits of knowledge that constitute the knowledge frame, that is, the value system to which they belong. The members of a cultural community "possess" these value-system knowledge frames—they know what objects or actions are included in each value system respectively, and they know what segment of the spatiotemporal or behavioral universe falls within the boundaries of each. They also know the subsets of cultural norms and to which value system each subset belongs. Since they share these knowledge frames, they all would have an intuitive approximation of the set of standards or rules that could appropriately be invoked in a given (problematic) circumstance. Likewise, they would know the point of view to be adopted when presented with a particular evaluatum.

2.2.3 Justification of evaluations and prescriptions

Taylor (1961:223) asserts that "prescriptions are justified in the same way that value judgments are justified," and that justifying a prescription is tantamount to justifying a set of value judgments. Thus there is a common logic for all evaluative and prescriptive discourse.

The logical relationship between evaluations and prescriptions on the one hand and justification on the other is straightforward. Justification is related to an evaluation or prescription as its *reason* (Taylor 1961:76) or *warrant* (van Dijk 1977:155); that is, justification is the reason for accepting or concurring with an evaluation or for doing a prescribed act.

Justification, however, has a complex logical structure of its own. Taylor (1961:77) proposes that there is a unified pattern of thought for all justification, and that there are four general phases in the overall process: verification, validation, vindication, and rational choice. All of these are "essential steps" in the entire process of justifying a value judgment.

We *verify* value judgments by appeal either to standards or to rules which we have adopted. We *validate* standards or rules (that is, we justify our adopting certain standards or rules) by appeal to higher standards or rules. The adoption of standards or rules which themselves cannot be validated by appeal to any higher standards or rules results from our decision to accept a whole value system. We *vindicate* our accepting a whole value system by appeal to the way of life to which we are committed. Our commitment to a way of life can be justified in terms of *rational choice* among different ways of life. [Ibid.]

Taylor suggests that this is the logical structure of all normative discourse, but I believe that the only kind of normative discourse that would manifest this structure would be a philosophical, ethical treatise such as *Zen and the Art of Motorcycle Maintenance* (Pirsig 1974), or an extremely comprehensive sermon. In ordinary normative discourse the logic is truncated. Verification and (optionally) validation are sufficient justification for evaluations and prescriptions in ordinary normative discourse. In fact, in a community that is a cultural isolate, such as the Ga'dang community was until very recently, it is questionable whether there was even the logical possibility of vindication and rational choice, since there were no known alternative value systems or ways of life.

2.2.4 Normative versus empirical justification

Taylor claims that "the validation of standards and rules, which is essential to the justification of value judgments, is not a part of scientific reasoning" (1961:110). Apparently this claim is made because the application of standards and rules in the case of scientific reasoning is believed to be beyond questioning. Baier (1958:75) implies as much:

We have seen that value judgments can be verified just like factual claims, but that in value judgments we make claims that give rise to a further question, namely, whether the criteria employed are the right ones. Factual judgments are decisively confirmed if they are empirically verified. Value judgments, on the other hand, must be not only verified but also validated. It is not enough to show that, *if* certain criteria *are* employed, then a thing must be said to have a certain degree of "goodness"; we must also show that the criteria *ought* to be employed.

Taylor (1961:80) agrees with Baier with respect to the greater need for justification in the case of value judgments:

It is clear that we have not succeeded in justifying a value judgment merely by showing that the evaluatum does or does not fulfill certain standards or rules. Another question immediately arises. Are those standards or rules appropriate ones for judging an evaluatum of that sort? We must not only justify the claim that, given the standards or rules, the evaluatum has a certain value. We must also justify the application of those standards or rules in the given circumstances. This is where validation comes in.

But is it true that "another question immediately arises" and that the appropriateness of the standards and rules must be validated? I will argue that this is not necessarily the case.

I contend that the difference between justification of value judgments and factual/empirical judgments is the degree of *sedimentation*, that is, institutionalization (Ihde 1977:147), of the standards or rules being applied. We have been led to believe that the standards and rules of the Western scientific tradition are beyond questioning because of their great degree of sedimentation. But as Kuhn (1970:43) has pointed out, the members of an interpretive or scientific community share a paradigm, and from this they abstract certain isolable elements and deploy them as rules. The rules, and the paradigm from which they derive, are only beyond question during a period of "normal science." They are open to question when anomaly is discovered that shows the paradigm to be deficient.

Thus, during a period of scientific revolution, even the so-called factual judgments may require the full-blown process of justification, including verification, validation, vindication, and rational choice. On the other hand, in a thoroughly integrated and stable cultural community, a value judgment may require only verification to be fully justified, because the standards and rules that are appealed to in justifying the evaluation are fully "sedimented" and considered beyond question. In this case, no validation requirement is imposed, much less vindication or rational choice.

The distinction that was made between value judgments and empirical judgments is therefore not valid. Both are normative processes. The difference is in the degree of sedimentation or acceptability of the standards or rules applied. Normative discourse, within the context of an established paradigm (scientific or cultural), requires only verification of evaluations or prescriptions.

2.3 The logic of Ga'dang normative discourse

There is a three-part logic involved in Ga'dang normative discourse: (1) assume a point of view; (2) evaluate or prescribe; (3) justify. The justification constituent of the Ga'dang logic does not include vindication and rational choice, which Taylor views as necessary for the complete justification of evaluations or prescriptions. The usual justification is a statement of a standard or rule that is a part of the system of norms known and accepted by the community. (Since chapters 6-9 deal with the analysis of Ga'dang normative discourse, the examples given in this chapter to illustrate the three-part logic will be brief.)

2.3.1 Ga'dang points of view

A Ga'dang point of view is the set of values relevant to a certain class of evaluata. To assume a point of view is to evaluate according to the particular set of values. Taylor suggests that the concept of points of view is universal (1961:108). True, all cultural communities do have points of view, such as moral, aesthetic, political, scientific, mathematical, and historical. But it is not necessarily the case that the set of points of view is identical across cultures, and it certainly is not the case that the membership of each normative category is identical. Thus, in the analysis of normative discourse, one must look for the points of view emic to the culture and determine what objects or actions may appropriately be evaluated according to each point of view as evidenced in the surface structure of text or lexicon.

This section includes all the Ga'dang points of view that have been identified on the basis of evaluative lexical pairs. These pairs denote the two opposite poles of an evaluative continuum. Each point of view has its own continuum. In most points of view there are also other adjectives, which express midpoints on the evaluative continuum. But in some cases an evaluatum must be either one or the other of the opposite evaluative lexemes, as in the economic point of view. In these cases, the lexemes may be modified to express different points on the continuum.

Figure 2, which lists all of the points of view that have been identified and the evaluative lexical pairs appropriate to each one, is not an exhaustive list. Nor is it necessarily true (though it may be) that each emic point of view has a corresponding evaluative lexical pair. The extremes of value and disvalue of a given point of view may be expressed by propositions, for example, in the case of a religious point of view, 'that which pleases God' versus 'that which God abhors'. It is to be expected, however, that a conventional point of view have lexical realizates as well, such as 'righteous' versus 'sinful' corresponding to these propositions.

The normative points of view of a speech community are likely to be taxonomically arranged (as in fig. 2). All Ga'dang points of view can be classified as moral, physical, or behavioral. These are broad types of points of view; specific points of view are subsumed under these categories. I give a name to each point of view simply to indicate the situations in which it is appropriately employed. Probably there is further taxonomic ordering of points of view, but an ethnocognitive survey (cf. Frake 1962) would be required to discover its structure.

The evidence for grouping certain points of view as moral ones has to do with whether or not the character of a person is involved in the evaluatum. If someone's character is involved, the evaluation is from a moral point of view. It is not necessary that the evaluatum is the person's character per se. It may be particular actions or attitudes. But whatever the evaluatum, if done from a moral point of view, a positive evaluation reflects well on the person involved, and a negative evaluation reflects badly. For example, if a person misrepresents his goods in bartering, that would be evaluated as *narakkat* 'bad'. This is considered a moral type of evaluation, because it would necessarily follow that the character of the person could also be evaluated as *narakkat*. However, if a person's ability in folk dancing is *narakkat*, it does not necessarily follow that the character of the person may be so evaluated. If a person is evaluated as *ungkug* 'ignorant', this is not a moral evaluation; it does not reflect on the person's moral character. It follows that no physical object can be evaluated from a moral point of view.

Point of view	Positive extreme	Negative extreme
MORAL		
ethical	*nalawad* 'good'	*narakkat* 'bad'
social	*nannakam* 'kind'	*natansit* 'cruel'
PHYSICAL		
economic	*nangina* 'valuable'	*nalaka* 'cheap'
attributional	*nadammat* 'heavy'	*nalampaw* 'light' (etc.)
artistic	*ka'anggam* 'lovely'	*kangngayangngag* 'repulsive'
BEHAVIORAL		
intellectual	*nala'ing* 'clever'	*ungkug* 'ignorant'
linguistic	*natunung* 'fluent/correct'	*saliwad* 'awkward'
emotional	*nasiyanak* 'peaceful'	*nakungkul* 'confused/ riled'
behavioral	*annung/pangngat* 'proper/ appropriate'	*balyat* 'improper/awful'

Fig. 2. Ga'dang points of view and evaluative lexical pairs

The most generic of Ga'dang evaluative lexical pairs is *nalawad* 'good' and *narakkat* 'bad'. This pair is so generic that it can be used for evaluations from any point of view. Each specific point of view (except for the ethical) has its own more specific lexical pair, but *nalawad* and *narakkat* may substitute for the more specific terminology in any evaluation.

The moral points of view include the ethical and social points of view. The ethical point of view has only the generic lexical pair *nalawad* 'good' and *narakkat* 'bad' to encode the opposite poles of its evaluative continuum. The social point of view has the lexical pair *nannakam* and *natansit*. The

former means 'kind, courteous, possessing desirable or admirable character traits'. The latter means 'cruel, mean, hostile, antisocial'. Adjectives
such as *na'allak* 'compassionate' and *na'ituk* 'selfish' belong on the moral
continua (ethical and social), but an ethnocognitive survey would be
needed to find out where these and others rank on the Ga'dang scale of
good and evil.

The physical points of view include the artistic, economic, and attributional; these points of view are assumed when evaluating physical objects.
The artistic point of view has the lexical pair *ka'anggam, kangngayangngag*
to express the evaluative extremes. The first means 'likeable, lovely', and
the second means 'repulsive (lit., that which causes shuddering)'. This pair
relates to physical appearance. Either one of the pair can be used to
evaluate the appearance, for example, of clothing or of a young lady. In
evaluation, *kangngayangngag* is used figuratively; its literal sense (which is
the most typical collocation) means the feeling of shuddering caused by
eating too much pork fat.

The lexical pair *nangina* and *nalaka* express the evaluative extremes of
the economic point of view. The first means 'valuable, expensive'; the
second means 'cheap'. In this particular point of view, there are no other
evaluative terms to express degrees of value or cheapness. However, *nangina* and *nalaka* may be mitigated, as in *medyo nangina* 'somewhat
valuable'. Another unique aspect of this point of view is that either term
may be a positive or a negative value, depending on whether the evaluator
is the owner or a prospective buyer. For an owner to evaluate an object as
nangina is to express value or esteem for the object, but for a buyer to
describe the object in that way is a negative evaluation, namely, that the
object is overvalued.

The attributional point of view includes several pairs of evaluative
lexemes, all of which focus on the evaluation of some particular physical
attribute of the evaluatum. Examples of such pairs are: *natuyag* 'strong' and
nakafuy 'weak'; *nadammat* 'heavy' and *nalampaw* 'light'; *nabangog* 'fragrant'
and *nabansit* 'fragrant, stinking'. Of course, there are different emotive connotations or attitudes as part of the different value systems shared by members of the speech community. A person may be very emotionally detached
or ambivalent in evaluating something as heavy or light, especially if he
does not have to carry it. It is difficult to be emotionally detached, however,
in evaluating an object that is present to the senses as either fragrant or
stinking.

The behavioral point of view includes all of those in which the evaluata
necessarily involve some activity, whether cognitive, emotional, or physical.
These points of view are the intellectual, linguistic, emotional, and (for lack
of a distinct term) behavioral.

The lexical pair *nala'ing* 'clever' and *ungkug* 'ignorant' express the extremes of the intellectual point of view. The word *abul* 'deaf mute', used metaphorically to mean 'ignoramus', may substitute for *ungkug*. This point of view is termed *intellectual* for lack of a more generic term describing not only mental alacrity, but any kind of skill, whether cognitive, physical, or artistic. Because of the inclusive nature of this point of view, it would probably occupy a higher node in a representation of the emic Ga'dang taxonomy of values or points of view than would others of the action-oriented (behavioral) points of view.

The evaluative extremes of the linguistic point of view are expressed as *natunung* 'fluent, eloquent, correct' and *saliwad* 'awkward, contorted, ungrammatical'. These terms can be used only to evaluate linguistic acts, that is, utterances.

There are so many evaluative terms and expressions relating to the emotional point of view that it is difficult to be certain which ones express the extremes. However, the terms *nasiyanak* 'peaceful' and *nakungkul* 'confused, riled' are at least close to the extremes of the most and least desirable states of mind.

A fascinating feature of the emotional point of view is the proliferation of metaphorical expressions referring to feelings or states of mind. Most of the metaphors are noun phrases with *nakam* 'mind' as the head noun and modifiers which, when used literally, modify nouns that denote physical objects. *Nadammat a nakam* 'heavy mind' means 'anxious'. *Malo a nakam* 'hurt mind' means 'grieved, sorrowful'. *Nalampaw a nakam* 'light mind' means 'joyful, carefree'. Some of the other metaphors concerning the mind, though these may relate more to character traits than to temporary states of mind, are *nataggat a nakam* 'hard mind', which means 'obstinate, mean', and *natattaddan si nakam* 'tamped-down mind', which means 'gracious, full of good character'.

The behavioral point of view is unique in several ways. For one thing, the evaluatum must be a physically observable action or segment of behavior. For another, there are very strong connotations of cultural expectations or rules of behavior when evaluation is done from this point of view. If there is a point of view that is a hybrid of moral and behavioral evaluation, this would be it. That is, a negative evaluation in this point of view would not necessarily imply that the person whose behavior is being evaluated is a bad person. However, if that person continually, willfully performed actions that were assigned disvalue from this point of view, he probably would be evaluated as *narakkat a tolay* 'a bad person'.

The lexical pair that expresses the extremes of the behavioral point of view is *annung* 'fitting, proper' versus *balyat* 'inappropriate, improper'. In this continuum, the positive pole may be expressed either *annung* or its synonym *pangngat*.

It is possible that a point of view may have more than one pair of terms to signal the extremes of value or disvalue, that is, synonyms expressing both poles of the evaluative continuum. It is also possible that one pole of the value continuum of a given point of view may have just one lexical realization, while the other has two or more, for example, *nala'ing* 'clever' versus *abul/ungkug* 'ignorant', or *pangngat/annung* 'proper' versus *balyat* 'improper'.

2.3.2 Evaluation and prescription

A few examples from the Appendix will be presented in this section to illustrate the function of evaluation and prescription in Ga'dang. (The number cited is the number of the sentence as it appears in the Appendix.) This section will be deliberately brief, since the normative notional structure of the Ga'dang text and its surface realizations are the topics of chapters 7-9.

Evaluation in Ga'dang is performed within or according to the point of view relevant to the evaluatum. In sentence 53 of the Appendix, there is an evaluation (of the speaker's past state of mind) from the emotional point of view:

```
Odde nadammat-in angkwa-k sinoy ...
but  heavy-cmp   thing-my   then
```

'But my mind was heavy then ...' (i.e., 'I felt sad')

An evaluation from the ethical point of view is made in s.171:

```
On, kamali ta    lud.
yes erred  we.2 really
```

'Yes, we both really erred (i.e., morally or ethically).'

An evaluation from the ethical point of view is made in s.354:

```
Kunna mat    yan ino tuldu   a nalawad allaye.
like  really that the teaching rl good   man
```

'That is really good (i.e., ethically sound) teaching, man.'

Prescription is within the context of the point of view of an observed or projected circumstance. (This is the initial constituent of the notional "schema of prescription," which will be discussed in chaps. 3 and 8). Justification of the prescription will appeal to standards and rules included in the point of view relevant to that circumstance.

An example of a prescription is found in s.312:

```
E    kakkapan tam    mallakad si na'inggud.
and try          we.inc walk     in straight
```

'And let's try to do what is right.'

The projected circumstance in this case was found in the previous sentence, a hypothetical circumstance in which the participants were arguing and slandering. Although this was stated as a conditional or hypothetical circumstance, it was, in fact, a good description of the state of affairs that led to this discussion.

Another prescription is found in s.320, in which the projected circumstance is stated in the conditional clause within the same sentence:

```
nu palungu amma sikwam, ma'awag si  dayawan nu ...
if first    more to.you needed obj honor    you
```

'If he's older than you, it's necessary that you respect him'

2.3.3 Justification in Ga'dang

The justification of the two preceding prescriptions is found in their immediate context. In the case of the prescription of s.312 ('let's try to do what is right'), the justification follows in s.313, namely, accountability to God for our actions.

In the case of s.320, the justification follows in the same sentence. The full schema of prescription is:

```
nu palungu amma sikwam, ma'awag si  dayawan nu,
if first    more to.you needed obj honor    you

gafuse palungu amma sikwam.
because first   more to.you
```

'If he is older than you, it's necessary that you respect him, because he is older than you.'

Notice that the justification is the same as the projected circumstance. The only difference is *nu* 'if' versus *gafuse* 'because'. This is begging the question but is not problematic because, for the Ga'dang people, the rule is implied by the fact (at least in the case of such a thoroughly internalized social value as the age theme). As long as evaluation is being done according to the social point of view (which entails moral obligation), the very mention of the age-differential concept justifies the prescription. In fact, the prescription is the expression of the rule conventionally associated with the age-differential concept.

The justification in Ga'dang normative discourse consists of a statement of the warrant or reason for evaluating or prescribing something. However, it is often true that the evaluation or prescription does not logically follow (in the strict sense) from the statement of justification. Thus the "inform reason" appearance of the justification statement may really be the invoking of a theme or norm (see chap. 3). The evaluation does not follow logically, but it does conventionally; that is, it follows because the conventions or expectations of the cultural community are that it should.

The logic of Ga'dang normative discourse is not syllogistic and not even very sound by strict standards of analytic logic. Sayers (1981) makes a similar observation concerning Wik-Munkan discourse. Huttar (1977:30) notes that "apparent differences in reasoning styles do hinder cross-cultural communication." The prescriptive science of logic that Westerners have inherited from the Greeks is not descriptive of universal reasoning styles. The Ga'dang norm, for instance, is not analytic reasoning, but rather a dialogical or conventional logic.

Goody and Watt (1968) claim that emphasis on analytical, logical thought processes is a consequence of literacy (see chap. 3). A close examination of Ga'dang normative discourse will reveal a great number of "logical fallacies," if judged by Western norms of sound logic. There are fallacies of diversion, begging the question, unwarranted assumptions, and irrelevant appeals to pity, tradition, questionable authority, or public opinion (Damer 1980). But if the arguments offered as justification of evaluations and prescriptions are acceptable to the participants in the discourse, they are valid justifications (Brooks and Warren 1970:171). If the reasoning is accepted, the point can be said to be proved (McCrimmon 1976:209).

Taylor's schema of the logic of normative discourse does allow for appeal to standards and rules that are cultural conventions. But in his view, this does not constitute a complete justification of an evaluation or prescription. The further steps of validation, vindication, and rational choice are required. But not so for the Ga'dang community (at least in that major part of it which is still preliterate), for in their normative taxonomy there is no Western scientific point of view. And it is the Western scientific point of view that assigns maximum value to syllogistic logic and rationality. Goody and Watt (1968:53) see this as one of the consequences of literacy. Although analytic, syllogistic thinking was not invented by the Greeks, they did invent the point of view that made them the prescribed modes of thought.

Taylor defers to the norms of his society by continuing with further steps of justification in normative discourse until he reaches one (namely, rational choice) that is compatible with the Western value system. What really happens in Western culture if justification becomes elaborate (as in

Taylor's schema) is that we continue to verify our judgments or prescriptions by appeal to higher and higher ranks of rules or norms until the highest rank is reached. That highest rank, at least according to the conventions of some Westerners, is rational (analytical, logical) or empirical verification and is required before a point can be said to be proved.

3   Psychology of Persuasion

There have been many studies of persuasion in psychology and related disciplines, and almost as many definitions have emerged. But all of them have much in common. "The inescapable fundamental thesis of persuasion is that it is a process of influencing the behavior of the persons who are being addressed" (Oliver 1968:94).

Kelly (1982:64-65), in discussing persuasive communication, that is, receptor/response-oriented communication, emphasizes *effect*, "the achievement of the desired response resulting in positive change." He quotes several authors on this topic, one of whom is Bettinghaus (1973:10), who defines persuasive communication as "a conscious attempt by one individual to change the attitudes, beliefs, or behavior of another individual or group of individuals through the transmission of some message."

Such definitions imply a cognitive and/or behavioral change. This is an acceptable definition of persuasion with one proviso, namely, that *change* be understood as not necessarily requiring the abandoning of a previously held opinion, attitude, or belief. In most cases, persuasion probably does require the abandoning of one opinion or behavior pattern and the adoption of another. However, a study of normative discourse reveals that this is not a necessary component of persuasion. Persuasion may be employed concerning a subject that the addressee already believes. In this case, the addressee may be required to change only by rearranging his cognitive taxonomy, that is, assigning a higher degree of importance to a particular belief. The result of this taxonomic rearrangement would be that, when faced with behavior options, the individual's choice would be more likely to be governed by the "elevated" belief than by other beliefs which would formerly have taken precedence.

Thompson (1975:2) offers a definition of persuasion that has no implication of a cognitive or behavioral about-face: "Persuasion as a minimum requires two persons with either the one intending to influence the second or each of the two attempting to affect the attitudes, beliefs, or actions of the other." Thompson uses the words *influence* and *affect* rather than *change*, thus avoiding any implication that a substitution or replacement is required. This is an important distinction, as will be made clear in the following discussion of knowledge structures and normative frames.

3.1 Cognitive psychology and knowledge structures

The notion of a system of knowledge organization as developed within the discipline of cognitive psychology is called a schema. Neisser (1976:55-56) defines it in this way:

> A schema is that portion of the entire perceptual cycle which is internal to the perceiver, modifiable by experience, and somehow specific to what is being perceived. The schema accepts information as it becomes available at sensory surfaces and is changed by that information; it directs movements and exploratory activities that make more information available, by which it is further modified.... In one sense, when it is viewed as an information-accepting system, a schema is like a *format* in a computer-programming language. Formats specify that information must be of a certain sort if it is to be interpreted coherently.

This definition seems to attribute to the schema a consciousness of its own, but I do not believe it should be interpreted literally. In any case, the notion of schema laid the groundwork for the development of a theory of knowledge structures.

Those who were interested in programming computers to interpret or produce texts developed the new discipline of artificial intelligence (AI). These people took note of the concept of a psychological unit of knowledge organization (e.g., schema), realizing that the computer needed an information-accepting system simulating that of humans. Thus the notions of "frames" and "scripts" were developed, referring to kinds of knowledge structures (Metzing 1980). The theory of knowledge structures was considered so significant by Schank and Abelson (1977) that they suggested a discipline to deal exclusively with these considerations: cognitive science, a field at the intersection of psychology, artificial intelligence, and linguistics.

In artificial intelligence and in cognitive science the psychological units of knowledge organization are referred to as frames or scripts. The concept of *frame* is explicated in the work of van Dijk (1977:159):

> The notion of *frame* [is] a theoretical primitive, cited as one explanatory component of linear and global coherence. The concept, which has been coined in recent work in artificial intelligence, belongs to cognitive theory. It denotes a conceptual structure in semantic memory and represents a part of our knowledge of the world. In this respect a frame is an *organizational principle*, relating a number of concepts which by *convention* and *experience* somehow form a "unit" that may be actualized in various cognitive tasks, such as language production and comprehension, perception, action and problem solving.

Knowledge structures constitute a corpus of expectations that are activated in particular contexts. These expectations embody the function of the knowledge structure, namely, to provide the information needed to interpret any input, and to know what, if anything, should be done in response. Knowledge structures include "the strong expectations which make reality understandable" (Schank and Abelson 1977:10). Lehnert (1980:83) defines this process as "expectation-driven understanding,... a process of generating expectations and recognizing when an expectation has been substantiated or violated."

If there is a distinction to be observed in the literature between *frames* and *scripts*, it is that *frame* is a generic designation for knowledge structures, whereas *script* refers to knowledge structures related to stereotypical segments of human behavior, that is, sequences of events or actions, verbal or nonverbal. Frames provide us with information about how to interpret stimuli, whether or not we perform any action as a result. Scripts provide us with information about what we should do next in a given context (or what customarily occurs), whether the action be verbal or nonverbal.

3.2 Knowledge structures related to persuasion

People in society do not need to be persuaded of what has already become conventionalized. Frames and scripts are conventional knowledge structures and are accepted by the members of a society. This is not to say that it is impossible to question the validity of the knowledge structures, but as a rule people do not focus conscious attention on them. They are a priori assumptions regulating the function of a society.

The function of knowledge structures is therefore very similar to that of norms (standards and rules). In fact, scripts are the cognitive organizational units by which we group our societal norms relating to behavioral options. Scripts include the information we need to behave in the culturally acceptable way.

Frames are conventionalized knowledge structures, each one including the knowledge of what value to place on the physical objects or actions that fall within its sphere of knowledge. Thus the evaluative points of view discussed in chapter 2 are culturally shared knowledge frames.

Persuasion relies on both kinds of knowledge structures. In any context in which one wants to persuade another, a script will provide the information of how to go about it. For example, if the Ga'dang informal litigation script is being activated or actuated, each community member involved will know how it is initiated, where to sit once the litigation gets under way, who should speak first, who should speak next, who should not speak, how to get the floor, how to recognize when the purpose has been achieved, and when to leave, to mention just some of the known stereotypical actions of the litigation script (see sec. 6.3).

The role of scripts in persuasion is to specify how the procedure is to be conducted. The person to be persuaded will recognize what is happening because of sharing the particular script with the communicator, and will know that acceptance or rejection or a change of behavior is being requested or expected. The role of frames, on the other hand, is to specify the types of propositions considered relevant as reasons or warrants for particular evaluations or prescriptions.

Both frames and scripts are normative because both have to do with societal expectations or conventions. Only frames, however, are inclusive of value systems or normative points of view.

Scripts do not provide us with all the information necessary to effect the persuasive task. Scripts are too general for that. There is also a corpus of cognitive units available to be selected from for the particular task at hand. Since the particular task is specific, the general script does not specify all the details.

Thus, in addition to scripts, Schank and Abelson (1977) posit the theoretical primitives of "goal" and "plan." The goal in normative discourse is to persuade someone of something. However, if a goal is not explicit in the discourse, a prior goal or purpose may be inferred, such as to produce a certain type of behavior in the addressee or to contribute to social harmony. The process of persuasion must have its cognitive effect on the addressee, however, before the more tangible goals can be achieved. Thus we speak of persuasion as the goal of normative discourse.

The speaker may employ one of several known plans in pursuit of this goal, or any goal. "A plan is intended to be the repository for general information that will connect events that cannot be connected by use of an available script or by standard causal chain expansion. A plan is made up of general information about how actors achieve goals" (Schank and Abelson 1977:70).

When the goal is persuasion, one is likely to employ one of what Schank and Abelson call the "persuade package of planboxes" (ibid.:83), which includes *ask, invoke theme, inform reason, bargain object, bargain favor*, and *threaten*. To this list, Walker (1983:22) adds *invoke precedent* and *invoke experience*. I will add still another, namely, *invoke norm*. It is possible that other plans should be included in this list, such as *predict consequences* (Rusher 1981:105). In any case, this should be regarded as an etic list; the particular types of plans employed by any speech community need to be discovered or confirmed by analysis of normative texts.

In the Ga'dang text in the Appendix, *invoke theme* and *invoke norm* are the plans employed in pursuit of the normative goal. *Predict consequences* is also used, but the consequences predicted are so closely tied to norms or themes of high emotive content in the culture that this usage could be included in the categories of norm or theme.

Sentences 208 and 209 of the Appendix provide a clear example. The meaning of these sentences is "It will be shameful if we don't tidy up our way of life; it won't be just Buton or Andits who will be made to look ridiculous, but all of us church members." The predicted consequence is being made to look ridiculous, but this is part of the shame theme, which is the most powerful theme in the Ga'dang culture (Noble 1975).

3.3 Persuasion as perpetuation of normative frames

It will now be made clear why a cognitive or behavioral about-face is not a necessary component or result of persuasion. But first, consider what happens when a radical change of opinion or behavior is required.

Belief is a closed or stable state of mind, and doubt is an open, unstable state of mind (Maranda and Maranda 1979:255). Human beings prefer the stable state of mind and will always interpret or behave according to known frames and scripts unless there is pressure not to. Persuasion, which aims to effect change in the addressee, must overcome the inertia of the stability of beliefs; that is, it must first create doubt. It must force an interpretation that deviates from the current script/frame; it must force some modification, if not rejection, of that script/frame. The plans that are likely to be employed when a substantial cognitive or behavioral change is required are: *ask, inform reason, bargain object, bargain favor*, and *threaten*.

The typical use of persuasion in normative discourse, at least in the Ga'dang community, does not involve the rejection of the conventional scripts or frames, but rather their perpetuation. This type of persuasion involves convincing someone that his or her behavior does not measure up to the conventional norms of the society and that it ought to be modified to conform. The fact that the individual already knows the conventional beliefs or norms is attested to by the fact that in the normative discourse itself the norms are cited as reasons or warrants for accepting evaluations or obeying prescriptions, and these are accepted as valid reasons. Their validity as facts is not questioned, nor is the appropriateness of applying them in the given context. In this type of normative behavior, beliefs stay constant and behavior is urged to conform. Social pressure (i.e., weight of public opinion) is brought to bear on one who deviates from the behavioral scripts acceptable to the society.

3.4 Ethnopsychology and neuropsychology

Recent findings in neuropsychology, in particular the so-called split-brain theory, suggest some interesting possibilities for ethnopsychology and cognitive anthropology. These possibilities were outlined by Paredes and Hepburn (1976) and touched off a minor furor of discussion, which was published in subsequent issues of *Current Anthropology*. This line of inquiry will be considered here, to determine what, if anything, it can offer by way of explanation for the cultural differences in strategies of persuasion or the practice of normative discourse.

3.4.1 Neuropsychology and hemispheric specialization

It has been only three decades since the beginning of the pioneering work on "split brains" (in which the two hemispheres have been surgically severed at the corpus callosum). This surgical procedure, known as commissurotomy, was done to relieve the symptoms of epilepsy, and it proved effective for that purpose. The earliest and perhaps the best known of those who have been involved in this research were Bogen, Gazzaniga, and Sperry. Sperry received the 1981 Nobel prize in medicine for his work, which has been described as "spawning a revolution in popular psychology and philosophy" (Naunton, *Dallas Times Herald*, March 26, 1983).

The procedure yielded an unanticipated result, namely, a substantial amount of knowledge about the differing functions of the two hemispheres of the brain. Once the productive area of inquiry was identified, many experimental procedures were devised to test the hemispheric functions in subjects who had not had brain surgery. Some of these procedures were: dichotic seeing or hearing (presenting visual or auditory stimuli only to the right or left side); thermistors (devices for measuring temperature increases in right and left hemispheres independently); and dye in the blood stream, which could be traced to determine if certain types of stimuli produced more activity in one or the other of the brain hemispheres.

The research is far too voluminous even to survey here. Dingwall (1981) produced a bibliography of 1,100 works on language and the brain dealing with hemispheric specialization, most of them written in the 1970s. Surveying perhaps 100 of these works, I found only one that was skeptical of hemispheric specialization. The others all agreed to the principle, though the details of their findings differed and at times conflicted on minor points. What I present here is a brief resumé of that for which a general consensus exists: certain broad categories of cognitive functions known to be centered predominantly in one hemisphere or the other.

Figure 3 lists the cognitive functions that have been identified as related. This list is a compilation from several such lists from the work of Thompson (1975:70), Paredes and Hepburn (1976:125), Akmajian, Demers, and Harnish (1980:320), and McGee-Cooper (1982:6). These authors in turn were compiling the findings of previous researchers. The far-reaching influence of the brain hemisphere research is evident here; note that Thompson is a neuropsychologist, Paredes and Hepburn are cognitive anthropologists, Akmajian et al. are linguists, and McGee-Cooper is an educator.

There is some degree of synonymity between some of the terms in a single column of figure 3. These are not intended to be discrete categories

Left hemisphere	Right hemisphere
symbolic or verbal	visuospatial
logical or analytic	synthetic perceptual
sequential or linear	holistic or nonlinear
rational and factual	emotive and intuitive
propositional	appositional or gestalt
language skills	nonverbal ideation

Fig. 3. Cognitive functions related to brain hemispheres

of cognitive function, but rather general areas. Nor is it intended that each hemisphere is capable only of the kinds of functions listed below it but rather that there is a strong tendency toward that type of localization or hemispheric specialization.

> While it is the right hemisphere that is viewed as uniquely specialized for holistic, synthetic processing, the left hemisphere must surely utilize such processing modes in extracting meaning from words, sentences, paragraphs, and the like. On the other hand, while it is the left hemisphere that is viewed as conceptual and logical, the right hemisphere has been shown to be capable of logical and conceptual operations. [Gazzaniga 1978:48]

A vast amount of empirical research underlies the generalizations in figure 3 concerning hemispheric specialization. The methods of dichotic listening and seeing, thermistors to measure brain hemisphere temperature differential, and dye in the blood stream to determine location of activity in the brain have already been mentioned. Other sources of empirical findings have been patients with surgically split brains or brain damage on one side or the other. It has been found (Nebes 1977:99) that patients with right hemisphere brain damage were likely to have difficulty perceiving spatial relationships and were prone to spatial disorientation, even becoming lost in familiar surroundings. They were baffled by mazes and maps and unable to copy geometrical shapes. This research supported the visuospatial cognitive orientation of the right hemisphere.

Dr. Elliott Ross has demonstrated the involvement of the right hemisphere of the brain in emotive cognitive functions. He observed hospital patients who had damage to the right hemisphere of the brain as a result of strokes and were subsequently unable to communicate emotion via the prosodic features of speech, though vocabulary, grammar, and articulation remained normal (Ross and Mesulam 1979). The patients were also unable to communicate emotions through facial, limb, and body gesture (ibid.:148). It was not that the stroke victims did not have emotional feelings; they did have them and were frustrated at not being able to express them. But a part of the mechanism for the expression of the emotions had been damaged in the right hemisphere of the brain.

Krashen (1977:107) asserts that the left hemisphere has "been shown to process both linguistic and nonlinguistic information in characteristic ways: It is analyzed, linearly arranged, temporally ordered (i.e., according to time of occurrence), and represented as propositions." He adds that for most people, nearly all right-handers and many left-handers, the left hemisphere is dominant for language. He cites research that reported more loss of speech from left hemisphere lesions than from right hemisphere, and temporary loss of speech resulting from anesthetizing the left hemisphere, but not the right.

Describing the results of some dichotic listening experiments, Krashen (1977) reported that there was a reliable right-ear superiority in reaction time, accuracy, and recall when verbal stimuli were presented. This right-ear advantage is believed to be an evidence of greater left hemisphere involvement, since stimuli from the right ear and eye are transmitted to the left hemisphere of the brain.

Krashen (1977) cites the work of Zurif and Sait (1969) showing that grammatical structure of sentences is analyzed best by the left hemisphere. He also cites the work of Gordon and Carmon (1976):

> In their experiment, subjects identified symbols for which they had just learned verbal labels (digits), such as dots representing binary numbers. As the experiment progressed, subjects showed a shift from right-hemisphere processing (left visual field superiority) to left-hemisphere processing (right visual field superiority). Gordon and Carmon suggest that the left hemisphere's advantage "for naming or codifying produced the reversal" (p. 1097). As the subjects learned the names of the symbols they saw, the left hemisphere played a larger role in their identification. [Krashen 1977:114]

The work of Ley and Bryden (1979:127-37) substantiates the findings concerning the localization of emotive cognitive functions in the right hemisphere of the brain. Drawings of faces expressing emotions were presented to twenty test subjects, and it was found that there was significant superiority of the left visual field (therefore right brain hemisphere) in the recognition of character and emotional expressions. Different experimental procedures were employed and these conclusions further substantiated in the work of DeKosky et al. (1980) and that of McKeever and Dixon (1981).

3.4.2 Hemispheric specialization, culture, and cognition

Paredes and Hepburn (1976:121) suggested that the research in hemispheric specialization might be "the Rosetta Stone by which such intriguing, yet troublesome, ethnographic curiosities as Trukese navigation and 'nonlineal codifications of reality' could be translated into general scientific terms." They called attention to the radical differences from culture to culture in cognition and problem solving, noting that "what is rational in one culture is not necessarily rational in another" (ibid.:122). Their thesis is that individuals may become habituated to a right- or left-hemisphere-dominated cognitive strategy, and that it may become characteristic of the cultural community.

> Whether or not it is true that different cultures (including class and occupational "cultures") differentially reinforce right- and left-hemisphere-dominated cognitive processes, it seems fairly obvious that the two kinds of processes are differentially evaluated in different societies. Perhaps the best example is the tendency of Westerners to regard only what appear to be manifestations of left-hemisphere functions as "real" intelligence. [Ibid.:127]

An example of a culture that does not employ left-hemisphere-dominated cognitive processes to nearly the same degree that Western culture does is the Wik-Munkan group of Australian aborigines. Sayers (1981) cites an example of a brief persuasive Wik-Munkan text that has no explicit logical link and suggests that "the implicit information in this text needs to be supplied to make it a logical Western (Aristotelean) argument." As an explanation for the difference, Sayers claims that what is known by the aboriginal comes from perception, not logical thinking.

The great danger in this consideration is in resurrecting the notion of "the primitive mentality." Fortunately, the value of right-hemisphere-oriented cognitive processes is now beginning to get its due respect, as in the work of McGee-Cooper (1982), Ferguson (1976), and de Bono (1970). The right hemisphere is known to be more creative and artistic, although less logical, but there need be no pejorative implication in this.

Neither Sayers nor Paredes and Hepburn offer any explanation of why these differences in cognitive processes exist. Thus Chisholm (1976:319) responded to the work of Paredes and Hepburn in this way:

> Their attempt to show how differences in hemispherical functioning may parallel cross-cultural (or individual) differences in cognitive styles may, however, be premature. My own feeling is that before this interesting question can be fruitfully explored, a number of problems must be squarely addressed. Among these problems is the paramount one of causality. Is there any a priori reason even to attempt to find similarities between the vague and nonquantifiable descriptions of supposed hemisphere-specific cognitive functions and the equally vague characterizations of cross-cultural differences in cognitive styles? Even if it were conclusively demonstrated that differences in hemispherical cognitive functioning exactly mirrored cross-cultural (or individual) differences in cognitive style, this would represent only a very mysterious and intriguing correlation—with the standard warning that no causal relationship should be inferred. Paredes and Hepburn seem to be

more concerned to show that this correlation exists than to explain why it should, although the opposite strategy might prove more enlightening.

Chisholm's point is well taken. If the differences in hemispheric specialization exactly mirrored cross-cultural cognitive styles, it would be mysterious. I suggest that there is no exact mirroring, and that the causal explanation of the cross-cultural differences is this: the inclination to employ right-hemisphere cognitive functions is characteristic of orality, and the inclination toward predominantly left hemisphere cognitive functions is characteristic of textuality, a consequence of literacy (Goody and Watt 1968). Furthermore, the inclination to the right hemisphere functions is somehow prior and more natural. It is a characteristic of children in literate societies up to the time they become literate (McGee-Cooper 1982:28).

Empirical research is cited in *Brain/Mind Bulletin* (April 19, 1979) showing that, of fifty-two children tested, the poorer readers and dyslexics showed an inclination to process visual information with a holistic and context-bound coding strategy, whereas good readers processed it analytically. It was found that even for poor readers, the left hemisphere was dominant in reading, but less so than for the good readers. In other words, the poor readers had a greater inclination to process visual stimuli in the right hemisphere of the brain, which, being less analytical and sequential, is less suited to the task.

More convincing evidence concerning the dominance of the left hemisphere in literacy is presented in two articles by Silverberg et al. (1979, 1980). In the experiments of these authors, tests were administered to many students who were just making the transition to literacy. The text subjects were Israeli students, twenty-four in second grade (age 7) and twenty-four in third grade (age 8). It was found that twenty-three out of twenty-four second-graders responded faster to target words presented in their left visual field, which feeds to the right brain hemisphere, than to the same target words in their right visual field, which feeds to the left brain hemisphere. In contrast, twenty out of twenty-four third-graders responded to the same stimuli faster in their right visual field than in their left (Silverberg et al. 1980:102). Moreover, the difference in the response time was described as "highly significant." Clearly the left hemisphere of the brain is better suited for literate tasks, and literacy readily becomes a predominantly left hemisphere function. The authors report:

> The switch in dominance was due to a dramatic reduction in response time (150 msec) to stimuli appearing in the right field contrasting to virtually no change in response time to stimuli in the left. Therefore, it is apparently not correct to describe the shift as a manifestation of some functional loss in the right hemisphere gained by the left, but rather a vast improvement in

left-hemisphere processing skills while those of the right hemisphere remained constant. [Ibid.:103]

3.4.3 Orality, literacy, cognitive orientation, and persuasion

The Greek civilization is "the prime historical example of the transition to a really literate society. In all subsequent cases where the widespread introduction of an alphabetic script occurred, as in Rome for example, other cultural features were inevitably imported from the loan country along with the writing system; Greece thus offers not only the first instance of this change, but also the essential one for any attempt to isolate the cultural consequences of alphabetic literacy" (Goody and Watt 1968:42). The primary consequence is posited to be the change from mythical to logico-empirical modes of thought (ibid.:43). The authors are careful to point out that there is no absolute dichotomy relating mythical thought to a primitive mentality not capable of logical thought. Rather, they suggest that "writing establishes a different kind of relationship between the word and its referent, a relationship that is more general and more abstract, and less closely connected with the particularities of person, place and time, than obtains in oral communication.... It was only in the days of the first widespread alphabetic culture that the idea of 'logic'—of an immutable and impersonal mode of discourse—appears to have arisen" (ibid.:44).

Plato and Aristotle are the founders of the prescriptive science of logic. They not only conceived of the possibility of a system of rules for thought, but they specified what these rules were. "This logical procedure seems essentially literate" (Goody and Watt 1968:53), because writing liberates the mind from the immediacy of the present context and the limitations of memory. Long and complex logical argumentation is difficult to create and deliver orally and even more difficult to assimilate or comprehend in oral communication.

The work of Goody and Watt establishes a link between literacy and logical modes of thought. The work of Tannen, on the other hand, asserts a relationship between orality and emotive cognitive processes. Tannen (1982:18) refers to writing as autonomous language, and oral communication as non-autonomous language. She contrasts the two in this way:

> Autonomous language ... focuses on the content of communication, conventionally de-emphasizing the interpersonal involvement between communicator and audience. Ideally, the audience is expected to suspend emotional responses, processing the discourse analytically and objectively. When relationships between propositions are explicit, the reader or hearer supplies minimal connective tissue from background knowledge and shared context. By contrast, non-autonomous language purposely builds on interpersonal involvement and

triggers emotional subjective responses, demanding maximum contribution from the audience in supplying socio-cultural and contextual knowledge.

What these authors have written suggests a correlation between orality and right hemisphere cognitive functions on the one hand, and literacy and left hemisphere functions on the other. The well-documented work of Ong (1982:36-56) lists several more contrasts between oral and literate societies; the similarity of the list in figure 4 to the one in figure 3 (hemispheric specialization) is very revealing.

We may draw the conclusion that literacy versus orality is the causal explanation for the correlation between certain cross-cultural differences in cognitive processing and the hemispheric specialization of the brain. Literacy promotes logical, analytic, objective, abstract thought, whereas orality promotes emotive, situational, holistic, subjective thought.

Bringing together these concepts from cognitive science, neuropsychology, and the orality/literacy contrast, we can explain the crucial difference between Western and Ga'dang normative discourse: The conventional persuasive plan in Western normative discourse is *inform reason*, and the conventional plan in Ga'dang normative discourse is *invoke theme/norm*. This

literacy	orality
logical	emotive
subordinative	additive
analytic	aggregative
concise	redundant or copious
objectively distanced	empathetic or participatory
abstract	situational

Fig. 4. Characteristics of literate and oral traditions

may also be postulated, tentatively, to explain the difference between normative discourse in all literate societies versus all oral ones.

The essence of the *inform reason* plan is the logical relationship that exists between the evaluation or prescription and the reason offered as justification. This is compatible with left hemisphere cognitive functions and with the characteristics of a literate tradition. The essence of the *invoke theme* or *invoke norm* plan is emotive and holistic, not necessarily related to the evaluation or prescription in a strict logical way, but rather related to the whole fabric of society (e.g., "if you accept this evaluation/prescription, we will have group harmony"). This is compatible with right hemisphere functions and oral traditions.

This is not to say that the literate or the oral society precludes the use of the plan that is typical of the other, but each is inclined to use its own conventional plan. Much of normative discourse in Western society comes clothed in the surface structure of expository discourse, in which *inform reason* is the standard interpropositional relationship. But it is not unusual to encounter *invoke theme/norm* in the context of oral communication in Western society. Even in this context, however, *inform reason* is more likely to occur than it is in Ga'dang normative discourse, because of the permeation of the literate tradition in the West. One consequence of literacy is a near reverence for rationality and logic. It is the Westerner's intellectual legacy from the Greeks and is a firmly entrenched normative Western value (Samovar 1981:42).

4 Sociology and Ethnology of Normative Behavior and Persuasion

In considering normative discourse and persuasion, the relevant contributions from one discipline overlap with those from another. Some sociological and ethnological factors have already been discussed. Others will be treated here, and also in subsequent chapters, especially chapter 6.

A speaker is likely to engage in normative discourse when he assigns a negative evaluation to the behavior of another person or when there are evaluations in conflict. Depending on the social relationships between the people involved, the discourse may be a rebuke or exhortation (monologue) or a dispute of some kind (dialogue). In this chapter we focus on dispute. Monologue is discussed in chapter 6.

4.1 Conciliatory dispute settlement

Black and Mileski (1973:11) relate two kinds of dispute settlement: therapeutic and coercive.

> Therapeutic dispute settlement is a conciliatory process in which an effort is made to restore relationships torn by conflict. Dispositions of this kind are especially common in tribal societies, where most social ties are intimate and permanent. On the other hand, coercive dispute settlement is adversarial, pitting one party against the other, declaring a winner and a loser, and thus is likely to harden the conflict and destroy any future relationship between the parties. Such adversarial dispositions are most frequent where disputants are strangers to each other in an impersonal context; this type of disposition is characteristic of modern courts of law.

In the Ga'dang context, especially within a single village, there is no such thing as an impersonal context. True to Black and Mileski's generalization, dispute settlement among the Ga'dang is typically of the therapeutic (i.e., conciliatory) type, aimed at restoring relationships.

In a more recent work, Black (1976:5) presented a taxonomy of four styles of social control, in which therapeutic and conciliatory were distinguished, though both are subsumed under remedial. The remedial styles of social control are contrasted with the accusatory, which include penal and compensatory styles. Figure 5 is from Black's work.

In this taxonomy, the Ga'dang informal litigation would clearly fall in the category of the conciliatory style of social control. Black (1976:5) says of this style that "the ideal is social harmony. In the pure case, the parties to a dispute initiate a meeting and seek to restore their relationship to its former condition. They may include a mediator or other third party in their discussion, together working out a compromise or other mutually acceptable resolution."

	Penal	Compensatory	Therapeutic	Conciliatory
Standard:	prohibition	obligation	normality	harmony
Problem:	guilt	debt	need	conflict
Initiation of case:	group	victim	deviant	disputants
Identity of deviant:	offender	debtor	victim	disputant
Solution:	punishment	payment	help	resolution

Fig. 5. Black's taxonomy of styles of social control

4.2 Consensus as the goal of Ga'dang normative discourse

Black and Mileski view law as a system of behavior and means of social control; they note that legal systems ideally are founded on a principle of "social eudaemonism, the ethic of group happiness" (1973:2). In the conciliatory type of social control typical of tribal societies where interpersonal relationships are close, the perpetuation of these relationships may be vital to group survival. The group need not be a small one to hold this value, however. Christopher (1983:55) observes that "in their heart of hearts, the Japanese people as a whole have only one absolutely immutable goal, which is to insure the survival and maximum well-being of the tribe.... Probably the single most important thing to know about the Japanese is that they instinctively operate on the principle of group consensus." Christopher draws a sharp contrast between this group affirmation and the values of Western society, where individuality is valued highly. It is also true that the Japanese prefer mediation and conciliatory dispute settlement, whereas confrontational or adversarial dispute settlement is typical in the West.

Martin and Colburn (1972:171-72) offer the following list of criteria for determining the degree of pressure to conform or to seek consensus: size (the smaller the group, the stronger the pressure to conform); frequency of contact (the more the members of a group interact, the stronger the pressure to conform); time (the longer the period during which members of a group have known each other, the stronger the pressure to conform); participation in decisions (the more individuals participate in making decisions, the more likely they are to accept these decisions); group centeredness (group-centered egalitarian groups exert stronger pressures to conform than leader-centered groups); cohesiveness (the more the sense of solidarity and feeling of "we-ness," the higher cohesiveness of the group, the stronger the pressure to conform); clarity of group norm (the less ambiguous the appropriate group norm, the greater the pressure to conform).

According to these criteria, the Ga'dang people have close to the greatest possible degree of pressure on them to conform. Thus the function of normative discourse in Ga'dang is to achieve or restore consensus. In fact, one of the strategies in the pursuit of this goal is to enhance the clarity of group norms by reiterating and reconfirming them. The logical relationship of the norm to the issue at hand need not be particularly clear as long as the norm itself is clear.

5   Normative Discourse

The text analysis presented in this and the following chapters is an exercise in discourse analysis (de Beaugrande and Dressler 1981, chap. 2). It focuses primarily on the text in the Appendix, and references to that text will be made by citing the appropriate sentence numbers (e.g., s.2-10). Reference will occasionally be made to other texts also, and relevant sections from them will be included here, since they are not in the Appendix.

5.1 Classification of texts

The notion of similarity between texts implies a classification of text types. Such classifying is the logical and appropriate starting point for discourse analysis. True, it is not strictly speaking the starting point, since it inherently involves analysis; but it should be the first-priority analytical procedure. Longacre's analogy (1983:1-2) points out the importance of classification of texts:

> We can, if we wish, compare California oranges with Florida oranges, but it is less useful to compare California oranges with Washington apples. We may compare sentences from narrative discourse in language A with sentences from narrative discourse in language B, but it is misleading to compare sentences from narrative discourse in language A with sentences from expository discourse in language B.

Longacre's concern here in comparing certain types of texts from two or more languages is to make generalizations and suggest universal features that will be of use in further linguistic investigation. Classifying text types is equally important for the analysis of an individual language. It may be even more important, since any generalizations concerning higher-level rules, that is, rules that function on the discourse level and may override the rules of morphology or clause-level grammar (Walrod 1979:44), are likely to be incorrect or too general to be useful if not identified within a particular discourse type. Furthermore, one of the aims of textlinguistics is to determine and describe the grammar of a given discourse type in contrast to the grammar of other discourse types.

5.1.1 A taxonomy of text types

There is no single heuristic for classification of texts. At first, guesswork and intuition may be relied upon. This can be fairly accurate if close attention is paid to the situational context in which the text was uttered. It presupposes some knowledge of the kinds of things speakers do with language and of the types of discourses that have been observed in human languages.

Once texts have been intuitively and tentatively classified, comparisons may be made to determine the characteristic surface structures of each. This may lead to some reclassifying of texts. Longacre (1983:3-6) posits four broad notional types of discourse: narrative, procedural, behavioral, and expository. Each of them may have several subtypes.

Because of embedding or skewing, few texts are purely one or another discourse type in their surface structure. Skewing occurs when a speaker encodes his notional discourse type in an alternative surface type, for example, exhorting or prescribing with a narrative. The social relationship between speaker and hearer is perhaps the most obvious reason for skewing of this type.

The concept of four broad types of discourse proves useful in classifying texts in Ga'dang, though there are some texts that are problematic or borderline as to classification. Three discourse types in Ga'dang have already been described in *Discourse Grammar in Ga'dang* (Walrod 1979), though certainly not exhaustively. Behavioral discourse was omitted from that work because of lack of data. It was a productive omission, since it necessitated further data collection, broader research in theory, more text analysis, and this presentation of results.

Longacre distinguishes behavioral discourse from the other three types by characterizing it as "minus in regard to contingent succession but plus in regard to agent orientation" (1983:3). It shares the feature of plus agent orientation with narrative discourse, and it shares the feature of minus contingent succession with expository discourse. Exhortation, eulogy, and political speeches are cited as examples of behavioral discourse.

5.1.2 The normative discourse type

While the label *behavioral* is appropriate to the kinds of texts I have been working with, I am using the term *normative* in its place. There are two reasons for this choice. First, *normative* has a tradition of use in other disciplines, such as axiology and logic (Taylor 1961), ethics (Frankena 1963:9-15), sociology and law (Donald Black 1976, chap. 6), and political philosophy (Ryan 1980). Similar uses are found in psychology, cognitive anthropology, and communication theory. The second reason for choosing *normative* is that its traditional uses, while not identical from one discipline to another, tend to be generic, potentially including all the kinds of texts which we would call behavioral, and perhaps more.

Normative discourse, then, is any discourse of an evaluative, prescriptive, hortatory, imperative, or eristic (i.e., disputatious) type. It fills approximately the same notional space as behavioral discourse in Longacre's schema.

It might be argued that a simple evaluative text such as the following is purely expository: "Running is good. It helps the body. It helps the soul."

However, if we examine the speaker's intention or the implicit performative, we would find that the thrust of the communication is, "I am recommending to you that you should run." This underlying structure does have agent orientation, even though the surface structure does not. I am assuming that any evaluative utterance, though it may appear to be pure exposition, has a purpose of affecting, influencing, altering or modifying in some way the knowledge, beliefs, or (more frequently) the behavior of another. Thus it is not distinct at the notional level from the other subtypes of normative discourse, which clearly have such a purpose. Again, a speaker's choice of encoding a recommendation to do physical exercise as an imperative, evaluation, or narrative about someone who benefited from it may depend on the speaker's social rank or relationship to the audience.

5.1.3 Embedded normative discourse

Grimes (1976:55-56) has observed:

> Some of the information in narratives is not part of the narratives themselves, but stands outside them and clarifies them. Events, participants, and settings are normally the primary components of narrative, while explanations and comments about what happens have a secondary role that may be reflected in the use of distinctive grammatical patterns, as in Munduruku. On the other hand, in nonsequential texts, explanatory information itself forms the backbone of the text, and narrative sequences may be used to illustrate it.

Grimes does not account for this phenomenon in terms of embedding or skewing between notional and surface structure text types, but it can be described in this way. Longacre (1983:13) refers to this as the embedding of one discourse type within a different discourse type. Grimes points out correctly that a speaker's evaluations may be encoded by lexical choice within a narrative, for example, in the choice of modifiers such as *loyal* versus *traitorous* (1976:62). In such cases, where the scope of the evaluation is probably a noun or verb, it would be counterintuitive to posit the embedding of normative discourse within the narrative. However, when a narrator encodes an evaluation in the form of a sentence or paragraph, which can easily be bracketed off from the rest of the discourse (and may need to be in order to properly analyze the grammar of narrative in the language), then this should be viewed as embedded normative discourse. Supporting such an analysis is the fact that such evaluations are likely to have a broad scope, referring to a major section of the narrative or to all that follows or precedes (especially if the evaluation is initial or final in the discourse). Furthermore, evaluative sentences or paragraphs have distinctive grammatical patterns in the context in which they are embedded; in fact, they conform closely to the grammatical patterns of normative discourse.

Jones (1983, chap. 4) has observed some of these phenomena and described them as "author comments." Author comments necessarily involve "a temporary departure from the main train of thought in a text" (1983:77). Author comments are most frequently expository or normative (*behavioral* in Jones's work); expository and normative discourse types are not arranged according to temporal succession, and neither are author comments as a rule. An author "may suspend his argument temporarily to explain a certain part of the discourse" (ibid.). This would be an instance of an expository comment (explanation) embedded in a normative text (argument). It is also common to embed normative comments (particularly the evaluative type) in expository discourse, or any other type. Jones refers to this type of embedding as opinion comments (1983:79). All of Jones's examples of opinion comments are clearly evaluative, therefore normative. In the sentence *Canned tuna is expensive* (toward the end of a *Consumer Reports* article comparing tuna), the word *expensive* assigns somewhat negative value to the price of tuna, since consumers would prefer that it not be expensive. It is not as bad an evaluation as *outrageous* or *exorbitant*, but it is on the negative side of center on the continuum of possible evaluations of prices.

Jones's typology of author comments also includes explanatory, incidental, and thematic comments. The following was cited as an example of an explanatory comment: "Bill Belden in the single was fortunate in that he foresaw the difficulty (evidently aware of the NAAO record of niggardly supporting lightweights) and long before the trip arranged to use a shell that he was accustomed to, from the same women's team." The parenthetical clause is the author's comment according to Jones (1983:82):

> Note the author-opinion overtones in this comment, which suggests the possibility of hybrid comments—comments which have more than one function.

His point is well taken. While the author's comment does serve to explain the action of Bill Belden, it is clear too that the author is assigning disvalue to the behavior of the NAAO ("niggardly"), and the author is assuming that Belden acted as he did because he made the same evaluation. The assigning of value or disvalue to an evaluatum is a subjective thing. The accountant for the NAAO might have described the same behavior as astute.

Incidental and thematic comments may also have a normative notional structure. In one of the incidental comments cited by Jones (ibid.:84) are the words *it is a sound scientific procedure*; one suspects that the entire incidental comment was intended to serve as a vehicle for this evaluation.

Thematic comments are a special case because of their importance in normative discourse (cf. sec. 8.2).

Perhaps not all author comments can be analyzed as the embedding of one discourse type in another, but many can be viewed in this way. Jones (1983:87) points out that author comments are clearly marked in discourse. At least some of this distinctive marking can be explained in terms of embedding, which involves a sudden switch to the grammar of a different discourse type.

Illustrations of the embedding of one text type in another are found in many places in the text in the Appendix. It is a normative discourse. However, the first speech of Andits (s.29-165) is predominantly narrative in structure, though thoroughly normative in content. The imperative of s.80 ("We should get rid of this kind of thing") is a return to the normative discourse style of the whole litigation. The notional normative discourse type is being directly realized in s.80, whereas in s.69-79 there is a skewing between normative notional structure and narrative surface structure. The imperative of s.80 is followed immediately by the unmistakably normative paragraph, s.81-83.

An example of a second level of embedding (normative discourse embedded within narrative) is found in s.75-76. This section is bracketed with a typical feature of the grammar of narrative discourse, namely, the quotative formula at the beginning of s.75 and at the end of s.76, in simple past tense. But within those brackets is the reported speech of the speaker himself, and that speech is purely normative. There are three clauses, all of which are nonverbal: 'It's his custom. He has no consideration because he is still a child.' These clauses are clearly evaluative. They assign a negative value to the behavior narrated in s.69-74 but mitigate the harsh evaluation by offering some excuse for the behavior on the basis of the youth of Buton, the agent of the narrated actions. The clause *gagangena* 'it's his custom' is frequently used to explain away and overlook the naughty behavior of a young child. Its use here referring to Buton is true mitigation, not a veiled insult, even though Buton is over twenty, because it is Buton's age in comparison with the speaker Andits's that is in focus. The pluralization of the word *anak* 'child' in s.76, is apparently ungrammatical in any type of discourse, narrative or normative included, because it is in the second clause of the sentence, which is providing an argument in support of the first clause, where the second person singular pronoun is the subject. Thus the second clause should read 'because he is still a child', and in fact that is the free translation I have given it. But Andits did use the plural form, and I interpret this as further mitigation of the harsh evaluation, namely, by directing it at a class of people rather than an individual. A more literal translation will demonstrate the mitigation: 'He has no consideration, because they are still children' (and this is a characteristic of children in general).

5.1.4 Reported speech in embedded normative discourse

There is a feature of the embedding in s.75-76 that warrants further explanation. It has to do with reported speech, which often functions at the discourse level rather than sentence level, as Larson (1978) clearly demonstrated. When a normative comment is embedded in a narrative surface structure, which is indicated here by the quotative formulas, there is no truth requirement for the quotative formulas themselves. That is, the reported speech need not actually have been spoken out loud to anyone. It is often just the unarticulated conclusion or evaluation that the speaker had formerly come to, but it is given as a quote. It appears that in the Ga'dang oral society a citation of what someone said (even if it was said by the same person who is citing it) functions to authenticate the utterance, just as a citation of a written work does in a literate society.

There is a clear example of this normative function of reported speech in s.16 of the Appendix, in which Sanggoon prefaces a quoted sentence as a reported thought ('this is what I thought before') and finishes the same sentence with the reported speech formula ('I said'). There are other examples where speakers claim to have said something with no indication to whom it was said. (In normal Ga'dang narrative discourse, the addressee of any reported speech is explicitly identified or can readily be construed from context.)

Thus, in s.77 it is unclear whether Andits is claiming to have told Paregaru the words quoted in s.75-76, or to have told Paregaru the whole anecdote of s.72-74, or both. (It cannot include s.71, since Paregaru was a part of that discussion and did not need to have it reported to him.) This distinctive function in normative discourse of reported speech as a citation to authenticate makes s.77 ambiguous. But the ambiguity is not problematic, since whether or not Andits said it to Paregaru or drew an unspoken conclusion would have no bearing on its use here as an evaluative comment embedded in narrative.

A shortage of verbs to describe states of mind might account for the use of the verb *kun* 'to say' when the content of the quote was thought and not said. But there is no such shortage: There is the verb *dandam* 'to think' used by Sanggoon in s.16, and there is the verb *arig* 'mistakenly think', used when the opinion held proves to be erroneous. Andits used *arig* in s.120 and s.124-25: 'I thought that we were to summarize all that we had studied. Not so.'

There are also numerous nonverbal expressions to describe states of mind or emotion. Using *uray* 'will, volition' in the prepositional phrase 'in my will' means 'I had it in mind to ...' or 'I intended to ...' (cf. s.111). The word *nakam* 'mind, heart' has a multitude of uses, most of them metaphorical, to describe states of mind or emotion, for example, s.218: 'I really felt that (insulted) in my mind/heart'. Other common expressions are *antu ino nagyan so nakam ku* 'that is what was in my mind' ('that's what I was thinking') and *antu ino gakkad ino nakam ku* 'that was the purpose of my mind' ('that was my purpose').

Thus the use of the reported speech formula (with the verb *kun* 'to say') when the content of the reported speech is an evaluation not necessarily spoken to anyone prior to its being reported, is a feature of the grammar of normative discourse in Ga'dang (see "dialogue paragraphs" in sec. 5.2.2). This normative use of reported speech differs from that in narrative not only because no addressee is identifiable, but also because there is no specification of the time and place of the reported speech. Narrative discourse provides spatial and temporal settings and identifies participants, including the addressee of any reported speech.

5.2 Classification of dialogue

Before further discussion about the theory of normative discourse and its application to the analysis of Ga'dang texts, it would be useful to determine where dialogue fits into the classification of texts, and what effect it might have on our theory.

Surprisingly, what seems like a simple matter of definition turns out to be a substantial theoretical issue. Is dialogue a proper object of discourse analysis or textlinguistics? Or does it belong to the study of behavior? And does dialogue involve just two people, as the morphology of the word implies, or does it include the verbal interaction of any number of people? If more than two participants are allowed (by definition) in dialogue, then what if people come and go during the course of a discussion? What would be the boundaries of the discourse or text in that case?

5.2.1 Two-participant minimum in discourse

Paul Ricoeur, in a lecture given at the University of Dallas (McDermott Series, April 22, 1981), observed that books on a library shelf are potential texts. They become actual texts when somebody reads them. This is true for any kind of linguistic interaction, spoken or written. It is required by definition for any datum identified as a discourse or text that it involve at least two people. There must always be a speaker-and-hearer, writer-and-reader, or encoder-and-decoder. There may be more than one of each, but there must be at least one of each. It is theoretically possible that there is no other hearer/reader/decoder than the textlinguist himself (though this would be unusual), but there still must be one in order for the datum to qualify as a text. In other words, any text or discourse necessarily involves communication, which in turn logically implies an encoding of meaning and an interpretation of meaning.

This is a fine distinction similar to the question of whether a tree falling in the forest makes noise if no one hears it. In fact, the tree falling cannot be a datum for any analysis unless there is an observer or instruments that record the event and later provide an observer or analyst with the information.

This brings up the question of whether one person can utter a monologue and then analyze it as a text or discourse himself. He can do so only by recording it (if only in memory, though this is limited), and then bracketing the recorded text as an object of analysis. In this case it does become a text, since the encoder has now become the decoder as well. Of course, few people are likely to analyze texts that they produce for no one but themselves. In such a case, the analyst is "being two people," both encoder and decoder, assuming a position toward the text as though it were produced by another and he were the receptor. A poet or author could also assume such a position toward a manuscript he had produced.

5.2.2 Dialogue versus monologue

Since monologue involves two people, it cannot be distinguished from dialogue simply on the basis of one participant versus two or more participants. The difference is that in monologue discourse, one person does all the talking, and one or more people just listen, whereas in dialogue, two or more people take turns talking and listening. Pike (1967:442) posits the unit *utterance-response* as the minimum unit in conversation: "As its crucial component it would contain an exchange between two speakers." Since this is true of written (reported) dialogue as well as live conversation, I use the term *dialogue* to refer to either written or oral texts.

This definition suggests the possibility of treating dialogue as merely a concatenated string of monologues. But while the feature of taking turns to speak serves to distinguish the two, it is certainly not the only distinction. Other features are unique to dialogue, such as cataphoric or anaphoric reference to other utterances of the dialogue. In monologue, on the other hand, there are no other utterances in the immediate linguistic context to anticipate or refer back to. Furthermore, in dialogue we frequently find fragmentary sentences that would be unacceptable in monologue but are acceptable in the context of other utterances in dialogue.

Longacre comments further on the relationship of monologue and dialogue (1983:44):

> The importance of dialogue is not just that it helps us explain a few apparent anomalies. Rather we must view dialogue as a basic function of language:

viz., conversational interchange between people, communication. Seen from this point of view it is monologue that is the special development. Prolonged self-expression in which one person speaks to a group of people who take the passive role of hearers is clearly a secondary development.

In the same context, Longacre posits the units of monologue to be morpheme, stem, word, phrase, clause, sentence, paragraph, and discourse. The units of dialogue are utterance, exchange, dialogue paragraph, and dramatic discourse.

However, the rule of thumb in the analysis of the Ga'dang text in the following chapters is that *utterance* is a unit between paragraph and discourse. That is, an utterance is composed of one or more paragraphs, and a discourse is composed of one or more utterances. Utterance is "the unit bounded by what a single speaker says" (Longacre 1983:43). Thus a monologue discourse is *ipso facto* a single utterance. If the speaker in his monologue reports a number of utterances spoken by a number of other people, these are reported utterances embedded within the utterance of the present speaker. It is not uncommon for linguistic units to have embedded in them other units of the same level or a higher level of the hierarchy. Thus a paragraph may embed within a sentence in reported speech, and an utterance or whole discourse may embed within a paragraph. If all are being spoken (reported) by one person, they constitute a monologue.

In other words, the monologue is a single utterance by one person, although it has reported utterances embedded in it. Dialogue discourse necessarily has two or more utterances spoken by two or more speakers.

Dialogue paragraphs in the Ga'dang text occur only in the context of reported speech. In this context, the reported dialogue is somewhat idealized or regularized, and some of the interutterance cohesives are omitted. The reported dialogue is then made to cohere by use of the quotative formula: the verb *kun* 'say' plus noun or pronoun. The dialogue reported within the boundaries of a single paragraph has a conceptual unity.

In the actual dialogue of the appended Ga'dang informal litigation (i.e., not reported dialogue), all utterances manifest some surface characteristics of paragraph boundaries, indicating that they are not part of a paragraph begun in another utterance, except for seven of the briefest utterances (s.171, 182, 218, 315, 347, 362, and 367). These contain none of the features of paragraph boundary, so there is no evidence to support the claim that they are separate paragraphs. In fact, these utterances are "back channel responses" (Hall 1983, chap. 3). They are unique in that they are not considered to be a speech turn, since the floor has not been relinquished during a back channel response. Examples of back channel responses are murmurs of assent, sentence completions, verbatim repetitions of a word or phrase, or brief paraphrase. These could be considered to be a continuation of the paragraph begun in the previous utterance. But since back channel responses are not considered to be speech turns, such an utterance, paired with the preceding one, is not a real conversational exchange.

Exchanges have notional structures such as question-and-answer, proposal-response, or remark-evaluation (Longacre 1983:49). In the text of the Appendix, each constituent of such notional exchanges has some surface structure feature indicating that it is a paragraph in its own right. For example, the answer in s.170 begins with a preposed noun phrase, a paragraph-initial structure (see sec. 7.3.2), as does the response constituent of s.263, and the evaluation of s.354. Each of these examples is in an exchange relationship with the previous sentence or sentences. Thus an exchange necessarily involves two or more utterances, but each utterance in an exchange is also a paragraph in its own right, except in the case of a reported exchange.

The units of discourse in Ga'dang are morpheme, stem, word, phrase, clause, sentence, paragraph, utterance, exchange, and dialogue. A dialogue discourse potentially makes use of all the levels of the hierarchy. The monologue, on the other hand, makes use of the levels up to the utterance level, although, as mentioned, it is possible to embed the units of dialogue discourse within monologue discourse.

The term *normative discourse* serves as well for dialogue as for monologue since each—a whole dialogue or a whole monologue—is of a particular notional discourse type (in this case, normative) and the whole unit has a macrostructure, the constituents of which are marked in the surface structure. The individual utterances of the dialogue discourse unit are constrained by rules imposed by the grammar of the unit as a whole. No utterance is a discourse in itself, but each is a part of the whole linguistic unit, the normative discourse.

In this study it will be demonstrated that an entire, lengthy dialogue discourse in Ga'dang that is normative in notional structure may be skewed at some points in surface structure, that is, encoded in the surface structure of other discourse types. The explanation of why this skewing takes place is a part of the description of the structure of normative dialogue. Skewing and embedding are characteristic of dialogue (see sec. 5.1.3), making dialogue (usually) a composite of text types.

To summarize, the crucial difference between monologue and dialogue (Pike 1967:442) is that more than one person speaks in dialogue (notwithstanding the unusual case—usually in written texts—of one person conducting a dialogue with himself, behaving as though he were two people; cf. sec. 5.2.1). Dialogue is very different from monologue, especially in that the latter has less embedding and skewing; in other words, monologue is more consistently one text type throughout.

5.2.3 Dialogue and the taxonomy of texts

There is a fixed social relationship between speaker and addressee(s) in monologue. If that relationship requires some skewing between the notional structure that the speaker intends and the surface structure used to encode the intention, the skewing will be in effect through the whole monologue.

In dialogue, however, the surface structure of different utterances can be severally classified as narrative, procedural, expository, or normative (normative being more inclusive than Longacre's behavioral category; see sec. 5.3). It follows that the grammatical characteristics of the respective surface structure discourse types can be identified in dialogue, even when embedding or skewing occurs. The dialogue unit itself may be of a single notional discourse type (e.g., normative, as is the text in the Appendix), even though some utterances or parts of utterances within it may have the surface structure of another type. These embedded or skewed surface structures are filling slots in the macrostructure of the normative discourse or in one of its constituents.

There are ways of recognizing that a particular surface discourse type is a skewed realization of a different notional type. At times the means of determining the skewing are surface features, such as the embedding or sandwiching of one discourse type within grammatical features of another discourse type. At other times, the clues that indicate skewing are pragmatic, to be found in the situational context.

5.2.4 Dialogue in its broader context

Dialogue fits into the broader context of a theory of human action and behavior. Pike (1967:32) suggested that "language events and non-language events may constitute structurally equivalent members of classes of events which may constitute interchangeable parts within larger unit events."

Any linguistic communication necessarily involves at least two people, speaker and hearer(s), and it is less natural for one to do all the talking and the other(s) to do all the listening. Dialogue is the most natural unit of linguistic communication; thus Pike (1978) views performative interaction (dialogue) as the appropriate starting point for the analysis of verbal behavior. Longacre elaborates (1983:337):

> It is probably misleading to think of language as embedded in simple fashion within the still broader context of human behavior. Verbal activity does not embed in nonverbal activity like an egg in a paper bag. Rather, to a large degree man's verbal activity informs, interprets, and structures his nonverbal activity. Patterns of human activity are very complex and language cannot be left out of account at any turn. At any event, however, any given stretch of verbal activity must be considered to be part of broader situational and

behavioral patterns which are not exclusively and often not even primarily verbal.

The idea of developing a more comprehensive theory of actions of two or more people that would hold equally well for verbal or nonverbal actions has been explored and formalized by Nowakowska (1979). The primitive concepts of the theory are elementary actions, concatenated actions (strings of actions), duration, idling, outcomes of strings of actions, and results of pairs of strings of actions. By assigning a symbol to each of these primitive concepts, Nowakowska is able to give an algebraic representation of any dialogue. There are some rules in the theory that idealize dialogue compared with normal conversation; for example, one speaker is not allowed to interfere with another speaker. Each participant must be either acting or idling (i.e., speaking or listening). The theory also requires that for a string of utterances to constitute a dialogue each subsequent utterance must be "significantly" related to the preceding utterances. (Sequences of utterances not so related do not qualify as dialogues.) Overt signals of this type of relation between utterances are called dialogue markers, "those phrases which refer to earlier or subsequent parts of dialogue, announce the inference, etc." (Nowakowska 1979:197).

Certainly this is not all there is to be said about dialogue and a theory of actions (see van Dijk 1977, chap. 6), but it does demonstrate the possibility of viewing dialogue from the perspective of a more generic theory of human actions, actions which may occur simultaneously or in sequence, which have beginnings and end points, and which have resulting states different from initial states. (In the case of dialogue, the differing end state is likely to be cognitive or behavioral, rather than a physical state.)

Some of Nowakowska's concepts (though not the algebraic formulation) will be employed in chapter 7 in the discussion of the beginnings and endings of the litigation unit and the units of which it is comprised and in the discussion of the duration of the units, the noninterference feature (i.e., turn taking; see Hall 1983, chap. 3), the initial state of anger and fragmentation, and the achievement of the end state, namely, consensus.

The fact that this verbal behavior unit restores consensus, social order, and generally acceptable attitudes and behavior among the participants is seen as a verification of Longacre's statement that "to a large degree man's verbal activity informs, interprets, and structures his nonverbal activity" (1983:337). The normative function of the Ga'dang litigation is very clear. It helps to structure societal relationships and interactions. Indeed much of dialogue has a normative function, in structuring society, persuading people to conform to the already existing structure, or perpetuating the status quo (see sec. 5.3).

5.2.5 Dialogue and normative discourse

Dialogue is the most natural vehicle of normative discourse. There are few situations, at least in an oral society, in which normative monologue is appropriate; and since orality is prior to literacy, both logically and chronologically (Derrida et al. notwithstanding), there is a sense in which dialogue is most natural for normative discourse.

Hall (1983:23-25) demonstrates that for the Western Subanon all "judicial behavior," accusation, or argumentation is cognitively subsumed under the generic term of *bintung* 'dialogue'. Rosaldo (1980:188) reports that in the northern Philippines the usual way of negotiating anger (normative behavior) is through the *purung*, a public oratorical debate. Kawashima (1973:59, 62) views rule by consensus and mediation (a particular type of dialogue) as the primary means of dispute settlement (normative behavior) in Japan. There, as in many countries where shame is a significant cultural value (Noble 1975, chap. 11), mediation is a preferred mode of normative behavior. Goody and Watt (1968:48-53) assert that in a nonliterate (oral) society "the cultural tradition functions as a series of interlocking face-to-face conversations," and that "the reasons which Plato, or his spokesman Socrates, gives for holding dialectic to be the true method of pursuing essential knowledge are very close to the picture [given by Goody and Watt] of the transmission of the cultural tradition in oral society." Thus we expect that in an oral society normative discourse (one of the main functions of which is to transmit or perpetuate the cultural tradition) will typically be in the form of dialogue rather than monologue.

In a literate society, normative essays are not uncommon; they may be, in fact, the most common type of normative discourse. The sermon genre is a normative monologue, but it is probably a consequence of literacy and has more in common with literacy than with orality. Many sermons are "the speaking of what is written to be spoken as if not written" (Gregory and Carroll 1978:37-47). There is, of course, no such genre in a nonliterate society; there is no such genre in Ga'dang, which is just becoming a literate society. (There is a sermon genre developing, but it has more in common with oral discourse than with written.) In the following section, it will be noted which of the subtypes of normative discourse may naturally be encoded in monologue form in Ga'dang.

5.3 Characteristics of normative discourse

This section describes primarily the notional characteristics of normative discourse. Surface structure features will be discussed in chapter 7.

5.3.1 The communication situation

Jones (1983:12-15) presents a taxonomy of communication situations, differentiating sixteen types of language communication based on their distinctive features. He suggests four classificatory features and posits a different type of communication for each of the sixteen possible combinations of the presence or absence (+ or -) of the four features. The features are: face-to-face encounter (face), use of the vocal-auditory channel (voc), turn taking (turn), and spontaneity (spon). All of these features would be present (+) in Ga'dang litigation, although it would be slightly less spontaneous than many casual conversations, for the participants in the litigation arrive with some rough idea of what they might say, at least for their opening statements. So the Ga'dang litigation would be 4 + according to Jones's criteria, but this would not serve to distinguish it from almost every other type of linguistic behavior in Ga'dang.

Two exceptions in Ga'dang to the 4 + type are the narration of folktales and "advising," an infrequent speech event usually directed to young people about to be married. These are minus turn taking and at the low end of the scale with regard to spontaneity. Folklore is at the low end of the scale with regard to a normative component. (Monologue discourse thus plays a small role in Ga'dang normative behavior, which has weighty implications for translation of normative texts.)

Almost all normative discourse in Ga'dang (and perhaps any oral society) would be of the 4 + type (face-to-face conversation/dialogue). Thus, other features of the communication situation would have to be referred to in order to distinguish litigation from less formal argumentation, and to distinguish any eristic discourse from nonconflict normative conversations. Designated versus nondesignated turn taking (Hall 1983, chap. 2) would be one possible distinguishing criterion. The presence of a community leader at the discussion (one not directly involved in the conflict) would be another.

In a literate and technological society, there are many possibilities for normative discourse other than the 4 + type. They include lectures, sermons, moral and ethical books, essays, and monologues on radio or television.

We may conclude that if a taxonomy of communication situations is to be a viable approach to discourse analysis, a different one may be needed for an oral society than for a literate society. More likely, any proposed taxonomy would function only as a limited etic grid, and the emically contrastive features of the communication situation in a particular speech community would have to be identified for each language studied.

5.3.2 Agent and addressee orientation

Normative discourse is oriented to the addressee. Furthermore, since some attitude or action is being recommended or commanded to the addressee, it is also agent oriented. The addressee is to be the agent of the commanded action, though the action may be only cognitive. *Agent* is being used in a generic sense, since, for example, if the addressee were commanded to go to sleep, he would be an experiencer, sleep being something experienced passively, rather than actively. Thus agent orientation is intended to include the roles of actor, knower, experiencer, and other similar roles.

Addressee and agent orientation are notional structures. The usual surface realizations in normative discourse are second person pronouns. Other surface realizations are possible, however, especially in the case of mitigation (see. sec. 7.5).

5.3.3 Contingent succession and projected time

Actions and agents are notional requirements of the command elements of normative discourse. But contingent succession is not a requirement. A number of commands can be strung together with no requirement as to the order of performing the actions.

Projected time is a notional requirement, since it is not logically possible for a speaker to command someone to do something that the speaker knows is already done. He may utter a surface imperative in such a case, but he is doing something other than commanding, such as joking. Even with the command "Continue what you are doing" there is plus projected time, because the temporal range of the action commanded is "from this point in time forward." In fact, in the absence of some explicit or pragmatic constraint on the time of performing the action, the default (i.e., assumed) time frame of a command is "starting now." The default end point would be at the end of the time that it takes to do the action. In some commands, such as "believe this," there is no terminus.

5.3.4 Normative component in all communication

There is some normative component in all linguistic behavior, if only to maintain the social status quo or effect a minute cognitive change in the addressee. All linguistic communication could be ranked on a scale or cline of degrees of normativity. Typically, narrative would be the least normative, and procedural, expository, and normative would be respectively higher on the scale of normativity. Subtypes of normative discourse would fill out the high end of the scale, with direct command or imperative at the top. Folklore is at the low end of the scale with regard to a normative component. It is not used to command or exhort, but rather to reinforce cultural values implicitly.

Scientific papers, though idealized as expository ("it is true that ..."), are in fact often normative ("you should believe that ..."). Although they have the surface structure of objective, expository statements of fact or observation, which would be midrange on the scale of normativity, they may really be very near the top, especially in the context of a theoretical clash between separate schools of thought within a discipline. Of course, it is also possible in such a context for the so-called scientific papers to become normative even in surface structure, for example, as tirades against another point of view rife with evaluative terminology. Without a normative component, scientific papers would probably not be written. Writers want readers to see things from their point of view, and believe as they do.

A curious paradox in science is the case of the advocates of biological determinism or mechanism, who hold that human cognition and behavior are determined by biological or environmental factors beyond one's control. How do these people account for the fact that they write articles and books to influence other people to adopt their point of view? And surely these people would not defend their views vigorously and persuasively to those who did not believe them, would they?

5.3.5 Mitigation of normative discourse

A discussion of mitigation necessarily involves some discussion of surface structure features, as well as social and political relationships (deference) that call for mitigation. Some of these things will be mentioned here, then elaborated in following chapters.

Two methods of mitigation are frequently used: (1) the disguising of normative discourse in other text types (for example, narrative or expository; and (2) the disguising of the addressee in something other than or more generic than a direct reference to the person.

The first of the two methods also includes the selection of a subtype of normative discourse (see sec. 5.5) that is a less direct realization of the command or exhortation, that is, a subtype which would directly realize an intention lower on the scale of normativity than the speaker actually intends. For example, an evaluation ("it would be good if X") often encodes an implicit exhortation or command ("do X"). This type of realization (skewing to a less normative surface structure) could be a portmanteau realization of the normative intention and an attitude of deference (Martin and Colburn 1972, chap. 8), if the speaker is inferior in social rank to the addressee.

The second type is also very common: the use of a first person dual or inclusive pronoun (e.g., "we should do X"). Since almost any speaker believes himself to be right and not in need of exhortation, this usage is a mitigation in the interest of social eudaemonism or harmony. It may also be a realization of deference.

5.4 Notional structure

The discussion of the notional structure of normative discourse includes not only semantic information, but also features of the communication situation, such as speaker's intention and social relationships. The interaction of a speaker's intentions and his awareness of his social relationships affects his purpose (what he hopes to accomplish by speaking) and the implicit or explicit performative he chooses to encode that purpose.

5.4.1 Implicit performatives

Usually the performative in normative discourse ("I command/order you ...") is implicit. For the majority of people in any speech community there are few communication situations in which it is socially appropriate to make the performative explicit.

There is also a range or scale of normativity for the performatives of normative discourse. To command is not the only possible intention. To recommend is another possibility. The generic term *prescription* can be used to refer to any notional structure of the order/command/recommend group. Taylor (1961:191) suggests that the basic concept of normative discourse is *ought*. That is adequate for the types already mentioned, but not for other types still to be treated. Any discourse that realizes an intention *primarily* to affect or change the beliefs or behavior of others or to bring about or maintain a desired social structure, is a normative discourse. Other discourse types have normative components and share some of these intentions, but not as the primary speaker's intention.

This more comprehensive definition of normative discourse covers some types of utterances which otherwise are very hard to classify as to discourse type, such as "how ya doin'," "what's happening, bro," and the Ga'dang *wara tabbim?* 'do you have betel nut?' This is the category of social banter. Yawindo's comment, *mabisin akun* 'I'm hungry' (s.265 in the Appendix), when it appeared that the litigation was terminating, is in this category. (It is the approximate equivalent of the idiom "let's buzz off.")

These utterances are intended to maintain (or perhaps improve) the social ambience. They are lighthearted and contribute to relaxed social interaction. If there is an implicit prescriptive element, it would be something like "let's be friends," "let's continue being friends," or (encoded by certain intonation patterns) "let's get to be better friends."

5.4.2 Prescribe or command versus recommend or suggest

Prescribe and *command* are the notional structure of stronger normative discourse. Exhortation and imperative are their direct realizations.

Other surface realizations are possible (see sec. 5.5) due to portmanteau realizations of prescription plus some feature of social setting.

Prescribe and *command* are high on the normativity scale even within normative discourse, while *recommend* is midpoint, and *suggest* or *advocate* would characterize "less tense" normative interactions in which the degree of difference of attitude or opinion between communicator and addressee is perceived by the communicator to be little or none. Perpetuation of the social status quo is one thing that speakers implicitly advocate by means of the social subtype of normative discourse.

5.4.3 Volition and purpose

Discourse expressing the notions of volition or purpose, choice or intention, is difficult to classify. A statement such as "I will be going to the library this afternoon" is narrative with plus projected time as to notional classification, but "I intend to be involved in the peace rally" or "I chose to boycott the lecture" appears to be normative, implying an evaluation of possible courses of action at a given point in time and selection of the one deemed best on some scale of values.

Most evaluative discourse has implicit prescription, which is easy to recognize. "Running is good" is a prescription or recommendation. It is more difficult to recognize any prescriptive element in "I chose to boycott the lecture," but it may involve a prescription: to believe, do, or behave as the speaker did. Thus, explicit statements of volition or purpose are tentatively classified as normative.

5.5 Surface subtypes of normative discourse

The following surface subtypes are presented in the order of least normative to most normative. This is not to say that the speaker's intentions in any given instance are necessarily so ranked. But given no interference from social setting or social relationships, the order would hold.

Since these are surface types, they could as well be numbered as named. In a sense, that would be more accurate, since their names (*social, evaluative, prescriptive,* and *eristic*) refer to their notional structure. However, as with most other surface structure units, it is a useful mnemonic to give them names reflecting the notional structure that they typically realize.

5.5.1 Social

Social banter and any utterance of a purely social, stereotypical nature typically has a question-and-answer or utterance-response structure. It occurs in the context of dialogue or it initiates dialogue.

5.5.2 Evaluative

Evaluative discourse may be monologue in many languages, but in Ga'dang it is customarily dialogue. This discourse subtype tends toward the surface structure of expository discourse, since it is characterized by nonverbal clauses such as 'it is good that ...'. But while the clause itself is nonverbal, the evaluatum is likely to be realized in an embedded relative clause that is verbal, since the beliefs and behavior of others are the expected evaluata of normative discourse; for example, 'it is good that he agrees with me' or 'it is good that he mowed the lawn'. This subtype is typically minus projected time, but not necessarily so, as in 'It would be good if he would mow the lawn', which in terms of surface structure is evaluative.

If there is a parallel of this subtype in Doležel's schema of narrative modalities, it would be the axiological modality—discourse focusing on goodness, badness, or indifference (1975:95).

5.5.3 Prescriptive

Generally, prescriptive discourse may be either dialogue or monologue. Of the four subtypes it is the one most likely to be monologue, or rather one-sided dialogue. In Ga'dang, however, it is typically dialogue, though as the culture moves from orality to literacy, prescriptive discourse may be increasingly monologue.

Prescriptive discourse is the most clearly agent and addressee oriented, minus contingent succession, and plus projected time. Verbal transitive and intransitive clauses, imperative in form, are typical of this subtype. There is a sense in which this is the purest form (the standard) of normative discourse.

Doležel's deontic modality, the notions of obligation, prohibition, and permission (*must, must not, may*), would be realized by prescriptive discourse. The epistemic modality might also be subsumed here (knowledge, belief), but only when combined with the normative component (*should know, should believe*).

5.5.4 Eristic

Eristic discourse is necessarily dialogue. It involves evaluations and prescriptions in conflict (differences of opinion about what has been done or what ought to be done). Argument, dispute, and any type of dialogue dispute resolution fall within this classification. The appended text is an eristic discourse, and its surface structure will be examined in detail in chapter 7.

5.6 Litigation as normative discourse

The Ga'dang litigation is viewed as one unit of verbal behavior because it has an identifiable beginning, nucleus, and end. The beginning occurs when the people assemble at a prearranged place and begin to speak. The end occurs when they stop speaking and disperse. This is an inexact description, since they assemble and disperse in a relaxed fashion over a period of several minutes, during which time casual conversation not a part of the litigation goes on. But this is not problematic. As with any unit of behavior, there is some indeterminacy as to the exact point in time when one activity ends and another begins (Pike 1967:77), and since there are several participants, there is some overlap as to exact arrival times.

Besides this unit of behavior, there is a more clearly defined unit of language, the eristic discourse itself. Linguistic signals marking the beginning and end make precise identification of the boundaries possible (see chap.7).

Whether we focus on the unit of behavior or the unit of language, we are dealing with a normative unit. Vygotsky (1962:4) defines a unit as "a product of analysis which, unlike elements, retains all the basic properties of the whole." Hwang (1981:23) has elaborated on the importance of focus on wholes, since the parts cannot be adequately analyzed or described apart from reference to the whole. Her intention is that we should focus on the whole discourse as a unit of verbal behavior.

The litigation is a unit of normative behavior. Within that unit, the linguistic unit is a normative discourse. At a still lower level, there are utterances within the normative discourse, and there are segments of narrative and expository discourse embedded within these utterances. But the whole unit is normative, and the embedded segments fill slots in the normative discourse, or in the units which make up the normative discourse.

Since we are dealing with a behavioral unit and a linguistic unit, the following chapter examines both sociopolitical structures and linguistic structures. The extralinguistic structures that are a part of the situational context exert some pressures on the form of the linguistic unit and its component parts. Thus the notion of higher-order rules, which we observed to be influencing the morphology and syntax within a discourse, is in effect across the boundary of verbal and nonverbal behavior, and we are forced to examine the larger, nonverbal context of the discourse in order to find explanations for the phenomena within the text. The whole endeavor has become interdisciplinary.

6 The Ga'dang Text: Notional Structure

The text in the Appendix is an instance of Ga'dang folk litigation. From a corpus of several recorded folk litigations (recorded with the permission of persons involved) I selected one to focus on here. Other texts will be referred to at times to give additional evidence for a conclusion or to show contrastive features of other discourse types.

6.1 Units of normative discourse

Two types of discourse are described in sections 6.1.1 and 6.1.2: *tarabbag*, which is of the eristic subtype of normative discourse, and *tuldu*, which is of the prescriptive subtype. (The text of the Appendix is of the eristic type.)

6.1.1 Formal versus informal litigation

The text in the Appendix was referred to by the participants as *tarabbag* 'discussion' or *mattatarabbag*, which literally means 'reciprocally answer'. Buton, the younger of the two litigants, occasionally referred to it as *kasu* 'case', which is the term for a formal litigation. But this *tarabbag* lacked at least one feature of a *kasu*, namely, that the litigants did not have designated advocates, *mallalat*, to represent their interests and do most of the talking for them. Another feature distinguishing this *tarabbag* from a *kasu* is that there was never any consideration of levying a *multa* 'fine/penalty' against one litigant to be awarded to the other.

It may be misleading to describe Andits and Buton, the two who had misunderstandings with each other, as litigants, since this was not a formal case. Nevertheless, the term is used to distinguish them from the other participants in the *tarabbag*.

The main thing that their discussion had in common with formal litigation (*kasu*) was a local official as moderator (barrio councilman Sanggoon). In a similar discussion on another subject and on another occasion with different participants, Sanggoon was again the moderator, and he rendered a decision including a *multa*: one litigant was to give one water buffalo to the other. The decision was considered binding and, as an afterthought, was written on a piece of paper. This case was considered a *kasu* even though the litigants did not have designated advocates, which indicates that the *multa* 'fine/penalty' is a more crucial distinctive feature between the *tarabbag* and the *kasu* than is the *mallalat* 'designated advocate'.

To make it clear that the discussion in the text of the Appendix was not a *kasu*, Sanggoon cited his position as president of the church leaders (s.4). He reminded everyone before rendering his decision and exhortation that the discussion was "according to faith, not according to Ga'dang customs" (s.191-93).

6.1.2 The informal litigation unit

The boundaries of the litigation unit are signalled in the situational context and in the surface structure. One indication of unit boundaries is any change of activity (Pike 1967:77) or change of actor.

In the situational context of Ga'dang litigation, the indication of a unit boundary (marking the beginning of the litigation) is the change of activity of the people involved: They all walked to a prearranged meeting place and sat down. It is true that the prearrangement involved some activity related to the unit being studied, but this is true of any activity we focus on—we could always find it to be related to some larger behavioral context. Thus the prearrangement is just one of several features leading up to and bringing about the litigation unit. The disagreement itself would be another; it is also a logical prerequisite to the litigation.

In the linguistic surface structure, the signal of the beginning of a litigation is a statement by the moderator (the one who regulates the discussion, renders a decision, and tries to effect a consensus). His statement includes the purpose of the discussion or statement of the problem and the names of the principals (anyone aggrieved, accused, or directly involved). This is often in the vocative form, addressing the principals directly and articulating the problem succinctly. Sentence 1 in the Appendix is an example: 'Now then, Buton, whatever is the misunderstanding between the two of you, discuss it'. Another litigation began: 'Our coming here was to talk about ...' and went on to summarize virtually all the publicly known facts about the case, naming everyone involved and telling how they were involved—requiring a sentence of fourteen clauses!

Such straightforwardness is highly unusual among the Ga'dang and in the Philippines in general, where smooth interpersonal relationships are sought at almost any cost and great care is taken not to cause anyone to lose face. One expects a good deal of circumlocution, which is common when addressing issues of a problematic nature or where feelings are at stake. But here in this situation the opening statement is directly to the point, a clear indication that this is the beginning of a particular behavioral and linguistic unit.

In the interest of preserving smooth relationships, no blame is placed in the opening statements. Negative evaluations are studiously avoided at this point and in the early part of the proceedings. They creep in gradually as the discussion progresses. Impartiality is stressed by anyone who can conceivably claim it; the moderator himself must be impartial or at least appear so.

6.1.3 The normative monologue

While the normative monologue (called *tuldu* 'to teach/advise') is not the main focus of this study, it is worth commenting on, because certain features of normative discourse are more clearly identifiable in this text type. A *tulgu* can be given only by a speaker who has considerably more social rank than the potential addressees. A father, grandfather, or patriarch in the clan typically has such rank. The age difference requirement and the kin requirement may be diluted if the advisor has greater social prominence for some other reason, such as wealth or political alliances. But the advisor must still be older.

The occasion for this type of discourse is that the person to be advised is facing some major event in life, such as going away to school or getting married. The content of the discourse revolves around what is acceptable behavior in the new situation. The constituents of the discourse are address, global theme, prescription, and closure.

The address and global theme are always encoded in the first sentence of the discourse, and almost always in noun phrases or subordinate clauses preposed before the main verb of the sentence. This is a marked sentence order in Ga'dang, since the main verb is usually the first constituent.

The address usually consists of a pronoun and either a common noun or a proper noun, for example, *ikkayu abbing* 'you.pl child (you children)', or *ikka Tabbagon* 'you Tabbagon'. This initial pronominal and nominal reference to the addressee results in a triple reference in one sentence, since the addressee will also be referred to pronominally as a suffix to the main verb of the sentence (which will be the prescription, or the first of a series of commands making up the prescription). There may be even more than three references to the addressee in the first sentence, as in the following example (references capitalized):

```
IKKAYU ABBING, gafu se nadatang ino kadokal DAW,  e    umang
you.pl child   because arrived  the bigness yours and go

KAYU   miskwela, amme YU    mangayoyung     so mesturu,
you.pl school    not  you.pl be.disrespectful to teacher

se  antu ino kakkungkul so piskwela'an.
for that the disruption of school
```

'You children, now that you have grown up and are going away to school, don't be disrespectful to the teacher because that disrupts the school.'

In addition to the address ('you children') and the global theme (advice topic: 'your going away to school'), the preceding example gives the first of several exhortations that make up the prescription constituent. This first exhortation displays the structure of the typical "schema of prescription," which has three constituents: projected circumstance; prescription; and justification (cf. the "hortatory point" in Brichoux and Hale 1977:76). In the case of the first prescription in an advice discourse, the projected circumstance is often the global theme or advice topic of the whole discourse (the projected circumstance being any situation that the advisor anticipates and wants to give some advice about). If the prescription constituent has additional command elements (prescriptions), the projected circumstance for these may be the global theme, but usually is some more specific circumstance such as 'concerning your behavior at your boarding place' or 'as you enter the classroom'. If it is the global theme, it is optionally reiterated preceding post-initial prescriptions.

In the few texts of this type that I collected, without exception there was a justification constituent (a supporting argument) following each prescription. If the command was given in the negative (don't do X), then the justification was just a negative evaluation of doing X: *se narakkat inay* 'because that is bad'. Or it gave the expected undesirable result of doing X as a reason for not doing it: *se kakkatawa ka* 'because you will be ridiculed'. However, if the command was a positive one (do X), then the justification was either a positive evaluation (e.g., *se antu ino nalawad a aggangwa* 'because that is good doing/behavior') or else it gave the expected desirable result (e.g., *takesi kunna, mali'nawan a masinggud* 'in order that it will be cleaned away and orderly').

The advice discourse proceeds with a series of instances of the prescription schema, not necessarily in any sequence of generic to specific or vice versa, but linked together in a coherent text by virtue of the fact that they are all related to the initial global theme or advice topic. However, there may be some taxonomy of order of importance of the exhortations in the speaker's mind. Two texts given to young men considering marriage (given by two speakers to two different addressees) provide some evidence of an emic order of importance. One young man was exhorted to be industrious and build a house. The other was exhorted to be industrious, build a house, and not cheat on his wife.

The closure of an advice discourse may be *antwen inoy* 'that's all', which is often used at the end of a monologue or at the end of utterances within a formal or semiformal dialogue. Or the closure may be a sentence explicating the normative intention of the monologue just uttered, as in the following example:

```
Antwen yaw  ino anggam ku a isapit sikwam ikkallay,
that    this the want  I to  say  to.you you.man

ta dingngaggan nu ammin yo   sapitan ku.
so listen      you all  this say    I
```

'This is all I want to say to you, man, so heed all I said.'

The three-part schema of prescription is the unmarked mode of prescription in Ga'dang. It is very standardized in monologue advice texts, which are relatively free of contextual or situational modifying influences. In the eristic discourse in the Appendix, the schema is not always fully realized in the surface structure. There are frequent marked realizations in which the justification is deleted and the projected circumstance is provided by prior context. (These will be discussed in more detail later.) There are some examples of unmarked (complete) realizations of the three-part schema in the Appendix (s.189-90, 320, and 343-36).

6.2 Multiple structures of social organization

The participants in the informal litigation of the Appendix were related to each other in several distinct but partially overlapping organizational structures. In this section the participants will be introduced and their relationships explicated according to each type of structure.

6.2.1 The people involved

The litigation was a semiformal attempt to settle a grievance between two Ga'dang men. The older of the two litigants, Andits, felt that he had been slandered and slighted by the younger one, Buton. Buton contended that he had been unjustly accused and maligned in public and made the brunt of malicious gossip. He claimed that he was innocent of wrong toward Andits. The situation had been heating up as the story made its rounds via the village grapevine. Finally a third party, Baggit, took the initiative and arranged for a local official to hear the case.

In addition to the three men already mentioned, four others were involved: Sanggoon, Laka, Yawindo, and Bayombong. Sanggoon was the closest thing to a magistrate in the proceedings. Laka was a sort of "magistrate emeritus," being the eldest man present. (He did not personally conduct the hearing for reasons explained in sec. 6.2.4.) Yawindo and Bayombong were pseudojurists, who through their kibitzing contributed to the reaching of a decision in the case and persuading all parties to accept it.

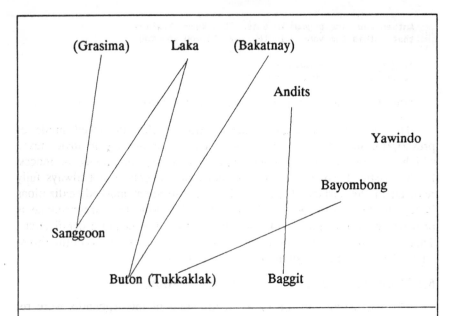

Key

Laka. Age 64. Husband of Grasima, former boyfriend of Bakatnay, father of Sanggoon and Buton, distant relative of all others.

Andits. Age 51. Father of Baggit, cousin of Bayombong, uncle of Tukkaklak and therefore Buton's uncle-in-law (a close relation).

Yawindo. Age 45. Distant relative of all others.

Bayombong. Age 40. Father of Tukkaklak, father-in-law of Buton.

Sanggoon. Age 37. Son of Laka and Grasima, half-brother of Buton, related to Andits but one generation younger, so refers to him as uncle.

Buton. Age 26. Son of Laka and Bakatnay, half-brother of Sanggoon.

Baggit. Age 22. Son of Andits, a distant in-law of Buton.

(Names in parentheses are persons not involved in the actual hearing of the case, but they show relevant relationships; lines have been drawn on the chart only to show relationships of direct descent.)

Fig. 6. Kinship relations of people involved in the litigation

6.2.2 Structure of kinship relationships

The participants in the litigation, Andits, Buton, Baggit, Sanggoon, Laka, Yawindo, and Bayombong, were related to each other by at least three partially overlapping and sometimes conflicting structures of social organization, namely, kinship, political, and ecclesiastical structures. Each structure has its own hierarchy and can be represented in something like an organizational flow chart.

The traditional Ga'dang social organization was a mixture of kinship and chiefdom structures, since many extended family units inhabiting remote areas of the forest had a kinship organization in which the patriarch of the group was the leader. In such a structure, Laka would be at the top of the flow chart, being the oldest and related to most, if not all, of the other participants. Figure 6 displays the kinship relationships between the people involved in the litigation.

6.2.3 Political structure

Traditional Ga'dang chiefdoms existed in a few areas that had a very good water supply and good available land for fifty to a hundred families. With this many families, there would be two or more men with approximately equal claim to leadership by the criteria of age and kinship relations, so other criteria were used to select a *patul* 'chief'. The *patul* would be the one with the optimum combination of verbal and physical prowess, the latter being measured by ability as a warrior-headhunter.

In this structure, Laka was the village chief about thirty years ago, when he was in his prime. If the pure chiefdom structure were still in effect, Laka might still be at the top, or at least above the other participants

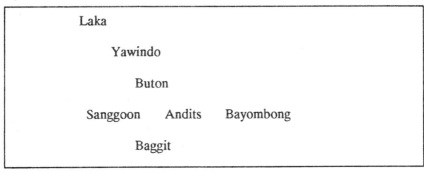

Fig. 7. Hyothetical authority hierarchy by traditional Ga'dang criteria, premium on physical prowess

in this litigation, though by now he would be barely hanging on. His leadership would be on the wane, and his most likely successor would be Yawindo, who, though he lacks the verbal prowess of Sanggoon or Andits, excels in physical strength.

There is a vestige of this type of structure still remaining among the Ga'dang people, and it is evident on occasion when men like Yawindo flex their muscle, figuratively and literally. As a result, Yawindo is treated with a little more respect than would otherwise be due him. Figure 7 displays this structure (with some guesswork on my part).

The other criterion of leadership potential in the traditional Ga'dang chiefdom, that of verbal prowess, has now become more important because of the transition currently taking place from chiefdom to state. In the structure that the Ga'dangs are moving toward, Sanggoon would be at the top of the hierarchical chart; he has a natural verbal prowess and the most education. Because of these qualifications he was coerced into running for municipal councilman in recent local elections, and he won easily. (There are one or two councilmen elected in each barrio of the municipality, and they serve on the council of the municipal mayor. They have authority to settle civil cases in their own barrio.)

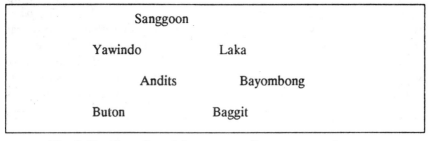

*Fig. 8. Ranking of participants according to present-day
political clout in the municipality*

Figure 8 displays the ranking of the seven participants in the recorded case according to their present-day political clout. Sanggoon is at the top, even though he is one of the younger men and probably has the least physical strength of any, being the smallest man in the group. Yawindo ranks high in this structure because of his friendships with men who hold public office in the municipality. Laka ranks high for similar reasons and because of his position of leadership in the past. The two very young men, Buton and Baggit, have virtually no political clout.

6.2.4 The church organizational structure

The participants are socially related to each other in a loosely structured church organization with several appointed leaders or elders (Andits
and Buton being two of them) and a president chosen by the elders from
among their own number (Sanggoon). Sanggoon is at the top of this organizational chart. He is also qualified to hear a case by virtue of his political position as a municipal councilman. However, the particular case in
the Appendix was billed as a function of the church organization, so
Sanggoon officiated since he was the president of the elders. The structure
of the proceedings was nearly identical (except for the *multa* feature—cf.
sec. 6.1.1) to that of two or three other recorded cases not involving church
members, in which Sanggoon was acting as councilman.

Sanggoon: president of the elders.

Andits, Buton: two of the elders.

Laka, Yawindo, Baggit: church members.

Bayombong: not a church member.

Fig. 9. Ranking according to church organizational structure

The overlap of traditional structures, recent political structures, and
church structures is evident in the text of the Appendix. Thus Sanggoon
felt obliged to explain (s.193) why he was the one officiating instead of his
father, Laka, who should have been officiating according to traditional
Ga'dang structure. The occasional references to operating according to
church structure (s.4, s.192, s.267) also distinguish the present discussion
from those that would be under the jurisdiction of the present-day political structure. It was important to make this distinction, since the situational context left it ambiguous. Sanggoon was qualified to officiate in either
church or political structure; but had the discussion been a function of the
latter, there likely would have been a *multa* imposed (settlement of money
or goods).

Figure 9 displays the organizational structure of the church as it relates to the ranking of the seven participants in the *tarabbag*.

According to church structure, Laka would be at the bottom, as would Baggit. But because of the fact of overlapping structures of social organization, Laka is treated with more respect even in purely church-related functions. This is readily observable in the case under consideration, in which monologues by Baggit come early in the case, are brief, and are primarily narrative though with an explanatory and evaluative intention. Baggit does inject a few brief remarks of the hortatory type, but these are largely ignored by the other discussants. Laka, on the other hand, reserves his contributions almost until the end, and then he articulates what is already obvious and not likely to be refuted. Laka's comments and exhortations (his speech is the closest to pure hortatory discourse) are heard carefully, and they elicit considerable response. The only person who treats Laka's comments in a somewhat cavalier manner is Andits, who is the only one present who is of Laka's generation, though a few years younger. Andits occasionally interrupts with a very audible yawn, hoping to encourage all to bring the case to a close.

Clearly the members of a community cannot totally divorce themselves from the influence of a different structure of social organization even when involved in a function predominantly organized by the church structure. Recognition of this is extremely important in text analysis. It accounts for the appropriateness of Laka's exhortations and the response to them. It explains the inappropriateness of Baggit's hortatory discourse in this context. Whatever exhorting or persuading that Baggit hopes to do needs to be veiled in expository or narrative discourse without explicit exhortations and imperatives.

6.3 Constituents of the normative discourse

In this section I focus on the unit as a whole and its function in the larger context of social interaction. The discourse level constituents will also be presented, both notional and surface structure, as well as the function of each constituent in the context of the discourse.

6.3.1 Initial state and final state

Initial state and final state are the first and last constituents of the litigation unit respectively (see sec. 6.1.2). They are realized in the surface structure by opening and closure and will be discussed in section 7.1. The initial state includes the disharmony and the reason for it encapsulated as a statement of the problem. It also includes the notion of what is to be done about it, which surfaces as a statement of purpose, such as 'We are here to discuss this matter.'

The social situation immediately preceding and still present at the beginning of the discussion recorded in the Appendix was one of social fragmentation—lack of harmony. The greatest disharmony existed between the two litigants, Andits and Buton. However, in this small, close-knit, oral society in which virtually everyone is related to everyone else, disharmony between two individuals had resulted in general disharmony. Such disagreements are not infrequent, yet the society abhors the disharmony and strives for social eudaemonism—the ethic of group happiness (Black and Mileski 1973:2)—or consensus (Christopher 1983:55).

The *tarabbag* 'discussion, informal litigation' is the mechanism employed to get from the undesirable initial state of disharmony to the desirable end state of consensus. The end state of the *tarabbag* of the Appendix was ostensibly consensus.

Ideally, consensus is the state to be achieved at the end of a discussion, one that will last from that point forward (at least with respect to the issues of the discussion). However, this ideal is seldom if ever achieved.

Notice that in the discussion, Buton, the younger litigant, does not speak in the last twenty-four out of the total thirty-nine utterances (see fig. 10). Thus he fails to explicitly endorse the consensus reached late in the discussion. This raises some question as to whether the consensus is unanimous and likely to last. On the other hand, his nonparticipation toward the end may be explained by his youth. (Neither Buton nor Baggit, the two youngest, participate toward the end.) Or it may be explained by the fact that he was somewhat cowed, having borne the brunt of the negative evaluations. Buton had included some conciliatory statements of good faith in his earlier utterances, especially in utterance 15 (UT15) of the *tarabbag*, in which he was somewhat self-depreciating and remorseful. These comments indicated that he was willing to accept reprimand and augured well for a lasting consensus.

6.3.2 The medial notional constituents

The medial constituents in the text of the Appendix (and other eristic normative dialogues as well) are: grievance; conciliation; evaluation; prescription; consensus. Each constituent within the discourse functions to contribute to the formation and longevity of the consensus, the purpose being to thoroughly persuade participants so that the problem and disharmony will not resurface. Often this purpose is not achieved, and a subsequent *tarabbag* is required to rehash the issues and try to lay them to rest.

The first post-initial constituent is *grievance*. The essential feature of grievance is negative evaluation. Accusation is certainly included, being a type of negative evaluation in which the evaluation may be left implicit, as in 'he did/said X', with no author comment to say that it was bad to do/say X. The speaker assumes that all others will also make a negative evaluation of X. The incidents or problems referred to will function as the topics

UT	S	Utterance Length	Location	Speaker
1	2	x	1-2	Bayombong
2	26	xxxxxx	3-28	Sanggoon
3	13	xxx	*	Yawindo
4	137	xxxxxxxxxxxxxxxxxxxxxxxxxxxxxxxxxxxx	29-165	Andits
5	141	xxxxxxxxxxxxxxxxxxxxxxxxxxxxxxxxxxxxx	*	Buton
6	1	x	166	Sanggoon
7	3	x	167-69	Buton
8	1	x	170	Andits
9	1	x	171	Buton
10	92	xxxxxxxxxxxxxxxxxxxxxxx	*	Andits
11	10	xxx	172-81	Sanggoon
12	1	x	182	Yawindo
13	8	xx	183-90	Andits
14	1	x	*	Baggit
15	34	xxxxxxxxx	*	Buton
16	16	xxxx	*	Bayombong
17	27	xxxxxxx	191-217	Sanggoon
18	1	x	218	Andits
19	24	xxxxxx	219-43	Sanggoon
20	1	x	*	Andits
21	48	xxxxxxxxxxxx	*	Baggit
22	19	xxxxx	244-62	Andits
23	2	x	263-64	Baggit
24	1	x	265	Yawindo
25	64	xxxxxxxxxxxxxxxx	266-329	Sanggoon
26	1	x	330	Andits
27	16	xxxx	331-46	Laka
28	1	x	347	Yawindo
29	1	x	348	Laka
30	1	x	349	Sanggoon
31	4	xx	350-53	Laka
32	1	x	354	Yawindo
33	4	x	355-58	Andits
34	3	x	359-61	Laka
35	1	x	362	Andits
36	4	x	363-66	Laka
37	1	x	367	Andits
38	2	x	368-69	Yawindo
39	1	x	370	Sanggoon

UT = utterance number (actual sequential order)
S = number of sentences in the utterance
Utterance length = approximately one x for each 4 sentences
Location = sentence numbers in the Appendix (* = omitted)

Fig. 10. Display of Ga'dang litigation utterances

UT	S	Location	Discourse function
1	2	1-2	False start, statement of purpose
2	26	3-28	M. purpose, evaluation, impartiality, start
3	13	*	Paraphrase of purpose, evaluation, impartiality
4	137	29-165	L. grievances, evaluation
5	141	*	L2. rebuttal attempt (defense), grievance
6	1	166	M. progression signal
7	3	167-69	L2. conciliation
8	1	170	L. conciliation
9	1	171	L2. conciliation, agreement
10	92	*	L. reject defense, refocus grievance
11	10	172-81	M. evaluate, begin to focus blame
12	1	182	Evaluation endorsed
13	8	183-90	L. endorsement, show of good faith
14	1	*	Extraneous
15	34	*	L2. plea of innocence, show of good faith
16	16	*	Evaluation, exhortation
17	27	191-217	M. judicial evaluation, prescription
18	1	218	L. press advantage
19	24	219-43	M. decision and supporting arguments (persuade)
20	1	*	L. motion to close
21	48	*	Reiterate, conciliate, in defense of L2
22	19	244-62	L. refocus the evaluation, citing public values
23	2	263-64	motion to close
24	1	265	Social banter
25	64	266-329	M. prescriptive peak, decision elaborated, argued
26	1	330	L. motion to close
27	16	331-46	P. evaluation, prescription
28	1	347	Paraphrase, toward consensus
29	1	348	P. evaluation, consensus
30	1	349	M. amplification paraphrase, consensus
31	4	350-53	P. amplification, prescription, consensus
32	1	354	Strong endorsement, consensus
33	4	355-58	L. reiterate grievance, put it to rest
34	3	359-61	P. positive evaluation of state of harmony
35	1	362	L. agreement, consensus
36	4	363-66	P. positive evaluation, closure, elicit consensus
37	1	367	L. confirm consensus, closure
38	2	368-69	Closure, social banter
39	1	370	M. closure, social banter

UT = utterance number (actual sequential order)
S = number of sentences in the utterance
Location = sentence number in the Appendix (* = omitted)
M. = moderator; L. = litigants; P. = patriarch

Fig. 11. Discourse function of each utterance

of evaluation and prescription in the following constituents, so the grievance constituent could be defined as a presentation of evaluata.

The grievance constituent also includes any answer to the grievance in the form of counteraccusations or rebuttal/defense. The defense is not so much calculated to defuse the disagreement as to counter what has been said. At this stage there is still confrontation rather than conciliation. However, the grievance constituent is prerequisite to consensus. This seems paradoxical, since grievances or accusations appear to work against consensus and harmony. But if the litigants themselves are to join in the ultimate consensus, they must be given opportunity to try to shape that consensus. This they do by relating incidents, utterances, and feelings that led to their own actions or present attitude. The content of the grievance constituent is thoroughly normative, consisting of evaluations of attitudes and actions of the speaker and others, and justification of those evaluations. Each litigant hopes that his evaluations of others and his justifications of himself will figure prominently in the shaping of the consensus.

The second medial constituent is *conciliation*. This is something of an about-face, immediately following the grievance constituent. (The text constituents are displayed in figures 10 and 11.) UT6-9 (s.166-71) form a conciliation cluster, immediately following the grievance of UT4 and UT5 (s.29-165). Show of good faith (UT13 and UT15) is subsumed under conciliation, but it is of a more social nature. The conciliation cluster of UT6-9 expresses personal good will, whereas the show of good faith is an expression of willingness to be evaluated and to suppress personal feelings or evaluations if they conflict with the evaluations of others. Personal conciliation paves the way for the litigants to agree with each other, whereas show of good faith paves the way for the litigants to agree with everyone else. Both are vital to achieving consensus.

The third medial constituent is *evaluation*. The topics of the grievance constituent are the evaluata in the Ga'dang informal litigation. The content of the accusations or explanations is evaluated. Evaluation is always done on the basis of norms. Norms may be *standards* by which things can be graded (good or bad) or ranked (better or worse), or they may be *rules* by which the evaluata are judged to be right or wrong, correct or incorrect (Taylor 1961:5-33). In either case, the norms employed in the Ga'dang litigation are those emic to the Ga'dang society, or to the subset of that society to which these participants belonged.

The fourth medial constituent is *prescription*. If an attitude or action has been evaluated and found to have disvalue, a prescription will be made. Numerous prescriptions may be included in this constituent, along with justifications. But prescriptions in dialogue, in contrast to the normative monologue (see sec. 6.1.3), are frequently given without justifications immediately following. One possible reason for such omissions is that the justification of each prescription is to be found in context in the form of the evaluations (in the previous constituent) which prompted the prescriptions. The second possible reason is that maximum deletion is in effect at the prescriptive (normative) peak of the discourse. This feature, and the variety of surface realizations of evaluations and prescriptions, will be discussed in sections 9.4 and 9.5.

Note that the evaluations and prescriptions were a necessary prerequisite to consensus in the Ga'dang litigation. Since the initial state of disharmony consisted of evaluations in conflict, there must be some adjudication of these and some statement by the society (represented by the participants in the discussion) as to which evaluations were correct, that is, in keeping with public values or norms, and had the best chance of contributing to group happiness.

The fifth medial constituent, and the last constituent before closure, is *consensus.* This consists of general agreement with the evaluations and prescriptions that have gone before, and statements that the initial problem or disharmony no longer exists.

6.3.3 Turn taking as utterance boundaries

Designated turn taking (Hall 1983, chap. 3) and noninterference (Nowakowska 1979:196) are features of the communication situation structure of this type of eristic discourse. These rules are not observed without exception, but they are observed far more than in casual dialogue. The net effect is to give order to the proceedings, minimize friction, and expedite the achievement of the end state (consensus).

Hall (1983:58) observed that in structured types of dialogue or litigation there is someone who has the responsibility of directing people to speak at the appropriate times. In the Ga'dang litigation, the moderator (Sanggoon) does this more than anyone else, but he is not the only one to designate when another should speak. For example, at the end of UT4, litigant Andits designated that litigant Buton should respond. Frequently there was no explicit designation, but the participants had a clear idea of who should speak and when.

There were even times when individuals designated themselves to speak. Yawindo did so in UT3 (not included in the Appendix): *Antwen inoy yo sapitan nu? Matubburan ku pay* 'Is that all you will say? I'll just add on.' Then Andits, in UT4 (s.29), designates himself: *Ana ino daretsu a assapitan ku* 'I have something straightforward to say.' Another example is s.266, in which Sanggoon says: *Antu ino masapit ku ke* 'I'll just say this.' Still another example is Laka's self-designation (s.331-32): *Kallay. Tubburan ku si bisang lamang* 'Man. I'll just add a little.'

The features of turn taking and noninterference made the transcription of the discourse and the identification of the utterance boundaries in it

Notional constituent	Realizations of the constituent
Opening	UT 1,2,3
Grievance	UT 4,5,10,(15)
Conciliation	UT 6,7,8,9,13,15,(21)
Evaluation	UT 11,12,16,17,18,(19),(21),22,27,(34)
Prescription	UT (17) 19,25,27,(31)
Consensus	UT 28,29,30,31,32,33,34,35,36,37
Closure	UT 0,23,24,26,(37),38,39

Fig. 12. Utterances realizing notional constituents

much simpler than transcribing casual conversation. The utterances are displayed in figure 10. Notice that the length of each utterance is displayed with approximately one X for each four sentences. Frequently, however, a single X represents an utterance of just one sentence in length.

6.3.4 Turn taking related to notional constituents

Utterances and notional constituents are not co-terminous. Nor can one constituent be defined as ending and another one beginning between any two particular UT's. There is overlap, but a gradual progression from one to the next constituent. This is accounted for primarily by the different perceptions of the different individuals of where they were in the process of litigation at that point. Some would try to go on to the next constituent, then others would go back to the previous one. But as a general rule, there are no two-constituent jumps. There may also be constituent transitions within one utterance.

While figure 11 displays the text with a capsule statement of the discourse function of each utterance, figure 12 displays the constituents of the macrostructure of the litigation and shows which utterances realize each constituent.

The utterance numbers in parentheses indicate utterances that contain elements of more than one notional constituent. Notice how the litigation slides from one constituent to the next, with considerable overlap at the borders. The reason for the overlap is the differing perceptions of the participants in the discussion concerning how far along in the whole litigation they were. In particular, UT20, UT23, and UT24 were untimely motions to close. The participants had misinterpreted UT19 as Sanggoon's complete prescription and decision. In fact, he had a lot more to say, which he did in UT25, and Laka also had several things on his mind to say before the discussion closed.

There are significant observations to be made concerning the relation of the notional structure to the utterances of the litigation. These observations provide insight into the process of persuasion and consensus formation in Ga'dang. Figure 10 shows that the long utterances are early in the discourse. In fact, the first 5 utterances of the total 39 contain 319 sentences, almost half the total (715) of the whole discourse. Furthermore, the total of the sentences that function as realizations of the grievance constituent (though in discontiguous utterances) is 404, more than half the total. This is an indication of the importance accorded to giving each litigant his chance to shape the developing consensus. It is also an indication of the therapeutic and conciliatory nature of getting the facts and evaluations out in the open. The "facts" can thus be evaluated according to the norms of the community, and prescriptions imposed if they are in order. This is much more satisfactory and pacifying to the litigants than dealing with the indeterminacies of suspicion, innuendo, and rumor, which contribute to uncertainty and doubt, an open, unstable state of mind abhorred by human beings (Maranda and Maranda 1979). On the other hand, knowledge and belief are closed, stable states of mind, comfortable and satisfying. This explains the therapeutic value of laying out the facts of the case and explains why so much of the exercise of pursuing a consensus is devoted to the grievance constituent.

Evaluation and prescription have a much more balanced share of the total number of sentences (about 146 and 108 respectively; there is some uncertainty since some utterances make a constituent transition). But notice that evaluation is realized by 10 utterances, whereas prescription is realized by only 5. This is a feature of the social structure of which the participants are members, namely that only Sanggoon and Laka are qualified or privileged to prescribe. Sanggoon speaks 88 sentences or more as realizations of the prescription constituent, and Laka speaks about 20. Sanggoon also speaks the majority of the sentences of the evaluation constituent, but the remainder are divided up between 5 other participants. It appears to be anyone's prerogative to evaluate, though the evaluations of some are taken much more seriously than those of others. Baggit's evaluations are almost completely disregarded. He is the youngest participant, and his comments are not referred to in other utterances, nor are they followed by anyone's endorsement.

The consensus constituent, which intuition indicates is the most important, actually occupies a very brief section of the surface structure. It is realized by only 20 sentences, but these are distributed within 10 utterances. All the older participants except Bayombong are vocal at this stage. (Bayombong may be somewhat miffed because his attempts to function as moderator or co-moderator were thwarted earlier.) But once consensus has been reached, on the basis of evaluations and prescriptions eloquently supported earlier, the purpose has been achieved, and little more needs to be said. Simply endorse the consensus, have your affirmative vote counted, and move to adjourn.

The closure constituent is the briefest of all, once everyone has reached a consensus. It really consists of only 4 sentences, the final ones, since earlier motions to close (UT20, UT23, UT24, UT26) were futile attempts. Participants had apparently misread the degree of satisfaction of some other participants. Or possibly they made the motions to adjourn to prompt Laka to make his contribution so the discussion could be completed.

A further observation concerning the opening and closure constituents relates to cohesive elements, those parts of the discourse that function primarily to make what follows cohere with what has preceded. While the surface structure realizations of the medial constituents include cohesive elements, the opening constituent has no immediately preceding linguistic context, and the closure has none immediately following. Thus in the opening, any initial cohesive element must form a bridge between the immediately following linguistic context and the immediately preceding nonlinguistic (social or situational) context. And if there are such elements in the closure, they must form a bridge with the following nonlinguistic context.

A discourse-initial cohesive element realizes the transition from the nonlinguistic onset of the behavioral unit of litigation (dispute settlement) into its nucleus, which is the linguistic unit of normative discourse of the *tarabbag* subtype. And a discourse-final cohesive element realizes the transition from the linguistic nucleus to the nonlinguistic coda or closure of the behavioral unit. We expect to find such cohesives initially and finally in discourse, since not only must discourses be *studied* in their behavioral, sociological, cultural, and psychological context (Longacre 1983a:338), they must also be *uttered* meaningfully in this larger context. (Chapter 7 presents the analysis of discourse-level surface structures, beginning with these cohesives.)

6.4 The backbone of normative discourse

In narrative discourse the backbone is the event line and the narrated events are related to each other by chronological linkage. In normative discourse the backbone is the theme and the linkage is logical. The themes around which normative discourses are organized are the topics of evaluation and prescription. The backbone (the main thread of development of the theme or themes throughout the discourse) consists of evaluations and prescriptions.

In the informal litigation of the Appendix, the global theme is the misunderstanding between Andits and Buton. *Misunderstanding* (lit., 'not reciprocally cause to understand') is the Ga'dang euphemism for strife, contention, or serious conflict. The word *misunderstanding* is used in s.1, s.3, s.10, and s.15 of the opening constituent of the discourse, the function of which is to articulate the global theme. There are secondary themes presented in the following constituents, some of which are the specific causes of the misunderstanding. But since the global theme is inclusive of the specifics, the global theme is the first topic of evaluation and prescription when the litigation reaches that point. Thus the general principles of what should be done in case of misunderstandings are presented, first in s.172-80 and again in s.194-202.

Following the initial articulation of the global theme in the opening constituent, the secondary themes are presented in the grievance constituent, that is, the presentation of evaluata. The litigant's personal evaluation of the information he is presenting is always unambiguous, either because it is stated, or communicated by intonation and manner of presentation. In any case, whether or not an evaluation can be immediately construed, any normative theme, whether it is the global theme or another, is a part of the backbone of normative discourse.

6.5 The normative peak

The normative themes are not developed in random order in the evaluation and prescription constituents of the discourse. Just as in the preceding constituents, they occur in the order of most generic to most specific topics of evaluation and prescription, then return again to the most generic.

The most generic theme is the least delicate of the normative topics, since it is the one on which there is the greatest (in most cases unanimous) agreement. Thus any articulation or discussion of such a theme is a low tension point in the discourse. On the other hand, the most specific or most focal normative topic is that which involves the greatest degree of disagreement, the greatest disparity of evaluations. This point of greatest conflict of evaluations is, of course, the point of highest tension in the discourse. It is also the normative peak, since it is the point at which the greatest effort is being made to persuade someone to change opinions or behavior. It is the point at which the greatest effort is being made to persuade someone whose opinion or behavior has been evaluated as unacceptable to conform to the particular norms that are being advocated.

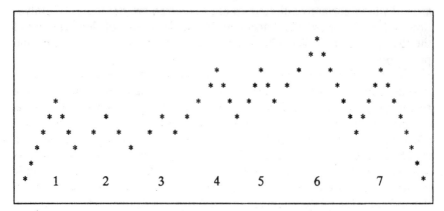

Fig. 13. Profile of the text in the Appendix

In the text of the Appendix, there is a normative peak for the discourse as a whole, found in s.300-4. There are also normative peaks within other utterances, functioning as the peak of that particular utterance, but not the peak of the discourse as a whole. One such secondary peak is s.210-13, and another is s.80-85. Figure 13 is a rough approximation of the profile of the text.

Seven peaks are identified in this Ga'dang litigation. Three of these are in the grievance constituent (peaks 1-3 in fig. 13). Peaks 1 and 3 are in UT4 and UT10 of the text, spoken by Andits, and peak 2 is in UT5, spoken by Buton. (Peak 1 is included in the Appendix, s.80-100.) Peak 4 of figure 13 is in UT17 of the discourse, spoken by Sanggoon; the peak section of this utterance is s.210-13 of the Appendix. Peak 5 is spoken by Andits and is virtually the whole of UT22 (s.244-62). Peak 6 is spoken by Sanggoon, UT25, s.300-4. Peak 7 is spoken by Laka and is a part of UT27 (s.341-46).

Note that peak 6 is the highest in figure 13. It is the normative peak of the whole discourse unit. The other peaks are the peaks of the utterances of which they are a part. As such, they may also function as the peaks of the normative discourse constituent of which that utterance is a part.

In a normative discourse, the peaks are not necessarily the points of greatest excitement, tension, or emotion. To some extent, the tension and emotion have abated before the normative peak. The litigants released a good deal of emotion in the grievance constituent early in the discourse. They are already somewhat more relaxed and pacified before the normative peak. If they were not, they would probably not be receptive to the evaluations and prescriptions of the normative peak uttered by the moderator.

Furthermore, whereas a climactic narrative builds up tension and excitement as it approaches its peak, in normative discourse the speaker tries to mitigate and assuage tension prior to the normative peak. Nevertheless, there is a decrease in mitigation in the vicinity of the normative peak. This is not to increase tension, which would be counterproductive, but to increase persuasiveness or normative force.

7   The Ga'dang Text: Surface Structure

Most of the Gad'dang discourse-level surface structures are discussed in this chapter. Some will be reexamined from other perspectives in the following chapters, and some additional ones will be introduced there.

7.1 The discourse unit in its behavioral context

Cohesion with the nonverbal context (see the last two paragraphs of sec. 6.3.4) is achieved discourse initially by the first sentence of the first utterance as, for example, in s.1 of the text in the Appendix:

```
Ara  antu Buton, e    nu sanna ino amme yu
okay then Buton  and if what   the not  you.pl

pakkinnawatan a  adwa, antu ino pattatarabbag daw
understand    rl two   that the cause.discuss you.pl

ta bakkan a  kunna sitan, a  wara kad     madingngadingngag
so not    rl like  that   rl exist perhaps being.heard

daw    so   tolayira.
you.pl from people
```

'Now then, Buton, whatever is the misunderstanding between the two of you, discuss it, so that it won't be like that (hearsay), what you may have heard from other people.'

There are several features working together in this sentence to effect the transition from the nonverbal context into the normative dialogue. The first is the vocative phrase *ara antu, Buton* 'now then, Buton'. The words *ara antu* always signal a major discourse-level transition, either initiating a discourse or making a transition between major constituents of a discourse. Either of the two words in isolation can function as a discourse-level cohesive, but not signalling such a major transition, as in s.170, 173, and 178: *Antu ino kun ku so da'bu* 'This is what I said a while ago.' (The word *antu* is usually translated 'this' or 'that'; cf. also s.166 and 188.) Most of these examples show *antu* in a phrase or clause that is functioning as cohesion between utterances. However, in s.1, *ara antu* initiates the dialogue.

The first complete clause of s.1 also functions as transition from the nonlinguistic context to the normative dialogue. 'Whatever is the misunderstanding between the two of you ...' is a *circumstance*, which will be immediately followed by a *prescription* (cf. "schema of prescription" in chap. 8). The circumstance functions as anaphoric cohesion. It refers to the whole situation that led to the litigation up to and including the initial state. Thus cohesion with the relevant behavioral context up to that point in time is effected.

On the other hand, the prescription ('discuss it') functions as cataphoric cohesion. It announces and anticipates the following dialogue. Thus the transition into the normative dialogue is effected. But this is not all. There is a *justification* constituent of the schema of prescription realized by s.1, which justifies the giving of the prescription: 'so that it won't be like that (hearsay), what you may have heard from other people.' This is both anaphoric and cataphoric. It refers to what has gone on before, implying that the initial state of the litigation (rumor, slander, hurt) is unsatisfactory, and that a different end state is to be achieved by following the prescription. Thus the purpose of the entire behavioral unit is alluded to, and the entire unit is made to cohere with its larger social context and the ethic of group harmony.

At the end of the normative dialogue, cohesion between the dialogue and the following nonlinguistic context is achieved in the final two sentences, s.369 and s.370. A few previous utterances had made it clear that the desired end state of consensus had been achieved (s.348-68), and in s.369 Yawindo announces that the discussion is finished and it is time to go. In s.370, Sanggoon recommends that some nonlinguistic behavior should immediately follow the end of the structured dialogue, namely, making coffee and washing hands. This not only makes the transition out of the structured dialogue, but also effects coherence with the larger context since washing hands together and drinking coffee together are symbolic of harmony.

7.2 Cohesion between larger units of normative discourse

Cohesives are those surface structures that effect cohesion between utterances. Here I will focus on cohesives that are internal in the dialogue, at or near the beginnings or ends of utterances. Most of the sentences that have this inter-utterance cohesive function are first or last in an utterance. Occasionally they are second or penultimate in the utterance.

7.2.1 Designated turn taking and cohesion

The term *designated turn taking* is used in a looser sense here than was intended by Hall (1983, chap. 3). Hall included in designated turn taking any formal dialogue situation in which one individual had the responsibility of directing others to speak, and also the situation in a dialogue in which any participant would designate who should speak next (a "passing on of the floor"). I expand the definition of the term to include any clear designation of the beginning or ending of an utterance, whether a preceding or following utterance, or the one the speaker is uttering at that moment. This definition is now so general in comparison to Hall's that it might seem of little use, but it does serve to contrast the discrete turn taking of the *tarabbag* from the unstructured, undesignated turn taking of casual conversation. If the *tarabbag* were contrasted to more formal litigation, finer distinctions would probably need to be made.

Four types of turn-taking cohesives can be identified, depending on whether the cohesive points forward or backward, and whether it points to the utterance of which it is a part or to another one. The four are: cataphoric, different UT; anaphoric, different UT; cataphoric, same UT; and anaphoric, same UT.

The first type is the cataphoric, different UT. It occurs at the end of the utterance of which it is a part, and it anticipates or designates the following UT. These cohesives occur early in the normative dialogue, in the opening and grievance constituents. In UT1, s.1, the designation is '(the two of you) discuss it', and in s.2 (the final sentence of UT1) it is 'just hear each other out'. At the end of UT2, virtually a whole paragraph (s.23-28) is devoted to this type of designation. In s.23, Andits is designated and told to speak in a certain way, that is, to speak his grievances, whatever they are. In s.24, Buton is designated and given similar instructions. Finally in s.28 the two of them are designated to tell and discuss their grievances. The two of them respond, following the order of designation in s.23 and s.24. Andits's response is UT4, s.29-165. A further example of the cataphoric, different UT cohesive is found at the end of Andits's speech in UT4. In s.163, Andits designates Buton with a second person pronoun:

```
Ara  sigi sapitan nu  pay  nu anya pay  anggam nu  sassapitan.
okay go   say     you just if what just want    you say
```

'Okay, go ahead, just say whatever you want to say.'

In s.164 Andits repeats the designation almost verbatim. Buton responds in UT5 (not included in the Appendix due to length and problems with the recording).

The utterance that follows such a designation automatically coheres with its linguistic context in the dialogue. It has been designated or predicted and is the "default" (i.e., expected) continuance. In all instances of cataphoric, different UT designations, the content of the following utterance also cohered with what went before. (Occasionally there is an utterance the content of which is only marginally coherent with the whole dialogue unit, but none of these are responses to cataphoric turn designations. UT14 was such an utterance, characterized as extraneous in fig. 6.)

The second designated-turn cohesive is anaphoric, different UT. This type is not uncommon in the normative dialogues studied, but there does not happen to be one in the text of the Appendix. In this type the speaker refers back to the utterance just completed, often simply asking if the speaker has finished what he wanted to say (another evidence that these are communication-situation oriented rather than content oriented). In UT3 of the *tarabbag* (not included in Appendix), Yawindo asks the previous speaker, *Antu-in inoy o sapitan nu?* 'Is that all you will say?' In another discussion, one speaker asks another *Awanin sapitan daw?* 'Do you have no more to say?' Still another speaker asked simply, *Awanin?* 'No more?' The speaker seldom waits for an audible answer to his question, since he is virtually certain before he asks that the other is in fact finished.

The third type of designated-turn cohesive is cataphoric, same UT. (This type may occur immediately following the second type, the anaphoric, different UT.) Referring again to UT3, after Yawindo asks, 'Is that all you will say?' he immediately follows with *Matubburan ku pay* 'I'll just add on.' However, this third type of cohesive need not be preceded by another one in the same UT. In UT27, s.331-32, Laka begins his utterance with *Kallay. Tubburan ku si bisang lamang* 'Man. I'll just add on a little.'

This third type of cohesive points forward to the remainder of the utterance of which it is a part. There is a particular form of this type of cohesive that has a very significant function in the normative dialogue. This form begins with the words *antu* or *antu yaw*, both of which can be translated as 'this'. Together they mean something like 'this very thing'. This form of the cataphoric, same UT cohesive is used only twice in the normative dialogue of the Appendix, once at the beginning of the evaluation constituent and once at the beginning of the prescription constituent. The evaluation constituent begins with s.191:

```
Antu yaw   ino dama-k pelang     kappay a  masapit.
this this  the able-I just.only  also    rl say
```

'This is what I am able also to say.'

Sentences 192 and 193 are somewhat parenthetical, so the above cohesive is paraphrased in s.194, *E kunna yaw yo masapit ku* 'And this is what I have to say.' The prescription constituent of the discourse begins with a similar sentence, s.266, *Antu ino masapit ku ke* 'This is what I say.' The words *antu* and *yaw*, or the two together, are used in cohesives in other parts of the discourse, but only in these two places as cataphoric, same UT cohesives. Other recorded normative dialogues have similar sentences leading into the evaluation and prescription constituents. In all instances observed they were spoken by the moderator, the one who officiates and mediates the litigation. Clearly this form of the cataphoric, same UT cohesive marks the beginning of important constituents of the normative discourse.

The fourth of this group of cohesives is the anaphoric, same UT. This type of cohesive announces the termination of the utterance of which it is a part. Thus it has the least overall cohesive effect in the dialogue. It simply provides the cue for others to begin to speak if they wish to. Examples of this type of cohesive are in UT4, s.165, and UT36, s.366, of the Appendix, and also in UT10 (not included). In UT10, Andits concludes by saying, *Antu-in inoy o sapitan ku* 'That's all I have to say.' The completive suffix *-in* is always a part of this cohesive, usually in the phrase *antu-in inoy* 'that's all'.

7.2.2 Content-oriented cohesives

The turn-taking cohesives described in section 7.2.1 tend to be person oriented or speech act oriented; they are more explicitly related to who is speaking rather than to what is being said. The types of cohesives described here and in sections 7.2.3 and 7.2.4 are more oriented to semantic content.

The more common type of the content-oriented cohesive is the "summarize content" type. An example of this is found in UT5, s.166, in which Sanggoon sums up in a sentence the whole previous utterance of Buton (not included). The sentence begins with *antu ino*, an anaphoric reference to what has immediately preceded, and is followed by a capsule statement of the content or an abstraction of the main theme of what preceded: 'That is what you know about the hurt your uncle felt toward you, man.' A similar content summary cohesive is found in the last sentence of UT25, s.329. It begins with the words *ira inay* 'plural that', that is, those things (that have just been said). In this case the cohesive does not refer to a previous UT, but to the content of all that preceded in the same UT.

While the content-summary cohesives are necessarily anaphoric, there is another content-oriented cohesive which is cataphoric. Its nature is to elicit content rather than summarize content. It is similar to the cataphoric, different utterance cohesive of the turn-taking type in that it designates the following speaker, but it is different in that it focuses on what is to be said. The whole of UT6 (s.167-69) functions as this type of cohesive: 'What, in fact, was my sin, uncle? Tell me....'

7.2.3 Paraphrase and endorsement as cohesion

The paraphrase cohesive is similar to the content-summary cohesive. The difference is that the paraphrase does not, as a rule, summarize a large segment of preceding text in capsule form. Rather, it paraphrases the content of the immediately preceding proposition or proposition cluster, or simply endorses it (e.g., 'yes/true/good/I like that'). Furthermore, the paraphrase cohesive tends to be the only sentence in its utterance. Thus it is not functioning to make its own utterance cohere with what preceded or what follows. Rather, it has a function of effecting cohesion at the level of the purpose of the whole litigation unit. It contributes to the achievement of the desired end state, consensus, by endorsing the evaluations or prescriptions of others.

There are 13 paraphrase cohesives in the litigation of the Appendix. None of them are in the first 170 sentences; 9 of them are in the last 25 sentences. This distribution, along with the content of the paraphrases, clearly shows the function of this type of cohesive to be that of advancing the discussion toward consensus.

The first example of this type of cohesive in the text is s.171 (spoken by Buton, the second sentence in the following example). It paraphrases the sentence before it (spoken by Andits):

```
Antu ino kun  ku so da'bu inoy, a  nu kamali na tata, kamali ta   adwa.
that the said I  at while then  rl if error  of one   error  we.2 two
```

'That's what I said a while ago, that if one of us erred, we both erred.'

```
On, kamali ta   lud.
yes error  we.2 really
```

'Yes, we really both erred.'

The simple endorsement is an even more common form of this type of cohesive. Sentences 182 and 183 are good examples, spoken by Yawindo and Andits respectively. Both sentences consist of just one word, *gakkurug* 'true'. The other examples of this type of cohesive are found in the Appendix, s.218, 347, 348, 349, 350, 354, 359, 362, 365, and 367.

7.2.4 The flashback cohesive

The flashback cohesive is anaphoric, but it does more than simply refer to what immediately preceded. In fact, it necessarily skips what immediately preceded and refers back to something earlier in the linguistic context. The key words are *so da'bu* 'a while ago'. The particle *so* is the marker of temporal or spatial location; *da'bu* means 'earlier'. This type of cohesive is usually at the beginning of an utterance. It is used not only for the purpose of cohesion in the discourse, but very likely is used also as a "citation to authenticate" (see sec. 5.1.4).

In s.170 (first sentence in the preceding example), Andits used the flashback cohesive *Antu ino kun ku so da'bu inoy* 'that's what I said a while ago'. Sanggoon used these exact words in s.173, and again in s.178, referring to some of his own earlier utterances.

7.3 Paragraph boundaries and the normative coda

Paragraph boundaries are of special significance in normative discourse. Several types of surface structures occur paragraph initially or finally, and their distribution plays an important role in the realization of the macrostructure of the whole discourse.

The rule of thumb concerning unit boundaries is that any boundary of a larger unit (i.e., of greater hierarchical ranking) is also, *ipso facto*, a boundary of all smaller or lower-ranking units. Thus an utterance boundary is also the boundary of a paragraph, sentence, word, etc. Therefore, the turn-taking cohesives discussed in the previous section will not be prominent in this discussion, even though they also signal paragraph boundaries. (This illustrates the economy and advantage, if not the necessity, of the discourse-oriented approach.)

Notwithstanding the general rule, the notion of a "dialogue paragraph" is a useful one. In the context of reported speech, a speaker or writer may report a dialogue within his own utterance. When the content of the reported dialogue is conceptually unified, the surface structure realization is likely to be a dialogue paragraph, as in s.136-40 of the Appendix. The types of surface structures at paragraph boundaries, their function as cohesives, and their function in the discourse as a whole will be discussed in sections 7.3.1-7.3.6.

7.3.1 Narrative paragraph markers in normative discourse

The most common type of narrative paragraph marker occurs initially in a narrative paragraph, signalling the beginning of some event or notionally related sequence of events (related in that they occur at a common place or in a relatively uninterrupted period of time, and usually involve the same participants throughout). The key words that signal the beginning of a narrative paragraph are *wara sin* or *wara so* (existential plus temporal or spatial location marker). A free translation of these words would be 'at the time of ...' or 'it happened that ...' or, if the definite past tense temporal location *sin* is used, 'after that had happened'. There are many examples in the text of the Appendix, as in s.51, *Wara sin gafu na yawe* 'At the beginning of this', or in s.69, *wara sin maragadi* 'at the time of cutting wood'. Other examples, including the abbreviated forms *waso* and *wasin*, are in s.103, 105, 109, 117, 119, and 141. At least fifteen paragraphs in the text open with a narrative paragraph marker.

The question is, what are these narrative paragraph markers, and the very narrative-looking paragraphs of which they are a part, doing in a normative discourse? Their function as cohesives between paragraphs is not in question, but why this type of cohesive in a normative text?

The answer is to be found in the content of the paragraphs they intro-
duce, and in their distribution in the whole discourse. They occur early in
the discourse, almost exclusively in the grievance constituent (prior to
UT11, s.172); and the semantic content of the paragraphs is made up of
events, utterances, reactions, and feelings—the things to be evaluated in
the overall normative exercise. (Thus the grievance constituent might also
appropriately be called presentation of evaluata.) Narrative surface structures are embedded within the realization of the grievance constituent of
the discourse.

The feature of the normative coda (see sec. 7.3.3) is evidence that
these narrative segments are embedded within normative discourse. It is
not simply a case of some narrative discourse followed by some normative
discourse.

7.3.2 Preposed noun phrases at paragraph boundaries

The normal order of clause-level constituents in Ga'dang is verb, subject, object. One method of introducing a new paragraph topic is to put
the subject noun phrase first in the initial clause. Whereas the narrative
type of paragraph cohesive (*wara so*, etc.) provides orientation concerning
time, place, and events of the remainder of the paragraph, the preposed
noun phrase tends to highlight the particular topic or theme to be
developed. The preposed noun phrase is characteristic of expository discourse, but is not uncommon in narrative, especially when the narrator
wishes to switch the focus of attention to a different participant.

In normative discourse, the preposed noun phrase is used to focus attention on an evaluatum that is about to be evaluated. As such, it is often
an anaphoric cohesive, referring to a topic that was mentioned in the
grievance or "presentation of evaluata" constituent. One example is in
s.148:

```
E    ira yaw  allay si gakkurug ino kalowan ino nakam ku ...
and pl  this man  in truth      the hurt      the mind  my
```

'And these things are really what grieved my heart, man ...'

This example is a part of the grievance constituent, so no extensive
evaluation of 'these things' is given, other than that they grieved the
speaker. In s.222, a preposed noun phrase introduces one of the major
topics to be evaluated: *e ino daffug ira kanu inoy a nasapit* 'and that water
buffalo that was spoken of'. Then follow three paragraphs concerned with
the evaluation of the buffalo incident in which Buton offended the neighbors by letting his buffalo wander loose and do some damage. Again in
s.282, the normative topic is introduced in a preposed noun phrase, *e anda
iyo paraparal ke* 'and about this slander'. This is the focal evaluatum from

the moderator's point of view, and it is repeated in another preposed noun phrase in s.295, as well as evaluated at great length.

7.3.3 The normative coda as paragraph closure

The normative coda is an evaluation or prescription signalling the end of a paragraph in normative discourse. There is typically some thematic reorientation immediately following it and opening the new paragraph, such as the preposed noun phrase announcing another evaluatum to be considered, or a new slant that the evaluation should take. The coda followed by a thematic statement is a clear indication of paragraph boundaries.

The normative coda is perhaps the most distinctive surface structure feature of normative discourse. The embedded narrative segments discussed earlier are distinguished from paragraphs in typical narrative discourse by the normative coda at the end.

Not all paragraphs that have normative codas contain embedded narrative structures. Nor do all paragraphs in the discourse have a normative coda, but there are at least twenty-eight in the informal litigation of the Appendix.

The normative codas are of two types, evaluative and prescriptive. The evaluative coda concisely expresses a judgment concerning an evaluatum (usually an action or behavior pattern). Evaluata may be judged good or bad, right or wrong, desirable or undesirable, or ranked better or worse. Of course, there are many ways to paraphrase each type of evaluation.

Sentence 21 in the Appendix is the normative coda of the paragraph s.17-21. The paragraph revolves around the fact that the two litigants did not take the initiative to bring about a solution to the problem, and it ends with s.21:

```
Amme    na ira inoy allay nad.
reject it pl that man   should
```

'It should not be like that, man.'

The word *ammay* (or *amme* when followed by a consonant) means 'rejection, disfavor, dislike, refusal'. Without affixation, as in the preceding example, it is not a verb. Verbless equative sentences, cleft sentences (Jones 1977:195), or predicate-adjective sentences are characteristic of expository discourse in Ga'dang. However, if the particle *nad* 'should/ought' occurs in such structures, they are normative sentences, not expository.

Sentence 21 is an evaluative coda, since no prescription is explicitly given. (The prescription is implicit: 'Don't behave like that.') It is considered an evaluative rather than a prescriptive coda for another reason as well, namely, that it is a verbless sentence.

The relationship between the two types of normative codas, evaluative and prescriptive, is that an evaluative coda implies a prescription and, conversely, every prescriptive coda necessarily presupposes an evaluation. However, despite this dependency relationship, the two are definitely not in free variation with respect to distribution in the normative discourse.

There are some evaluative codas in every constituent of the discourse. However, although a prescription is implied in every evaluative coda (and perhaps in every evaluation), the distribution of the prescriptive codas in the dialogue is restricted. There are few places in normative discourse where a prescriptive coda is appropriate: Prescriptive codas occur only in normative discourse peaks.

A prescriptive coda is a sentence containing a verb and expressing an imperative. Like the evaluative coda, prescriptive codas often occur with the particle *nad*, as in s.213:

```
Ino ammu yu     a  makadaral so angngurug tam,
the know you.pl rl able.ruin at faith     ours.inc

amme tam-un nad   a  pakakwan-in allay.
not  we-cmp ought rl to.do-cmp   man
```

'That which you know ruins our faith we should not do, man.'

However, whereas *nad* increases the normative force (see chap. 9) of a verbless sentence, it decreases the normative force of a prescription or imperative. In other words, the prescriptive coda with *nad* is a mitigated one, a prescription somewhat disguised as an evaluation. The preceding example occurs near the transition into the prescription constituent of the whole discourse. It is difficult to pinpoint exactly where this transition occurs, but it is clearly in the vicinity of s.213.

The peak of the prescription constituent is the peak of the normative discourse. In this context, there is an unmitigated prescriptive coda *Kakkapan tam* 'Try!' (s.304).

Another unmitigated prescriptive coda is in s.80, in the middle of the grievance constituent, which is not the peak of the normative discourse. However, the immediate context of s.80 is certainly a secondary peak of the discourse as a whole, clearly the peak of Andits's presentation of evaluata. Sentences 73-77 manifest the surface structure of a narrative peak (Walrod 1979:25-28). In this section, Andits presents (narrates) an account of an incident in which the behavior of Buton was very offensive to him. This is followed by the prescriptive coda of s.80: *Ariyan tam ira inay ira a banag* 'Get rid of that kind of thing.'

The two short paragraphs that follow s.80 (s.81-85) can be interpreted as amplifications of the prescription. These are immediately followed by the narration of another offensive incident in s.86-100, which is even more clearly marked with the surface structure of a narrative peak. Maximum deletion is in effect throughout this section, with virtually all surface structure cohesives and non-nuclear elements of sentences omitted. To observe the net effect of maximum deletion in truncated sentences, notice that in the first four pages of the appended text, there are about four sentences per page, but sentences 86-100 are so short that they all fit on approximately one page (see sec. 9.5).

In addition to the unmitigated prescriptive coda (s.80) in the peak of Andits's presentation of evaluata, there is an evaluative coda at the end of the peak section with the least mitigation possible. It is s.100, *Inammek* 'I rejected/disliked it'. Its free translation is 'infuriating', the strongest emotion. It was uttered with laryngealization (tense constriction of the throat), conveying more intense emotion than any other surface structure of the whole dialogue discourse.

Other evaluative codas are found in s.37, 50, 57, 58, 68, 243, and 294. Other prescriptive codas are s.262, 281, and 326.

7.3.4 Hypothetical circumstances as thematic cohesives

Another type of cohesive which may mark the beginning of a paragraph is a conditional clause expressing a hypothetical circumstance. In addition to functioning as a cohesive between paragraphs, this type of clause may also function as the initial constituent of the notional schema of prescription unit (see sec. 6.1.3). This constituent is called the *projected circumstance*. The nuclear and final constituents of the schema are *prescription* and *justification*.

The clearest example in the Appendix of a hypothetical circumstance functioning both as a paragraph-initial cohesive and a projected circumstance is found in s.235:

```
E nu gangngariyan si makkamali etam  se tolay etam ...
and if for.example obj err       we.inc for people we.inc
```

'And if for example we err, for we are just people ...'

The remainder of the paragraph consists of a sequence of three prescriptions and a justification or supporting reason. The prescriptions are: (1) don't be ashamed; (2) get a companion to go with you; and (3) go talk over the problem with the other party. The justification is: 'so that you won't forget about it, because if you allow it to go on, the problem will get worse'.

Other examples of the hypothetical circumstance as paragraph cohesive, but not as a part of a schema of prescription, are s.201, 202, and 207.

7.3.5 Change of addressee

A paragraph boundary may be signalled by an explicit switch of addressee within an utterance. These switches are of two types. One is a switch from nonspecific addressee to a specific addressee. The second type is a switch from a specific addressee previously mentioned to a different addressee. The first type involves a switch from addressing everybody in general and nobody in particular to addressing one or more persons specifically, as in s.319, *Mampe sikwam Buton* 'As for you Buton'.

Another example is found in s.59. In the previous paragraph, Buton was being talked about, referred to by name in s.51, and by third person pronoun *na* in s.52, 57, and 58. Then in s.59, Buton becomes the addressee, being addressed with the second person pronoun *nu*, which becomes *-m* when suffixed to a vowel-final stem.

The second type of addressee switch is encoded in a phrase preposed to the initial position of the sentence, as in s.328, *E ikka pay Andits* 'And you Andits'. The addressee was Buton beginning in s.319, and he was referred to by name again in s.327. In s.328 the addressee is Andits.

7.3.6 The cohesive cluster at paragraph boundaries

There are a few paragraphs that are introduced by a cluster of cohesive elements. These clusters begin with a conjunction that normally functions as a cohesive relating clauses within a sentence. Examples are *odde* 'but' in s.7, 63, and 337; *e* 'and' in s.225, 229, and 318; and *gampade* 'however' in s.229 and 230.

Following the lower-level conjunction is the paragraph-level cohesive of the narrative type, *wara so* 'it happened that'. Typically following the narrative cohesive is the preposed noun phrase type of paragraph-level cohesive. Examples of all three cohesives occurring initially in a paragraph are found in s.225, 229, 318, and 337. Sentence 229, in fact, has two of the lower-level conjunctions preceding the two paragraph-level cohesives:

```
E    gampade wara pay o   Buton ...
and however exist just the Buton
```

'And, however, as for Buton ...'

The use of these cohesive clusters is very significant in normative discourse. They are used to signal departure from the current "script," that is, departure from what would normally be expected to follow. The frequency of the conjunctions *odde* 'but' and *gampade* 'however' in the cohesive clusters is one evidence of the departure from script (norm). Another is the presence of something in the immediate context that is being contraindicated (to borrow a term from medical practice). Whatever that deviant (ab-*norm*al) behavior is, it is disapproved of, and the implicit evaluation is, 'This ought not to be done.' The cultural norms relating to behavior are "scripts" of proper conduct "prescribed" by the society.

7.4 Sentence, clause, and verb in normative discourse

Longacre (1982) has demonstrated that the tense, aspect, and mood of verbs can be related to a ranking scale in discourse. Each type of discourse has its own ranking scale; surface structures high on the scale are more prominent in the discourse. However, what is high on the scale for one type of discourse may be low for another. Thus a verbless clause may rank as the most prominent or important type of surface structure in expository discourse, but very low in narrative discourse.

Figure 14 displays the ranking of clause-level surface structures in Ga'dang normative discourse. The numbers listed opposite each type of structure refer to sentences in the Appendix; in the "negated" column are examples of the construction with negating morphemes.

The ranks in Ga'dang normative discourse are imperative, causative, compulsory, obligatory, volitional, epistemic, evaluative, and expository. They are listed in figure 14 in order of greatest normative force to least normative force.

The direct imperative is selected intuitively as the structure with the greatest normative force; thus it is the focal structure or "standard" of normative discourse. However, there are some good reasons to focus attention on the midpoint in the normative scale, the obligatory construction.

The obligatory construction consists of any form of imperative plus the particle *nad* 'ought', which occurs frequently in normative discourse. It does not indicate that there is no option but to do what is commanded; rather, it indicates that there is a moral obligation to do it. There are forty-four occurrences of *nad* in the text of the Appendix, far more than there are direct imperatives. In a society in which consensus, group harmony, and moral obligation are of paramount importance, the concept of ought-ness is almost on the level of coercion.

Three other features draw attention to the obligatory rank in Ga'dang normative discourse: (1) The obligatory rank is a watershed or dividing point; all higher ranks are prescriptive, and all lower ranks are evaluative. (2) The obligatory particle *nad* exerts a "middling influence"; that is, when it is used in lower-ranking constructions, their normative force is elevated, but when it is used with the higher ranks, their normative force is mitigated. Thus it causes other constructions to move toward the rank of the midpoint obligatory construction. (3) The order of the normative ranking of pronouns changes at this point. At the obligatory and higher levels, use of the second person pronouns outranks use of first person inclusive, which in turn outranks first person dual. Below the obligatory rank the order changes to first

Normative rank	Surface structure	Examples	Negated
imperative			
direct	non-past verb, 2nd prs	168,257,323	108,349
cohortative	n-p verb, 1st prs inc	80,300-4,325	213,326
bihortative	n-p verb, 1st prs dual	235,319	
causative	same options as imper. *+paC—an* caus vb affix	none in Appendix	
compulsory	same options as imper. *ma'awag* 'necessary'	274,320	
obligatory	same options as imper. *+nad* 'ought'	116,231,259	129,199
contrafactual	cond.cl, past vb *+nad*	57,58,175	
volitional	verbs of volition *anggam, ammay*	100,115,181,201	243,338
epistemic	vbs of cognition *ammu, awat, arig, dandam*	16,120-25,196,269	39,40,84
evaluative	same options as expos. *+nad* 'ought'	21,113,358	129,329
expository	verbless w/ embedded participle or clause, or simple verbless cl	148,179 37,79,159,348,354	209,229 232

Fig. 14. Ranking of clause and verb in normative discourse

person singular as having the greatest normative force, followed by first person exclusive, inclusive, and dual respectively, followed by second and third person.

Note that it is logically impossible to use the first person exclusive above the obligatory rank, since all ranks above are prescriptive, and it is impossible to utter a prescription that excludes the people being addressed.

The first person exclusive means 'my sidekicks and I, not including you to whom I am speaking'. See section 7.5 for examples of this pronoun ranking.

Notwithstanding the significance of the obligatory rank in the grammar of normative discourse, the direct imperative is still ranked as having the greatest normative force. There is an implicit moral obligation (an implicit *nad*) to obey any direct imperative, since these are uttered in normative discourse only by those who have the appropriate social status. An example of the direct imperative is s.168, *tuldwan n-ak* 'tell me (lit., teach you-me)'. There may be pronouns in the clause other than the second person, but the second person pronoun is the addressee, and the one expected to do what is being commanded.

The cohortative is like the direct imperative except that the addressee is 'all of us' (the first person inclusive pronoun). An example is s.302:

```
Kakkapan tam    tangngallan ino bifig tam ...
try      we.inc control      the lips ours
```

'Let's try to control our speech ...'

This type of construction is given a ranking below that of the direct imperative because the use of the first person inclusive is a kind of mitigation. As a rule, the speaker is not including himself as one needing the exhortation, but on the surface he includes himself to mitigate the command. The bihortative, the imperative directed at the first person dual (i.e., we two), is slightly more mitigated. The first person dual is very often used as a nonspecific reference to people in general, as in s.235: *e inta makitatabbag* 'let's go discuss it' (lit., and go.we.2 discuss).

The verb of the imperatives is minimally affixed for tense, mood, or aspect. However, any of the voice- or focus-marking affixes may be used in an imperative. In s.108, *amme-m mad-damit* 'don't speak' (lit., not-you nominative-speak), the nominative prefix *maC-* is used. (Upper case *C* final on a prefix indicates doubling of the first consonant of the following stem.) In s.168, *tuldu-an n-ak* 'tell me' (lit., teach-accusative you-me), the accusative suffix *-an* is used. The positional prefix *i-* may also be used with the imperative, as in *i-gamwang nu taw* 'bring (it) here' (lit., positional-bring you here). Aspectual affixes may also be used, as in s.25 where the prefix *makka-* encodes reciprocal action, and as in s.41 where the reduplication of the stem of 'example' encodes continuative action.

The causative construction is ranked just below the imperatives in figure 14. Not all causative constructions are imperatives. But if the clause is imperative in form, with the addition of the causative affixation to the verb and the reference to the person(s) to be caused to do something, they are causative imperatives and rank high on the normative scale. There is no example in the Appendix. The following example from a Ga'dang folklore narrative has an imperative in reported speech:

```
Pak-kanan nu  ino abbing si  u'git.
cause-eat you the child  obj worms
```

'Feed the child some worms.'

The compulsory construction ranks next below causative. It has the form of an imperative but is preceded by the words *ma'awag si* 'necessary', as in s.274 and s.320. Sentence 274 has an additional complication in that the advancement of a noun phrase to sentence topic position ('you the old.man in faith') results in a construction with the imperative *umara'ni* 'draw near' actually embedded in a noun phrase following the sentence topic. The result is a verbless construction rather than the usual form of the imperative.

The obligatory construction, which ranks next below compulsory, has the form of an imperative with the simple addition of the particle *nad* 'ought'. The position of the particle in the clause is not fixed, but it is never far from the imperative verb and usually follows the subject, which immediately follows the verb. An example is s.116:

```
Lawad-an    tam    nad   iyo madal ...
good-accus  we.inc ought this study
```

'We should improve this study ...'

The contrafactual (the unfulfilled obligation) is a variant of the obligatory. The difference in the surface structure is that the verb is in the past tense, as in s.58:

```
Onnu in-ang    na nad   sinapit sikwak ...
or   past-come he ought said    to.me
```

'Or he should have come and said to me ...'

An example of the contrafactual with an explicit conditional clause is s.175 in the Appendix.

The volitional construction, which ranks next below obligatory, involves the verbs *ammay* 'dislike, reject' and *anggam* 'like, accept' but only when they are used as verbs. (*ammay* and *anggam* both have common nonverb uses with a lower normative rank.) *ammay* must have some verb affixation to be used as a verb, as in s.100: *in-amme-k*, composed of past tense accusative prefix + 'reject' + first person singular pronoun, 'I hated that' (cf. s.201 and s.226). When *ammay* is unaffixed (other than as a suffixed pronoun), it functions as a simple negative, negating whatever verb it is juxtaposed to, as in s.243:

```
Se   amme-k pay anggam o    manata'wig ...
for  not-I  just like   the favoritism
```

'For I just don't like favoritism ...'

Similar to s.243 is s.338. It happens that in both these examples the verb *anggam* is the one being negated; thus both of these sentences are also volitional constructions but not by virtue of the word *ammay*. Notice that *anggam* does not require verb affixation to function as a verb (cf. s.115).

The epistemic construction, which ranks next below volitional, is a verb clause, but with verbs of cognition. The verbs of volition (the next higher rank) are not highly dynamic verbs, but the verbs of cognition are near to the least dynamic. The verbs of cognition are: *ammu* 'know', *awat* 'understand', *dandam* 'think', and *arig* 'mistakenly think'. They are used to make strong evaluations; they elevate the normative force of evaluations, as in s.269:

```
Ma'awatan  si  abbing ka, se  abbing ka kepay lud.
understood obj child  you for child  you still really
```

'It's understood that you are a child, for you are still a child.'

The evaluative construction, which ranks next below epistemic, is a verbless clause with the particle *nad* 'ought'. As with any verbless clause, this construction may have a participle or verb clause embedded within one or both of its nominal constituents. Evaluative clauses with embedded verb structures rank higher in normative force than those with no verb element. An evaluative construction with an embedded verb clause is s.129:

```
Ira inay allay ino amme tam    ira nad  a  pakakwan.
pl  that man   the not  we.inc pl  ought rl cause.do
```

'Those things are what we should not do, man.'

An example of an evaluative construction without an embedded verb element is s.21:

```
Amme na ira inoy allay nad.
not  it pl  that man   ought
```

'It should not be like that, man.'

The expository construction is the most static of all the constructions, a verbless clause. It is the lowest-ranked clause type with respect to normative force and is encoded in surface structure that appears to be pure expository discourse. But the normative function of such sentences in the text is clear because of evaluative lexemes in them; for example, 'that is good/bad' is evaluative, whereas 'that is big/little' is expository (value neutral). Value neutral expository sentences are not a part of normative discourse. They occur in a normative text only if they are embedded, possibly as an explanatory author comment.

Sentence 179 is an example of an expository structure with an embedded verb clause:

```
E    mepangngat ikkallaye a  balawan dakayu ...
and fitting    you.man   rl rebuke  I.you.pl
```

'And it's fitting that I rebuke you both ...'

An example of an expository construction without an embedded verb element is s.354. Note that the English translation includes a gerund (a noun formed by adding -*ing* to a verb stem), but in Ga'dang the verb stem *tuldu*, with no affixation, functions as a noun.

```
Kunna mat  yan ino tuldu    a  nalawad allaye.
like  sure that the teaching rl good    man
```

'That is really good teaching, man.'

Sentences are ranked according to the clauses and verbs in them, particularly those in the main clause. Non-nuclear clauses in normative discourse sentences may function as projected circumstance or justification of the main clause(s). High-ranking verbs/clauses with these peripheral clauses make up sentences which are thereby mainline in normative discourse. High-ranking clauses without these peripherals (i.e., one-clause sentences) may signal a normative peak (see chap. 9). On the other hand, low-ranking clauses with no peripherals are low in normative ranking in the discourse and low in normative force.

7.5 Pronominal reference and mitigation

Normative discourse is addressee oriented. Thus the unmarked form of pronominal reference is second person. It is the norm that the commands or prescriptions of normative discourse are addressed to the people being spoken to. This unmarked form of prescription would be that of the highest rank in figure 14, the direct imperative. However, although this is the unmarked form, it is rarely used in the informal litigation. Few commands are addressed to the second person, and even fewer to the second person singular.

The explanation for this is in the social setting. The social relationships between speakers and hearers make it inappropriate for most speakers to command using the second person singular, which is the most direct and most unmitigated form of command. It may seem strange to call a rarely used form unmarked, but the evidence for doing so is found in the advice type of normative discourse, in which the speaker must have social status clearly superior to the addressee(s). In the advice discourse, the second person is used exclusively.

The second person is used in the litigation in the Appendix, but only at appropriate places. One of the uses of second person is initial in the discourse when the litigants are addressed and the problem stated. In s.2, the pronoun *kayu* 'you.pl' is used. This is the nominative case pronoun. Also, in s.1 and s.2, the genitive second person plural *daw* is used. (In s.1 it is *yu*, the form that follows a vowel-final stem.) Then in s.4 the emphatic second person plural is used, *ikkayu*. The second person pronouns of this pronoun set are used as vocatives. Thus for the initial address of the litigants, and throughout the opening constituent of the informal litigation, the second person is appropriate.

Once the grievance constituent begins, the litigants refer to each other in the third person, even though at times their remarks may be intended as direct accusation or exhortation to the other individual. At highly charged points in the discourse there may be a sudden switch to second person, as in s.59. In the sentences preceding and following s.59, Buton was referred to with the third person pronoun. In s.59, suddenly he is directly addressed with the second person singular pronoun. Then again in s.72-100, which is clearly the peak of Andits's grievance speech, Buton is referred to with the second person singular throughout.

In the evaluation and prescription constituents of the discourse, even in some normative peaks, the prescriptions are directed to the first person inclusive *etam*, as in s.300-4, the peak of the whole discourse. Here we would expect second person, but in the interest of group harmony the prescriptions are made somewhat more general and directed to everyone. The deliberate avoidance of giving prescriptions addressed to the second person is illustrated in s.213, in which the projected circumstance is addressed to the second person ('whatever you know that ruins our faith'), but the command element related to and immediately following this clause, in the same sentence, is addressed to first person inclusive ('we should not do'). A similar example is s.235, in which the projected circumstance is directed to first person inclusive and followed by a series of prescriptions followed by first person dual, which is still more mitigated. The only instances in the discourse in which prescriptions directed to the second person are prominent occur in the prescription constituent (s.268-75 and 319-23) addressed to Buton, who is much younger than Sanggoon. Even some of these are immediately paraphrased and addressed to first person inclusive (s.325-26), to mitigate the force of the direct prescription to Buton.

In the same section, when the focus is turned to Andits's fault in the matter, there is no prescription directed to the second person. Rather, very low-ranking normative constructions are used: an epistemic with second person pronoun in s.328, and an evaluative in which a second person plural reference (to Buton and Andits) is made in an embedded clause (s.329).

7.6 Particles, conjunctions, and marking of the backbone

Several particles have more significant roles in normative discourse than in other types of discourse. For example, the particle *nad* 'ought' marks any sentence in which it occurs as a normative sentence. Furthermore, within a normative text, any sentence with the particle *nad* is mainline (high ranking) in the discourse. Some of the other particles also mark their immediate context as very prominent, for example, *lud*, *mat*, *ma'lud*, *kad*, *gampade*, *gampama'de*. Other particles do not in themselves mark mainline or prominent sentences, but any sentence in which there is a cluster of particles definitely has high prominence in the whole discourse or significant function in one of the discourse constituents.

Figure 15 lists particles and conjunctions common in normative discourse. The English glosses are inexact; particles are notoriously difficult to translate, partly because their meaning is so context sensitive.

In the lower right of figure 15 a few combinations of particles are given. These are only a small subset of the possible combinations. The meanings of the combinations are often very different from the meanings of the respective morphemes of which they are composed.

Particles		Conjunctions, etc.	
nad	ought	*gampade*	however
kad	perhaps, indeed	*gampama'de*	however indeed
lud	surely		
mat	in fact	*gakkurug*	truly
lang	only	*gakkuruwingke*	truly indeed
ke	just, still		
pay	just	*pelaman*	not too significant
man	again, more	*kepay*	still, yet
allay	man, friend	*ma'lud*	surely, surprisingly

Fig. 15. Normative particles and conjunctions

The normative/evaluative particles are useful in classifying texts or units within texts. Utterances or parts of utterances that appear to be narrative or expository are in fact filling slots in the normative discourse, and the normative particles are the proofs. This is especially true in normative dialogue. (The distribution and function of the particles, as well as their normative ranking, will be discussed in chapter 9.)

8   Strategies of Persuasion and Their Realizations

In the context of the Ga'dang litigation, persuasion is the mechanism for getting from the initial state of disharmony or conflict to the final state of harmony or consensus. The term *strategy of persuasion* is not used in any technical sense here, but as a general term for any means of persuasion, including features of the speech situation, psychological processes, and rhetorical devices.

It might seem warranted to include all of these means under *rhetoric* as defined by Aristotle: "the faculty of discovering in the particular case what are the available means of persuasion" (Cooper 1932:7). But there is a distinction between what I am calling rhetorical devices and the other means of persuasion. The difference is not that rhetorical devices are verbal and the others are not, for all of the strategies have verbal realizations in the discourse itself. (Of course, nonverbal features do contribute to persuasion, such as body position or seating arrangement, but they are not under consideration in this study; cf. Bloch 1975:5-10.) Rather, the difference is in whether the means of persuasion is purely the verbal craft itself (i.e., the skillful use of the conventional or grammatical structures of normative discourse) or is drawn from some structures of the larger behavioral context external to the verbal art. The former is the set of means of persuasion called rhetorical devices, and the latter is made up of all others.

The distinction between rhetorical devices and other means of persuasion is similar to the distinction Aristotle made between artistic and nonartistic proofs (i.e., means of persuasion).

> By "nonartistic" proofs are meant all such as are not supplied by our own efforts, but existed beforehand, such as witnesses, admissions under torture, written contracts, and the like. By "artistic" proofs are meant those that may be furnished by the method of Rhetoric through our own efforts. The first sort have only to be used; the second have to be found. [Cooper 1932:8]

The similarity between Aristotle's formulation and my usage here is that the means of persuasion other than rhetorical devices "existed beforehand" in the form of structures of social relationships and societal norms. These "have only to be used," albeit in the context of the structure of normative discourse. However, there is somewhat less compatibility between artistic proofs and rhetorical devices. Aristotle said that artistic proofs have to be found, which has to do with creativity or invention.

Rhetorical devices, on the other hand, do not have to be found—they are features of the grammar of normative discourse, not just stylistic nuances available only to those creative enough to find them.

As with any linguistic structure, there are degrees of proficiency in the use of rhetorical devices and normative discourse in general. Artistic ability or oratorical prowess is the ability to employ all means of persuasion and to express them in the form of a well-structured normative discourse.

8.1 Communication situation factors

Communication situation factors relating to strategies of persuasion include: social relationships between participants, social setting (i.e., the type of dispute settlement), and the mechanics of interaction and how they are used in the persuasive process.

8.1.1 Conciliation as social control

The two kinds of dispute settlement proposed by Black and Mileski (1973:11) are therapeutic and coercive (see sec. 4.1), the therapeutic being a conciliatory process. The importance of conciliation in Ga'dang informal litigation is clear. It is integrally related to the purpose underlying the whole behavioral unit. But is it a strategy of persuasion, or just the opposite: being persuaded or a willingness to be persuaded?

It is a little of both. Since the ideal in this type of informal litigation is social harmony, each disputant must subscribe to that ideal at least overtly. To have one's own evaluations given serious consideration in the formation of the consensus, one must express willingness to accept the evaluations of others. In a Ga'dang eristic discourse, to be persuasive one must show a willingness to be persuaded. Thus there is a conciliation constituent in the Ga'dang eristic discourse, and this is realized in the exchange between Andits and Buton (s.167-71). They both admit to having erred. In Andits's speech (s.183-90) he expresses willingness to be rebuked for wrong behavior.

The whole notion of the conciliatory type of social control implies persuasion to the same extent as the accusatory types—perhaps to an even greater extent. In both types, the disputants are likely to present their grievance or rebuttal as persuasively as possible. But in the Ga'dang conciliatory type the evaluations and prescriptions must also be argued for in order that all involved will be persuaded to accept them and consensus be achieved. In the accusatory type of social control, social harmony or consensus is not the ultimate aim. A decision is imposed and enforced, but some of the participants are very likely not to be persuaded of the validity or correctness of the decision, and there need not be any persuasive effort to make the loser agree to the decision.

8.1.2 Impartiality

Impartiality is a strategy similar to conciliation. However, whereas conciliation is a strategy appropriate for the litigants in a dispute, impartiality is a strategy for the moderator or mediator. He must convince the disputants that he is equally willing to give credence to the evaluations (grievances or rebuttals) of either of them. If his claim to impartiality is convincing, he is well on the way to persuading all parties involved to accept his evaluations and prescriptions and therefore reach a consensus.

Sanggoon, the moderator of the litigation of the Appendix, made two explicit efforts to establish his impartiality. The first is in s.14-16, in which he points out that the reason he did not initiate the *tarabbag* 'discussion' was to avoid any appearance of favoring one or the other of the litigants. An implicit show of impartiality follows in s.23-24, in which Sanggoon gives balanced instructions to the litigants to air their grievances.

The second explicit claim to impartiality is even more noteworthy because of its position in the whole discourse. It occurs in s.240-43 following soon after Sanggoon's focusing blame on Buton, the younger litigant. Beginning in s.190, Sanggoon had been expressing his evaluation of the grievances, being very reserved about expressing any strong negative evaluation. There is very mild negative evaluation focused on Buton in s.201, on Andits in s.207, and on both of them in s.210, followed by prescriptions not explicitly addressed to anyone in particular (s.211-13). After a few more innocuous remarks, finally a strong negative evaluation is directed at Buton in s.229. This is immediately followed by more evaluations and prescriptions addressed to everyone in general, and then comes the explicit statement of impartiality in s.240-43. It is clear that if Buton is to be persuaded to endorse the emerging consensus at that point, he must be convinced that he is not being discriminated against personally and that the consensus represents a fair and impartial application of the norms of the society.

8.1.3 Deference

Other criteria of credibility besides impartiality are social status, educational achievement, and upstanding character (cf. Aristotle's "ethos" in Cooper 1932:8). A person who has one or more of these characteristics is more persuasive than a person who does not. The reason for this is deference. "Deference may be defined as a listener's inclination to accept the speaker's position because he considers the speaker to be superior in position, ability, or attainment, rather than because of the merits of his argument" (Martin and Colburn 1972:189).

Three types of deference are identified by Martin and Colburn (1972, chap. 8): instrumental, personal, and social deference. Instrumental deference is submitting to another in order to attain one's goals (acquiring

something desirable such as praise or a reward, or avoiding something undesirable such as punishment). Personal deference is submitting to another
because of admiration for him or desire to make a favorable impression on
him. Social deference is submitting to another because of the social role
or status that he possesses.

Social deference is the type that occurs in the Ga'dang informal litigation. It surfaces in several ways. The most immediately apparent is in the
role of the moderator. The one who functions as moderator must have an
appropriate social role or status. Sanggoon has more than enough creden-
tials for this office. He is a municipal councilman, and he has the highest
educational attainment of those involved as well as the highest office in the
loose organizational structure of the church, of which the disputants are
also officers. However, according to the criterion of social status on the
basis of age, Sanggoon should defer to his father, who is present. Thus he
explains in s.193 why he, rather than his father, will present the evaluation
and prescription.

Sanggoon's evaluations and prescriptions are accepted and endorsed
as a statement of the consensus of the group. This is the expected culmina-
tion of the normative dialogue and is an evidence of social deference.

Not only do people defer to a credible source (one who is impartial,
of good character, and has high social status or role), they also defer to
one who employs the normative discourse type, especially the prescriptive
form. Since this is rightly used only by people who have the appropriate
status, a part of the meaning conveyed by the discourse type itself is that
the speaker is one who deserves deference. Thus, a way of managing
deference is to speak authoritatively.

Sanggoon effectively managed deference by taking control of the discussion at the beginning. Bayombong tried to capitalize on the deference
phenomenon by seizing the floor initially and uttering a standard *tarabbag*
opening (s.1-2), including instructions to the litigants to discuss the
problem. But his effort to manage deference and to figure prominently in
the eventual shaping of the consensus failed because he was outranked and
outperformed by Sanggoon. Sanggoon took over the floor in s.3 and gave
more detailed instructions to the litigants in s.22-28. He continued to
manage deference effectively, with an explanation of why he should be the
one to do most of the talking (s.193), and with occasional authoritative
pronouncements prefacing his evaluations and prescriptions, for example,
'This is what I have to say' in s.191, s.194, and s.266.

Features of normative discourse that rank high on the scale of normativity (see chap. 9) are also means of managing deference. Vocatives
(s.319, s.328) and direct imperatives (s.343-46) are examples of such high-
ranking features.

8.1.4 Cooperation and blocking

Cooperation and blocking are strategies of a somewhat mechanical nature in dialogue. As strategies of persuasion, they can be used to promote one's own evaluations and have them shape the developing consensus, or they can be used to thwart attempts of others to steer the consensus in an unacceptable direction. If the consensus is taking shape in an agreeable way, cooperation is employed. This may be done through the use of back channel responses such as murmurs of assent, words of agreement ('yes' or 'true', as in s.182-83, s.362, s.367), a statement of positive evaluation (s.354, s.359-60), or endorsement by repetition or paraphrase of a clause or sentence (s.347, s.349).

Blocking is done when the direction of the discussion or the developing consensus is unsatisfactory. UT22 (s.244-62) is a blocking speech spoken by Andits. It followed Baggit's utterance (UT21, not included in the Appendix) in defense of Buton's actions. Just prior to Baggit's defense of Buton, Buton's actions had been the target of a strong negative evaluation by Sanggoon (UT19, s.229). Thus Andits, who had a strong vested interest in perpetuating Sanggoon's negative evaluation of Buton's actions, blocked Baggit's effort to cast Buton in a better light. The sequence was as follows:

UT19.   Sanggoon gives his evaluation and prescription, critical of Buton in s.229.

UT20.   Andits, satisfied, moves to close.

UT21.   Baggit speaks in defense of Buton (a rambling, mostly narrative utterance of 48 sentences).

UT22.   Andits utters a blocking speech.

Andits's blocking speech is a somewhat impassioned recitation of public values or norms. The connection between this utterance and the preceding utterance is not explicit. It is only when UT22 is viewed as a blocking speech that it coheres well in its context. It refocuses attention on the norms, which Buton's behavior fell short of, as evaluated back in s.229, and it blocks Baggit's attempt to assign a more neutral evaluation to Buton's behavior.

8.2 Psychological strategies: knowledge structures

Psychological strategies of persuasion have to do with the form of argumentation that is emic to Ga'dang and with the knowledge structures (frames, scripts, and especially plans) employed in the persuasive process. The most frequent strategy is to employ the cognitive plan of *invoke theme* or *invoke norm* (see chap. 3). These are offered as reasons in support of evaluations and prescriptions, but the logical connection between them is sometimes difficult to ascertain. From an etic perspective, we can subjectively provide the missing premises on which the conclusions, evaluations, or prescriptions appear to be founded in order to translate them into a form more compatible with Western idealization of deductive or syllogistic logic. This may be productive analytically, but it should not be confused with the Ga'dang emic cognitive orientation.

Invoke theme and *invoke norm* are the plans most frequently used in Ga'dang persuasion (see sec. 3.4.3). They are very closely related but *invoke theme* is the more generic. Without making too much of this distinction, I suggest that a theme is more generic than a norm, but more specific than a point of view or value system. For example, within the social point of view, one of the themes would be the age-differential theme; and within that theme, one of the norms would be that the younger person must respect the older (s.320). Another would be that the behavior of older people can be excused because of the onset of senility (s.220-21). To invoke a theme is to bring a set of norms to bear on the discussion and is a powerful strategy. Most of the following examples are of invoking themes.

Youth versus age is the most often repeated theme in the text of the Appendix. There is a great disparity in the ages of the two litigants. Andits is twice the age of Buton. The theme is invoked in a number of ways, most often by the use of the terms *lakay* 'old man' and *abbing* 'child'. Buton is referred to as *abbing* even though he is far older than a child. It is not really insulting to him in this context; it is used here as a relative term in order to focus on the difference in age.

The age theme is invoked repeatedly in s.216-21 of the Appendix. In s.217, Sanggoon says that Andits was insulted because it was his son-in-law (therefore younger) who said those things. In s.218, Andits applauds the invoking of the age theme, saying that he really did feel insulted, because he was, in fact, an old man. Then in s.220-21, Sanggoon again refers to Andits's age and *kabaw* 'senility'. Andits was in no way senile, but this is a part of the age theme. When older people do something that might be offensive, they are often excused on the grounds of *kabaw*, whether their mental faculties have waned or not. Here Sanggoon, after having directed a balanced rebuke to both litigants, is providing an excuse for the older one based on the age theme. He is beginning to subtly direct more of the blame at Buton, the younger one.

In the following example (s.268-74), Sanggoon again invokes the age theme, but with a novel and persuasive twist. He shows how the greater responsibility for getting the problem settled rested with Buton for two reasons, both of which invoke the age theme but in opposite ways: (1) Because he was physically younger, he should go to Andits out of respect for the older to try to settle the problem by discussion; and (2) because Buton was older as a church member and therefore presumably more mature in his faith, he should for that reason as well take the initiative.

```
Massiki ikka Buton, abbing ka kepay si urem. Ma'awatan  si
even    you  Buton  child you still  in mind  understood that

abbing ka, se abbing ka kepay lud.   I  Andits, lakayin.
child  you for child you still really pm Andits  old.man
```

'As for you, Buton, you are still a child in mind. It's understood that you are immature, because you really are still a young person. As for Andits, he's already an old man.'

```
Ammem  tonan si i Andits, umara'ni sikwam, se i Andits abbing,
not.you wait for Andits come.near to.you for Andits child

lakay  si angngitatam, odde si tata'dag, ammek inammu sikwana,
old.man in sight.ours but in stand    not.I know   to.him

se  lakay  lud,   nabbalin me'anak.  Se nu si angngurug,
for old.man really finished be.child  for as to faith

abbing kepay.
child  still
```

'Don't wait for Andits to come to you, for Andits is a child. He's an old man as we can see, but as to his stand, what shall we say? He really is an old man. He's finished being a child, but as to faith, he's still a child.'

```
E   ma'awag  si  ikka a lakay  si angngurug ino umara'ni,
and needed  that you  old.man in faith    the come.near

gangngariyan si  nu wara duma'nga a buruburung.
for.example  obj if exist meet   rl problem/worry
```

'And it's necessary that you (Buton) who are mature in faith be the one to go to him, if, for example, a problem arises.'

Another very important theme is that of solidarity—social cohesion. This theme is frequently invoked with the words *Ga'dang* or *tolay* 'person'. In the Ga'dang world, the two words are almost synonymous. There is one utterance of Andits's that is saturated with this theme (UT19, s.244-62); it is an eloquent, impassioned, and persuasive speech. Its key words are those invoking the solidarity theme: 'we Ga'dangs' (s.244); 'us.incl' (s.245-46); 'in/among.us.incl' (s.248); 'we Ga'dangs' (s.259); and 'person' (s.261). The first person inclusive pronoun is also used in other sentences, reinforcing the theme. A free translation of Andits's solidarity speech is as follows:

244. How many of us Ga'dangs are there now?　　245. We are few now!
246. We are few now! 247. I don't want strife among us, but rather we should
put our minds in proper order. 248. Let's throw out our customs of vindictiveness or jealousy or evil. 249. Let's throw them out! 250. Let's get rid of
that anger thing, for what's the use of anger?

251. When I've been removed, who will see me then? 252. I just won't be
around then.

253. That is why if you err, or if I err, man, just scold me. 254. If I err, come
and tell me. 255. I won't say that it is slander. 256. But if I'm bad or angry,
bury my bones! 257. Kill me! 258. What good am I, man? 259. And I request
that we Ga'dangs behave well; however, if I really hate you, just remove me,
in order that there will be none to lead you into bad things. 260. That's what
I'm telling you. 261. I'm not even a person if I hate others. 262. It's you
children who should do what is good.

The solidarity theme may also be invoked by means of an idiom. The
following two sentences were uttered by Baggit and Buton respectively.
(They are not included in the Appendix, but s.169 in the Appendix is a
similar expression.) Baggit had just finished saying that they should feel
free to exhort each other because of their close relationship. He emphasizes
this point with the solidarity idiom (the first sentence):

```
Ma  allay, korokorwan      ak kad    a  tolay?
why man    other/different I  rhet.Q  rl person
```

'Why, man, am I an outsider?'


```
Ma, sanna da iyatal da ulitag a  mattuldu sikwak?
why what     ashamed  uncle to teach    me

Korokorwan       imman ke  tolay?
other/different  again just person
```

'Why should uncle hesitate to exhort me? Am I an outsider?'

In the previous example, still another theme is invoked by the mention
of *atal* 'shame'. Shame is probably the strongest possible theme or value
that can be invoked by a Ga'dang. Various forms of the word are used to
indicate shame, embarrassment, shyness, humiliation, respect, reserve, or
shamefulness. The theme common to most of the uses, if not all, is that of
a proper sense of reserve, a sense of propriety. To say to a person *awan a
atal nu* 'you have no shame' is the strongest of rebukes. It suggests forward-
ness, brashness, pushiness, immodesty, and a general lack of reserve or
decency toward other people, particularly toward those who most deserve
it by virtue of greater age or social position. A person without shame is

one who lacks the decency to feel remorseful or embarrassed for doing what is wrong or for failing to live up to societal expectations (i.e., shameless). *To have shame* (which seems convoluted to the Western mind) is the opposite of *shameless*; *to have shame* means to be decent, proper, reserved. It is an admirable and person-oriented virtue (Noble 1975). The following are two sentences from different contexts (the first is from s.208):

```
Ka''atatal etam     nu ammetam ma'inggud o  angngurug tam.
shameful   we.inc  if not.we  order/tidy   faith    ours
```

'We are shameful if we do not keep our faith in order.'

```
Amme nad      ma'atal i litag a  mattuldu sikwak, se  abbing dak   ke.
not  should ashamed   uncle to exhort   to.me    for child  his.I just
```

'Uncle should not be ashamed to exhort me, for I am his child (younger relative).'

It should be noted that Ga'dang discourse is not entirely without an inform reason persuasive plan. This is also frequently employed, but very often it is employed in form only, not in content. That is to say, the form is that which would be used to present a logical supporting argument, but instead a theme is invoked, as in the following example (from s.320). It is a pseudo inform reason, which again invokes the age theme.

```
Nu palungo amma sikwam, ma'awag si   dayawan nu,  gafu se
if first  more to.you  needed   that respect you because

palungo amma sikwam.
first   more to.you
```

'If he was first before you, it's necessary that you respect him because he was first before you (i.e., older).'

Baggit used a similar construction, an inform reason form that actually invokes a theme. This example also introduces the next major theme, which was often invoked in the litigation, the kinship theme, invoked with the word *kolak* 'sibling'.

```
E   kunna pe   sikwayu allaye, paparefu etam   pe   nad   a
and like  just you.pl  man     same     we.inc just should rl

awan a  pattatarukyan gafu-se ikkanetam, makkakarolak-etam.
none rl strife        because we.inc     are.siblings-we
```

'And just like you, we should likewise not argue, because we are all siblings.'

```
Nu wara pakkamalyan na tata sikwatam, se  makkolak eta,
if exist error       of one of.us.all for siblings we

makkatutuldu eta.
recipr.teach we
```

'If one of us makes a mistake, because we are siblings, we should just teach/exhort each other.'

Other themes with strong emotive associations are frequently invoked: *allak* 'pity, benevolence' (s.253); *nakam* 'character' (s.247); *kakkatawa* 'ridicule' (s.337); *napatata* 'unity' (s.333-34); etc. Many other words invoke very negative emotive themes or values: *bungot* 'anger'; *kamali* 'error'; *kalussaw* 'hatred'; *rakkat* 'badness'; *apal* 'jealousy'; *maral* 'ruin, evil, slander'; etc. All of these can be found in Andits's one utterance, s.244-62, and throughout the text of the Appendix.

One other strategy or plan that may belong in the invoke theme group is the volitional strategy. It at least contributes to the desired group harmony or consensus, though not invoking it explicitly. It is the strategy of saying, 'I like that' or 'I don't like that.' It appears that not everyone has the privilege of making this kind of statement; only the older participants do so in the text of the Appendix (cf. s.243, 247, 348, 360).

The text of the Appendix illustrates well the use of the invoke theme and invoke norm plans in Ga'dang argumentation and persuasion. In one way, however, it is atypical, because the set of rules being applied to verify or validate evaluations and prescriptions is made explicit. These are the rules of *angngurug* 'faith', and at certain points they are explicitly contrasted with another set, those of tradition (*gagangay tam si'in* 'our customs of long ago'), as in s.173 and s.192 of the Appendix. Where there is no incompatibility between the two sets, the rules are not explicitly mentioned.

In recorded texts that do not reflect the borrowing of sets of rules external to Ga'dang tradition, no reference is ever made to the set of rules that is being applied. Rules are cited, but there is no requirement that they be validated in any way. They are the a priori rules that govern all Ga'dang behavior.

Even in the case of applying the rules of faith, no justification of the rules is requested or offered. There is no appeal to higher sets of rules or to a rational way of life, as Taylor (1961) indicates is inherent to justification in normative discourse. There is simply clarification of which rules are being applied. Thus the process of justification of evaluations and prescriptions is short-circuited in the Ga'dang oral society. Any evaluation or prescription based on the norms or rules of the society needs no justification. In the traditional Ga'dang view, there are no other sets of norms and rules to choose from. Thus, invoke theme or invoke norm is sufficient justification for any evaluation or prescription.

There is a parallel here to the findings of Bloch (1975:16-28), who notes that when political oratory (social control discourse) is used the possibility of contradiction is minimized or nullified by the fact that the participants made one fundamental choice *ab initio*. Just choosing to take part in such a discourse binds the participants to accept what follows because of the social relationships of the people involved and the unquestionable nature of the conventional subject matter. Thus he concludes that such a discourse cannot proceed as a logical exercise:

> Logic implies that one postulated connection between units is more right than another because of the innate relation between the parts of the logical argument. One can therefore say that to be logical, an argument must be couched in a form within which contradictory or alternative arguments are possible but excluded, not because of the way they are said, but because they are untrue: to be logical an argument must be formally contradictable in order to show its logical nature. Normally any statement is open to contradiction and replacement and since this is so in ordinary situations argument and reason are possible. By contrast, formalized language rules out the two prerequisites for logic, the potential of one statement to be followed by a large number of others and the possibility of contradiction. [Ibid.:21]

Bloch suggests that highly formalized discourse of social control is "beyond logic, its force being traditional authority" (ibid.). This is the case with the themes and norms invoked in Ga'dang normative discourse. This discourse is not as rigidly standardized as that which Bloch describes, but the themes and norms that may be invoked are highly conventionalized and beyond the possibility of contradiction.

8.3 Rhetorical devices

Rhetorical devices are surface features that have some conventional markedness; thus they are more prominent and more forceful. All rhetorical devices elevate normative force. Several have been identified in Ga'dang normative discourse: schema of prescription, parallel structures, chiasmus, and synthesis or summary.

8.3.1 Schema of prescription

Schema of prescription is a persuasive strategy. It is a three-part construction (introduced in sec. 6.1.3) with the following constituents: projected circumstance, prescription, and justification. These constituents are each typically realized by a single clause, but any constituent may be realized by more than one clause (cf. s.343-46). A brief example of this schema is found in s.189-90: 'If I speak falsely, scold me, because I am (like) the devil if I do not obey'. In this instance, the speaker's real persuasive intent was to convince everyone to speak in an acceptable way, but he used himself as the hypothetical example in order to establish a general principle.

8.3.2 Parallel structures

The use of parallel structures is a persuasive strategy in which the same idea is repeated or paraphrased. The second half of the structure is more forceful than the first, if for no other reason than that it doubles the emphasis given to the proposition. This is the case in s.245-46, in which the latter is a verbatim repetition of the former, 'There are few of us now!'

There is also the positive and negative paraphrase (in either order), as in s.343-44: 'don't just wait; get up and go' (cf. Hall 1983:149).

Another parallel structure could be described as a prescriptive one-two punch, that is, a pair of prescriptions (or evaluations) in which the first would be mitigated and the second would be unmitigated or more direct. In the following example (from s.300-4 of the Appendix) there is a double one-two punch, a flurry of exhortations. In the first pair ('reform'), the second is obviously less mitigated than the first. In the second pair ('try'), the second is more concise than the first, so somewhat stronger.

```
Nu dama na  nad,    reforma.   Mareforma.
if possible should reform      reform
```

'If possible we should reform. Reform!'


```
Kakkapantam tangngallan ino bifigfigtam, aggangwatam.
try.we.inc  control      the lips.ours    doings.ours

Kakkapantam.
try.we.incl
```

'Let us try to control our speech and doings. Try!'

There are many examples of this ascending structure, the second being less mitigated than the first. The most subtle one observed was spoken by Baggit, the youngest discussant, and although the tone of the whole is very subdued, the intention seems to have been to point a finger of blame:

```
Massiki tan  nu awan a  sinapit nu, e pakoman taka.
even     that if none rl said      you   forgive I.you

Kunna na tan  nu sinapit nu, ammena bali.
although that if said     you  not.it matter
```

'Even if you said nothing, I forgive you. Even though you may have said something, it doesn't matter.'

This strategy may be used to soften the blow and avoid shaming anyone with too abrupt or harsh an approach. Thus it has a better chance of persuading, not to mention its more substantial effect as a verbal one-two punch.

8.3.3 Chiasmus

The structure of chiasmus is described by Hall (1983:166 ff.) as being made up of at least a four-part organization. A simple form of chiasmus would involve four consecutive clauses, the fourth being closely related to the first (e.g., paraphrase) and the third being similarly related to the second. Complex chiastic structure was discovered in a Balangao normative text (Shetler and Walrod 1983) in which the most general topic was named first, followed by a series of propositions in descending generality (i.e., more and more specific) until the normative peak was reached, and then the process was reversed, reiterating the paraphrased propositions in reverse order until the most generic was reached again.

An example of a somewhat different chiastic structure is found in s.225-28 of the Appendix. At the beginning and the end of this section the state of mind of Andits and Galat is described ('affected/disturbed' and 'ashamed'). Following the initial description of their being 'affected' is the reason for their state of mind, namely, that it would appear that they 'were not able to teach or control' their child (younger relative). This proposition is paraphrased in s.227, just before the paraphrase of their state of mind in s.228.

There is a great deal of chiastic structure—or something similar to it—in s.244-62. This section lacks the symmetrical ordering of propositions, but the topic of *bangkirit* 'strife, hostility' is mentioned early (s.247) and is paraphrased near the end of the utterance as *kallussaw* 'hate'. Between these two statements of the general topic of exhortation are several statements about getting rid of those feelings, getting rid of people who behave in that way, and doing what is good. Each of these statements is paraphrased at least once before the speaker returns to the primary topic, but there is not a symmetrical ordering in this case.

8.3.4 Synthesis

Nowakowska (1979:202) suggests that the strength of connectedness between utterances in a dialogue is proportional to the extent of multiple connections of that utterance with others. I suggest that an utterance that can summarize or synthesize what has preceded (or explicate the global theme of what is to follow) has the greatest cohesive effect.

In normative discourse, especially in a culture in which the aim of such discourse is to achieve consensus, such a statement has a great deal of normative force and is a good strategy of persuasion. Being able to articulate a consensus is a stepping stone to having unanimous agreement on it.

Sentence 243 of the Appendix is a synthesis statement of several preceding sentences (starting at s.236). A more significant summary statement is found in s.327-29, in which Sanggoon sums up all that has gone on up to that point in the informal litigation. Each party had heard the other out, and the problem had been put behind them, and, as a result, there should be nothing further to trouble their minds. This summary statement served as a claim to success for the discourse, a notice that group harmony had been restored.

9   Ranking on a Scale of Normativity

All of the notional and surface features described in previous chapters may be ranked on a scale of normativity; that is, there are certain features which have more normative force. Normative force is the degree of probability of influencing, affecting, or producing a cognitive or behavioral change in another. Note that *influencing* and *affecting* are included in the definition, as well as *change*. Thus the normative discourse type includes texts intended to perpetuate frames or values, as may be the case in the Ga'dang informal litigation.

An example in American culture is the high school football coach at a pre-game pep-talk uttering a prescription with great intensity, "Get in there and hit those guys." It was already the intention of the players to do so, but the coach's prescription is not without normative force. It perpetuates the frame and reinforces the players' resolve.

My ranking of the features of Ga'dang normative discourse is somewhat intuitive, but supported by substantial evidence from the text. Since the ranking is subjective, there is room for question. The question, however, is not whether these surface structures can be given a normative ranking relative to each other, but whether I have determined the Ga'dang emic order. My conclusions are drawn from the written text, the audio recording, remembered features of the communication situation, and knowledge of the Ga'dang cognitive grid and public values.

A more certain determination of the emic order could be obtained through a scientific survey in which the Ga'dang people themselves would be asked to rank written or recorded texts or text parts as to their persuasiveness or coerciveness. In the Ga'dang oral culture, it would probably not be feasible to have test subjects give a numerical ranking to each normative structure in a large set. But it would be possible to present structures in pairs and ask the subject which one seemed to be "the heaviest." If audio recordings were used, there would need to be some controls on intonation and on test subjects' perceptions of the status of the speaker, especially if the segments being compared were spoken by different people. (This suggests another, more sociolinguistic type of survey, to determine the effect of social status on persuasiveness.) But no survey has been done in Ga'dang, and the following rankings are based primarily on evidence from the text itself and comparisons with other texts.

9.1 Ranking of discourse types

All linguistic communication has some normative component (see sec. 5.3.4); there is always some degree of intention to influence, affect, or change. In normative discourse, it is the *primary* intention; thus normative texts rank highest on a scale of normativity. Expository discourse is near the middle, followed by procedural. Narrative discourse typically has the least normative force.

The normative scale is almost the inverse of the information scale (Walker 1983:12-16), in which normative discourse ranks very low, and expository discourse ranks high. It is also very different from the "most dynamic to most static" scale (Longacre 1982:177), which ranks narrative as most dynamic and expository as most static. Normative discourse would occupy a midpoint on this scale.

9.2 Ranking of grammatical features within normative discourse

Clause types, pronominal reference, and particles or conjunctions were shown to have a significant role in normative ranking (see secs. 7.4-7.6). A ranking of clause types was presented in figure 14. The pronominal reference ranking interacts with the clause-type ranking to multiply the possible normative ranks. The top four ranks of clause types are the imperative, causative, compulsory, and obligatory. Each of these realizes its strongest normative force if a second person pronoun is used with it. The normative force of each is somewhat mitigated if a first person inclusive pronoun is used, and is even more mitigated by a first person dual pronoun.

Prescription always outranks evaluation in normative force. Therefore a prescriptive coda outranks an evaluative coda at paragraph boundaries (cf. sec. 7.3.3). However, social relationships between speaker and hearer may require that the speaker use nothing more forceful than evaluation, in the paragraph coda or any other feature of discourse including text type.

The particles and conjunctions listed in figure 15 also have normative ranking. The particles *lud* 'surely', *mat* 'in fact', *nad* 'ought', and *kad* 'perhaps' (the rhetorical question marker) rank very high and tend to elevate the normative force of any construction in which they occur. The adverbs *gakkurug* 'true' and *gakkuruwingke* 'very true' also elevate normative force. The conjunction *gampade* 'however' and its more emphatic form *gampama'de* are extremely high in normative force. They signal a radical departure from what is expected, that is, a departure from the current frame or script. Thus, when used in normative discourse that describes behavior being evaluated (see s.152, s.229, s.316), it is pejorative, since behavior should conform to the norms or expectations of the society, not depart from them. Implicit in the use of *gampade* in normative discourse is the bringing to bear of the weight of public opinion (expectations) on the evaluatum.

In contrast to the particles just mentioned, others that are used in normative discourse have a low ranking of normative force: *pay* 'just', *ke* 'just, still', *lang* 'only', and *allay* 'man, friend'. They tend to mitigate the force of any construction in which they occur and thereby contribute significantly to achieving consensus and social harmony by defusing tensions.

The word *allay*, in particular, expresses and reinforces group solidarity. The closer the social relationship between male speakers and hearers, the more likely that the word will be used very frequently. Its use is an implicit assertion of close relationship. When uttered with laryngealization and lengthening it may be a mild rebuke or lighthearted chiding, very mitigated and inoffensive.

9.3 Ranking of pairs of evaluative lexemes

The pairs of evaluative lexemes presented in figure 2 are not necessarily the only evaluative lexemes within the point of view, but they represent the positive and negative extremes. I make no claim that there is a difference in normative force between uttering a positive evaluation of an object or action and uttering the opposite negative evaluation. It may well be that there is a difference. (Positive reinforcement of good behavior is believed by some to be more effective than rebuke of bad behavior.) But the evidence from the Ga'dang text is thin, only that the discussion ends with several very positive evaluations (not of the behavior that brought about the litigation, but of the consensus). But the uttering of a parallel, positive-negative *pair* of evaluations does increase the normative force (see sec. 8.3.2).

The pairs themselves in relation to other pairs of evaluative lexemes can be ranked. What this presupposes is a hierarchical ranking of value systems per se, that is, the points of view realized by the pairs of lexemes.

All moral evaluations (ethical or social points of view) outrank all aesthetic ones with respect to normative force. Note that *narakkat* 'bad', which may function as the negative extreme in the ethical point of view, is potentially much worse than *saliwad* 'awkward speech' (the aesthetic point of view). Anything that is described as *saliwad* could also be described as *narakkat*, but not vice versa.

Within the moral points of view are included all considerations of group survival, solidarity, and harmony, as well as the social structures of the group and the norms governing social interaction (e.g., the age theme).

Within the aesthetic points of view there is also hierarchical ordering. The behavioral, which borders on the moral, would rank the highest. Thus the evaluation of an action as *annung* 'fitting, proper' or *balyat* 'improper' would have greater normative force than an evaluation of that same action

as *nala'ing* 'clever' or *ungkug* 'ignorant'. If a Ga'dang boy playing basket-
ball were told that his playing was *ungkug*, he might be offended, but he
would probably keep playing. If he were told that his playing was *balyat*,
he would probably stop, understanding that it would be inappropriate to
continue, for instance, if someone in the nearby house was critically ill.

The ranking of the relative normative force of the aesthetic points of
view, and therefore the pairs of lexemes associated with them, would be
this: The behavioral and the emotional would be at the high end of the
scale; the intellectual and the artistic would be near the midpoint; and the
economic, linguistic, and attributional would be at the low end.

9.4 Schema of prescription and normative ranking

The schema of prescription is high in normative force even in its unmarked form, namely, with one clause realizing each of its three notional
constituents: projected circumstance, prescription, and justification, as in
s.189-90. The normative force is elevated, however, when the nucleus is ex-
panded, that is, when there is more than one prescription (see s.235, which
has four prescriptions in the nuclear constituent).

Still higher in normative force is a prescription by itself, without an explicit projected circumstance or justification (cf. s.211-12). Since the
schema of prescription is considered the unmarked or standard form of
prescription (see sec. 6.1.3), such prescriptions in isolation are considered
to be the result of deletion, which is common at a discourse peak in
Ga'dang normative as well as narrative discourse. Maximum deletion,
which is the deletion of all non-nuclear constituents of the schema of
prescription, as well as the deletion of all non-nuclear elements of the
clause realizing the prescription, signals the highest degree of normative
force (e.g., s.211-12: 'Reform, change! Reform, change!').

9.5 Grouping of high-ranking features at normative peaks

The feature of maximum deletion is a way of achieving maximum normative force. Maximum deletion in the context of a prescription results in
an unmitigated, direct imperative. Another way of achieving almost maximum normative force is a clustering of the highest-ranking normative features at or around the normative peak. In a normative discourse, the
clustering is to be expected, although there may be focal points at normative peaks where the "stripped down" imperatives occur, as in s.211-12,
s.301, and s.304.

The feature of maximum deletion contiguous to one of the rare
prescriptive codas was discussed in section 7.3.3. The prescriptive coda is
in s.80. The context immediately preceding and following s.80 has clearly
marked narrative discourse peak surface structure embedded in this normative discourse secondary peak. Thus s.73-100 is extremely high in

normative force, exceeded only by the primary peak of the whole dialogue, in which direct prescriptions (highest-ranking surface structures) are uttered by the moderator (highest-ranking in the social context).

To illustrate the grammatical feature of maximum deletion in Ga'dang discourse peaks, figure 16 compares the discourse peak in s.86-100 with the first sixteen sentences of the discourse. The first sixteen sentences average twenty-five words each, with three sentences of forty or more words. Sentences 86-100 average less than six words each, with five sentences of three words or less. It is interesting to note that the one sentence that skews the average sentence length upward in the peak section, namely s.95, is an author comment of an explanatory nature, embedded within this embedded narrative section (a second level of embedding). Without this one sentence, the average for the whole section would be exactly five words per sentence.

As already mentioned, in addition to the feature of deletion, which elevates normative force, there may be clusters of high-ranking normative features. In one sense, deletion works against the realization of other features so that where deletion is most prominent the clustering is somewhat minimized. However, most of the other features can still be realized in combination with deletion.

The strongest cluster of surface features would be: (1) deletion (deletion in normative discourse removes all low-ranking particles, which tend to mitigate, while high-ranking ones may remain); (2) imperative; (3) second person pronominal reference (if explicit reference is needed—usually it will be deleted since context makes it clear); (4) high-ranking evaluative lexemes; (5) location in a highly normative discourse constituent, for example, prescription, signalled by *kunnantu* 'therefore' or *antu yaw ino sapit ku* 'this is what I have to say'; (6) location at the peak of such a constituent.

The greatest concentration of these high-ranking normative features is at the peak of the Ga'dang litigation (peaks 5 and 6 in fig. 13). Utterance 22 (s.244-62), spoken by Andits, and s.300-4 in utterance 25, spoken by Sanggoon, manifest all six features. The one exception is that Sanggoon does not use second person in s.300-4, but he does use it in other places when directly addressing Buton, who is younger. Andits and Laka, the oldest participants in the discussion, are more free with the use of second person in their prescriptions.

Clusters of high-ranking features are not squandered. They are reserved for the crucial peaks of normative discourse, when the participants sense that consensus is within reach. The effect is dramatic, and the litigation moves quickly to a close. Anger is abated, fellowship is restored, norms are perpetuated, and, at least for the moment, life in the Ga'dang community is as it should be.

S.	Number of words per sentence
1.	xxxxxxxxxxxxxxxxxxxxxxxxxxxxxx
2.	xxxxxxxxxxx
3.	xxxxxxxxxxxxxxxxxxxxxxxxxxxxxxxxxxxxxxxxx
4.	xxxxxxxxxxxxxxxxxxxxxxxxxxxxxxxxxxxxx
5.	xxxxxxxxxxxxxxxxxx
6.	xxxxxxxxxxxxxxxxxx
7.	xxxxxxxxxx
8.	xxxxxxxxxxxxxxxxxxxxxxxxxxxxxx
9.	xxxxxxxxxxxxxxx
10.	xxxxxxxxxxxxxxxxxxxxxxxxxx
11.	xxxxxxxxxxxxxxxxxxxxxxxxxxxxxxxxxxxxxxxx
12.	xxxxxxxxxxxxxx
13.	xxxxxxxxxxxx
14.	xxxxxxxxxxxxxxxxxxxxxxxxxxxxxxxxxxxxxxxxxxxx
15.	xxxxxxxxxxxxxxxxxxxxx
16.	xxxxxxxxxxxxxxxxxxxxxxxxxxxxxxxxxxxxxxxxxxxxxxxxxxxxxxx
86.	xxx
87.	xxxxxxx
88.	xx
89.	xxxxxxxxxx
90.	xxxxxxx
91.	xxxx
92.	xxxxxxx
93.	xxxxxxxxx
94.	xx
95.	xxxxxxxxxxxxxxxxxx
96.	xx
97.	xxxxxx
98.	xxxx
99.	xxxxxx
100.	x

Fig. 16. Sentence length in non-peak and peak sections

Conclusion

Normative discourse is integrally related to the notion of social control. It is the most desirable means of effecting social control, for it verbally perpetuates the society's norms or operational rules. By it people may be persuaded to behave in ways acceptable to the community, rather than coerced, or harmed for not conforming.

The most important contributions of this work on normative discourse are as follows:

(1) Explication of the nature of the relationships between cultural objects, norms, and knowledge structures, and the way in which persuasion relates to them. Persuasion often requires that they be changed, but it may also serve to perpetuate them.

(2) Clarification of the logic of normative discourse. There is not a radical difference in kind between normative and empirical reasoning. The difference is in the degree of sedimentation of the "facts." As long as the degree of sedimentation is great enough, statements or arguments justifying statements will be accepted and not challenged; thus for all practical purposes the point is proved.

(3) Explanation of the cultural differences in cognitive processes. The findings of researchers concerning the lateral specialization of brain hemispheres (e.g., Thompson 1975) and the correlation of the difference between each hemisphere's cognitive processes and the difference between reasoning patterns from one culture to another (Paredes and Hepburn 1976) as well as differences between oral and literate societies (Goody and Watt 1968; Ong 1982) have been summarized and a causal connection established.

The conclusion is that literacy results in thought processes that are more abstract, analytical, and logical—less holistic, intuitive, and artistic. Thus literate people become habituated to thought processes that are predominantly functions of the left hemisphere of the brain. The people of oral societies do not have the same stimulus to develop cognitive habits of this type. Furthermore, people in literate societies tend to develop a high value for logical and analytic thought processes and are more susceptible to the kind of persuasion that appeals to this inclination. On the other hand, oral societies (or oral contexts within a literate society) lean toward persuasion that appeals to the emotive, intuitive, and holistic cognitive functions.

(4) Description of the notional and surface structure of Ga'dang normative discourse. The notional and surface structure of several Ga'dang

texts was analyzed, and some features of the grammar of normative discourse identified, beginning with the level of the constituent structure of the discourse as a whole. The aim of normative discourse of the informal litigation type in Ga'dang was identified as being to achieve or restore consensus and social harmony. The ways in which the text coheres internally and with its larger context were made clear, and the strategies of persuasion and their surface realizations were described. The "route" was traced from the initial point of disharmony to the end point of consensus.

(5) Identification of a scale of normativity. Certain strategies and surface structures in Ga'dang were identified as having greater normative force than others, that is, greater persuasive impact. These were ranked on a scale of normativity, although further research would need to be done to determine if all the rankings I have suggested exactly reflect the emic ranking in the Ga'dang mind.

One must have an internalized grasp of the structure of normative discourse in a language, and of the ranking of surface features on the scale of normativity, and of the points of view or value systems of the cultural community, in order to produce a persuasive text. If a text is produced which eloquently employs all of these features of normative discourse, it is virtually impossible for any member of that cultural community to hear it and not be persuaded. He is able to resist being persuaded only if he has made an a priori choice not to accept the basic assumptions on which the normative discourse is founded. No text, no matter how nearly perfect, can overrule an individual's free will and right to make such an a priori choice.

Appendix: A Ga'dang Litigation

Bayombong:

1. Ara antu Buton, e   nu sanna ino
okay then Buton and if what the

amme yu   pakkinnawatan a adwa, antu ino
not you.pl understand   rl two   that the

pattatarabbag daw,   ta bakkan a kunna
cause.discuss you.pl so not   rl like

sitan, a wara kad   madingngadingngag
that   rl exist perhaps being.heard

daw   so   tolayira. 2. Ay
you.pl from people   well

kadidingngag   kayu-n   kelamang, kunna
hear.each.other you.pl-cmp just   like

na tan nu gakkurug onnu awan.
it that if true   or   not

1. Now then,
Buton, whatever is
the misunderstanding
between the two of
you, discuss it, so
that it won't be
like hearsay, what
you may have heard
from other people.
2. Just hear each
other out, whether
true or not.

Sanggoon:

3. Kunnamantu, se   ana etam si
like.this   because be we.inc at

baggaw a bakkan a tumuk, akwan tam si
light rl not   rl dark   do   we.inc obj

nalawad, se   antu ino sapit na Dios, a
good   because this the say of God rl

"Nu wara amme yu   pakkinnawatan a
if exist not you.pl understand   rl

makkakarolak si angngurug sikwak,
be.siblings in faith   to.me

mattatarabbag kayu, ta makkapakapakoli
discuss   you.pl so reciprocally.forgive

kayu   so nalliwatan   ino tinaggitata.
you.pl obj committed.fault the each.one

3. It's like this
therefore; because
we are in light and
not in dark, we
should do good,
because God's word
says, "If there is a
misunderstanding
between you siblings
in faith, discuss
it, so that you will
forgive each other's
faults.

4. Ino kun i Bayombong, inoy, ikkayu
the said pm Bayombong, that you.pl

4. About what
Bayombong said, you,
Buton and Andits,

```
Buton, anni Andits, nabayin  nad    yaw a
Buton and  Andits  long.time should this rl

nebanag ku, se     ikkanak pay ino neyekwa
told    me  because me      just the placed

yu    a  kunnangke presidente yu     a
you.pl rl as.if    president  yours  rl

mamangngal sitaw a iglesia tam onnu
to.lead    this  rl church ours or

kapilya. 5. Udde inappa.k ino atal ku
chapel      but  took.I   the shame mine

allay, se     amme-ta kappe-lamang dama
man    because not-we.2 also-only   able

pamipittanan a itakkub    ino gagangay tam
cause.stop   rl throw.away the customs ours

a ginaga'dang. 6. E   aggataron    ak
rl of.Ga'dang     and continuous.wait I

sikwayu    allay, nu inya nad    sikwayu ino
for.you.pl man    if who  should of.you  the

umang makitatabbag sikwak mappe'afu ira
come  discuss       to.me about     pl

sitaw a problema.
this  rl problem
```

you should have told
me about this long
ago, because I am
the one you have
appointed to be like
your president, to
lead our church.
5. But I was
ashamed, because we
are just not able to
stop or throw off
our Ga'dang ways.
6. And I just
waited, to see which
of you would come to
discuss this problem
with me.

```
7. Udde wara allay so awan, kunnangke
   but  exist man  lm none    as.if

naddang ira yaw a  aw. 8. On  se
arrived pl  this rl day    yes because

atallan ku enin  mamabwat si tatarabbag,
ashamed I  the.one to.start obj discussion

a bakkan kayu-in    in makan nakam,
rl not    you.pl-cmp the whose mind

se      amme-rak   anggam a bibbiyan a
because not-you.I like    rl honor    rl

kunnangke afu   yu,   kun ku-n ke lud
as.if     leader yours said I-cmp just sure

allaye.
man
```

7. But when none
came, this day
arrived. 8. Yes,
because I was
ashamed to be the
one to initiate this
discussion, because
I really thought
that you might not
want to honor or
respect me, as
though I were one of
your leaders.

9. I Teklanon pelang ino sinatabbag ku
   pm Teklanon only   the discussed me

si'in a nappakabebutan nu ansanna ira ino
before rl questioning   if how   pl the

akkakokwa yu.   10. Udde awan a dama
welfare you.pl   but none rl ability

na nasapit mappe'afu sikwayu, a kunna payo
his to.say about   you.pl rl like just

ikkanak allay, se   nagyan ak lud sey
myself man   because was I sure at

Bagabag sin ikkayu a amme pakkinnawatan a
Bagabag when you.pl rl not understood   rl

matama.   11. E sinapit ke i Teklanon
father.son   and said   just pm Teklanon

sikwak si "Ino nad   nalawad nu wara
to.me obj the should good   if exist

kunna sitan a problema, ikka pe-nad
like that rl problem you just-should

ino kunnangke pikampattan da,   se
the as.if   mediator   theirs because

ikka pe lud o kunnangke ama   ra
you just sure the as.if   father theirs

sitaw a kapilya, a bakkan nad   o
here rl chapel   rl not   should the

ikkanak. 12. Se   ikkanak namat, Balangao
myself   because myself really Balangao

ak, e amme-k inammu ino gagangay yu   a
I and not-I know the custom you.pl rl

Ginaga'dang. 13. Napapya nad   nu
of.Ga'dang   better should if

kaparefu-k ira a Balangao," kun na mat
same-I   they rl Balangao   said he really

pay.
just

9. It was just Teklanon who discussed this with me before, asking about your welfare. 10. But he was not able to tell about your situation, and neither was I, of course, because I was at Bagabag when the two of you, older and younger relative, had the misunderstanding. 11. And Teklanon said to me, "What would be good when there is a problem like that would be for you to be their mediator, rather than myself, because it's you who is like their father in this chapel. 12. Because, as for myself, I am a Balangao, and I do not know your Ga'dang customs. 13. It would be better if they were Balangaos like me," he also said.

14. Ammu yu   allay nu sanna gafu
    know you.pl man   if what source

na a bakkan ak o   namagabaggi a
its rl not   I the whose.body rl

nappa'ayag sikwayu allay, se   tantaro
cause.call you.pl man   because perhaps

lang nu wara masapit daw   sikwak nu wara
only if exist say   you.pl to.me if exist

kada'nan na ino tatarabbag, e   nganan
start   fut the discussion and depict

daw   na lang si wara tata'wiyan ku
you.pl fut only obj exist favoritism my

sikwayu. 15. Kolak   takayu adwa si
to.you.pl   sibling I.you.pl two in

binaba'lag, anda bangngag ak ke so
flesh   and deaf   I just at

gafugafu na ira yan a amme yu
sources its pl that rl not you.pl

pakkinnawatan a matama.
understand   rl father.son

14. You know the
reason why I was not
the one to call you
together, man,
because one of you
might say to me that
I started the
discussion, and you
might just claim
that I have
favoritism between
you. 15. I am a
blood relative of
both of you, and I
have just been deaf
about the causes of
the misunderstanding
between you, father
and son.

16. Antu gafu   na a kinapakapan na
    this source its rl arrival   its

ira yaw a aw, se   antu ino dinandam ku
pl this rl day because this the thought I

si'in, "Nalawad nu wara i Mayik na a
before good   if exist pm Mayik fut rl

aggadingngag so ira a mattatabbag na a
listening   to them rl discuss   fut rl

matama,   se   antu mat Americano,
father.son because this really American

e   tantaro iyatal da,   anda ammu-k si
and perhaps respect they and know-I obj

awan a tata'wiyan na na sikwara a adwa,"
none rl favoritism his fut to.them rl two

nekun ku.
said I

16. That's why
this day has
arrived, because I
had been thinking,
"It would be good if
Mayik were here to
listen to the father
and son discuss,
because he is an
American, and they
might respect him,
and I know that he
has no favoritism
between the two of
them," I said.

17. Nu sanna ira ma'lud iyan a amme
    if what pl sure that rl not

yu langin dama pattatabban a adwa,
you.pl just able cause.discuss rl two

takenasi si'in, ta amme na nad
in.order.that before, so not it should

langin nappa'oddu, si'in kayu-n
just became.much before you.pl-cmp

kenad-in, paddambalan takayu.
just.should-cmp cause.meeting I.you.pl

18. Udde oddu ira-in in agoman ku, se
    but much pl-cmp the reserve my because

awan lud umang maddanug sikwak nu ansanna
none sure come inform to.me if how

ino gafugafu na. 19. Se "madyat ino
the source its because hard the

kunna yaw" kun ku ira-n kelamang.
like this said I pl-cmp just.only

20. Gampade bakkan a naggabwat so nakam
    however not rl came from mind

daw a adwa. 21. Amme na ira inoy allay
yours rl two reject it pl that man

nad.
should

17. Whatever it was that the two of you were not able to discuss, you should have arranged a meeting with me about it long ago, in order that it would not just increase. 18. But I was too reserved, because nobody came to inform me about the reason for it. 19. And I just said, "This is an intolerable situation." 20. However, it was not the initiative of you two. 21. Man, it should not be like that.

22. Antu gafu na a malla amme
    this source its rl like not

kad kayu nepabburuburung so awira a
perhaps you.pl caused.worry at days rl

inoy, e ayo etam to tangnganaw ya nu
that and here we.inc this midday pt if

sanna ira yan allay. 23. E sapitan nu
what pl those man and say you

Andits, nu "I Buton ma'lud kunnera ma'lud
Andits if pm Buton sure like.pl really

22. Since you were not concerned about it in the past, here we are this midday to look into those things, man. 23. So, Andits, you say, "This is what I really heard about Buton, man." 24. The same for you, Buton, say, "Like this and this is what I really heard about uncle, man, and I

yo   diningngag ku sikwana alle.".
the heard   I of.him man

24. Mampe   sikwam Buton, nu "I litag
    likewise for.you Buton if pm uncle

ma'lud kunnayaw a kunnayaw ino nadingngag
sure   like.this rl like.this the heard

ku sikwana allay, e nekalussa-k si
I of.him man   and hate-it.I in

gakkurug," kun daw.   25. Amme yu
truth   say you.pl   not you.pl

makka'atatal   a adwa se
reciprocally.ashamed rl two because

bakkan-in a kunna si'in a dama ta a
not-cmp   rl like before rl able we.2 rl

makkapulipulitika a massisiri. 26. E   nu
recipr.politic   rl to.lie   and if

amme yu   mattalaw a massiri ki Dios,
not you.pl fear   rl to.lie to God

anda amme yu   mattalaw a mamalapanday si
and not you.pl   fear   rl slander   in

sapit, kunnanatan nu nakasapit kayu   si
speech even.though if able.say you.pl obj

narakkat a mekontara so layag daw   si'in,
bad   rl against   at ears yours before

ibukkat daw   to   ingke'in ta
remove you.pl here now   so

makkapakapakoli   kayu. 27. Se   ira
reciprocal.forgive you.pl   because pl

inoy mat,   kamali ira na nanu kunna.
those really mistake pl fut when like.it

28. E   istorya kunnantu, mattatabbag
    and story.it therefore discuss

kayu   a matama,   ta ayo kami a
you.pl rl father.son for here we   rl

aggadingngag.
listening

really hated it,"
you say. 25. The two
of you, don't be
reticent, because
it's not like before
when we would scheme
and lie. 26. And if
you are not afraid
to lie to God, and
not afraid to
slander, even though
in the past you
could say bad things
that were offensive
to hear, get rid of
that at this time so
you can forgive each
other. 27. Because
we really err when
we do those things.
28. And tell it
therefore, discuss
it, you father and
son, for here we are
listening.

Andits:

29. Ana ino daretsu a assapitan ku.
    be the direct rl speech   my

30. Udde antu mat   kun ku, nu maga'naddan
    but this really say I   if interrupted

kad   pay yo korwan a sapite nepalawad
perhaps just the other rl words made.good

tam-un   na lang-in allay. 31. E   amme
we.inc-cmp fut only-cmp man   and not

na ra na langin payin   a ma'ari inoy
it they fut only.cmp just.cmp rl remove that

a aggadandamman tam. 32. Gampama'de
rl thinking   ours   however

nebuyawut ku ira mat   na. 33. Gampama'de
made.known I pl really fut   however

wara ira na dalidaliwangkit na. 34. E   nu
exist pl fut ignoring   it   and if

sin   binaba'lag si gakkurug, amme-k ira-n
since fleshy   in truth   not-I pl-cmp

kelang anggam si ikkanetam ira-n kelang
just   like   obj we.inc   pl-cmp just

yaw a naraletung si gakkurug alle.
this rl gathered   in truth   man

35. Awan a ammu-k si ituldu-k onnu
    none rl know-I obj teach-I or

abbe'bek   ku si abbing ku alle.
discipline I obj child my man

36. Udde antu-in gakkurug yaw o
    but this-cmp truly   this the

pappa'itan ku nad   so abbe'bek ku si
cause.see I should of discipline my obj

abbing ku si gakkurug alle, se   amme na
child my in truth   man because not it

ira nad   mepapatta   si gakkurug o iyaw
pl should be.repeated in truth   the this

29. I have something straightforward to say. 30. But this I say, if I get interrupted or cut off, let's just make it good, man. 31. And don't let it ruin what we've been thinking about. 32. However, I really did speak out about it. 33. However, it was ignored. 34. And by the former customs, I just would not want for us to have this meeting, and that's the truth, man. 35. I don't know of anything that I instructed or rebuked my child about, man.

36. But in fact that's all I should divulge about my rebuking my child, truly, man, because this kind of thing should really not be broadcast. 37. This is really true, man.

ira a   tarabafu. 37. Gakkuruwingke yaw
pl   rl work   true.really this

allay.
man

38. Sapitan da   allay nu sanna ino   38. They can say
    say   they man if what the   whatever they know
                                              about me, man. 39. I
ammu ra   a sapitan gumafu sikwak. 39. Awan don't know that I
know they rl say   about me   none said any of this.
                                              40. I just don't
a ammu-k si sinapasapit ku yaw. 40. Amme-k know of it, man.
rl know-I obj said   I this   not-I

pe   ammu alle.
just know man

41. Ma'annararig etam   nad   si   41. We should
    use.examples we.inc should in   circumlocute
                                              somewhat (i.e., use
sapit allaye, udde malo lang nu wara   examples), but we
speech man   but hurt just if exist   should not stretch
                                              it out, because then
sumalofu, se   amme na naggagarimpa yo   we won't reach a
increase because not fut come.together the   consensus.

nakam.
mind

42. Se   ikkanak mat   allaye,   42. As for me, I
    because myself   really man,   was married five
                                              times. 43. Twice I
namillima-k a nangatawa. 43. Namidwa-k a   had a child in
fifth-I   rl married   twice-I   rl   marriage. 44. This
                                              is what I was
nangabbing a nangatawa. 44. Antu ino   feeling in my mind,
had.child rl married   this the   man, when there was
                                              not agreement
nispirensyan ku so nakam ku inoy allay,   between me and my
experienced I in mind   my that man   younger relative,
                                              man. 45. None at
se   waso bakkan allay a nappaparefu ino all, man. 46. I
because upon not   man   rl caused.same the never encountered
                                              this before.
nakam o affunan   ke   alle.
mind the elder.younger just man

45. Awaningke allay. 46. Amme-k
    none.really man   not-I

napasa'bal yaw.
encountered this

47. Udde, anta!   48. Amme-k ira
    but, who.knows   not-I pl

kelang   mebuyawut. 49. Ikkayu kallaye, nu
just.only make.known   you.pl man,   if

anna pay ino makasapit sikwayu se
what just the able.say you.pl because

iyaw, naraletungan tam a iyaw awan a
this, gathered   we.inc rl this none rl

baggat na, nu amme ta   pelang   a
grain its if not we.2 just.only rl

masingguyang a massimpakoli lullamang,
part.ways   rl forgiving   really.only

se   nara'lang etam. 50. Nabalin-in
because facing   we.inc   finished-cmp

nad   yaw.
should this

47. But who knows?
48. I won't spread
around those things.
49. You all say
whatever you are
able to, because
this meeting of ours
will have no value
or result if we
don't part company
having forgiven each
other, because we
are here facing each
other. 50. This
should be finished.

51. Wara sin gafu   na yawe
    exist when source its this.p

allaye, one init   yu   allay
man.p   yes.p reheat.food you.pl man

Teklanon, agyan taw allay ira anni Tony,
Teklanon stayed here man   them and Tony

a medyu nadammat-in kena-in sapit i
rl medium heavy-cmp just-cmp words of

Buton toya a "Fuffutan nangke   ki
Buton here.p rl persevere fut.really pm

Teklanon, nu sannanganna ino pangwa so
Teklanon if what.depict the cause.do to

elder onnu lakay   to kapilya a
elder or   old.man this chapel rl

51. When this all
began, man, you and
(Tony) Teklanon were
reheating some food,
for Tony and the
others were here
then, and Buton
spoke somewhat
sharply, saying
"Let's demand of
Teklanon to tell us
what to do to an
elder of the church
who slanders." 52. I
don't insist that I
was the one he was
accusing. 53. But I
felt heavy-hearted
then, saying,
"Please let's not do
that because we

mamaraparal". 52. Sabagay, amme-k sapitan
slanders   Anyway,   not-I say

si ikkanak ino asipan na. 53. Udde
obj I   the accuse he   but

nadammat-in angkwa-k sinoy a "Bakkan abbu
heavy-cmp   thing-my then rl not   please

yan o angkwan daw   se   ang tam
that the do   you.pl because go we.inc

abbu to adal tam," kun ku sinoy.
please here study ours said I then

54. Ino nepassapit ku so "Nakoy alle."
    the cause.say I obj wow   man

55. Arangngan na lang-in mappaye.
    request.it he only-cmp really.just.p

56. "Amme tam-un   na lang-in disisyonan
    not we.inc-cmp fut only-cmp decide

nu sannanganna inoy," kun ku. 57. E
if what.depict that   said I   and

gini'na na nad   sikwak inoy nu bakkan nak.
felt   he should of.me then if not   he.I

58. Onnu inang na nad   sinapit sikwak si
    or   came he should said   to.me obj

"O, nafektaran i ulitag so sinapit ku."
oh affected   pm uncle by said   I

59. Kunsesa'ay amme-m   abbu sikwak
    why   reject-you please me

a nekun nu si matotaw ak gafuso   elder
rl said I obj lost   I concerning elder

onnu lakay   to kapilya? 60. Antu ino
or   old.man this chapel   this the

idaying na so nakam na nu ansanna
pain   his in mind his if how

kanu   mattuldu so tolay a
it.is.said to.teach to person rl

should go to our
place of study."
54. What I had said
was "Wow, man!"
55. He really
requested that
again. 56. "Let's
not decide what to
do about that," I
said. 57. And he
should have realized
that I felt
offended. 58. Or he
should have come and
said to me, "Were
you offended by what
I said, Uncle?"

59. Why did you
reject me, saying
that I was washed up
as an elder or
leader of this
chapel? 60. That was
the anxiety in his
mind when he asked
how to instruct
people who
slandered. 61. Why
didn't he just say
to me, "Uncle was
affected and I'm
coming to discuss

mamaraparal. 61. Kunsesa'ay se   amme na
slanders   why   because not he

lang-in sinapit sikwak si "Nafektaran i
only-cmp said   to.me obj affected   pm

litag e   ang ku tatabban"? 62. Amme na
uncle and go I   discuss.it   not he

lang-in kun nu bakkan ak o target na
only-cmp said if not   I the target its

ino sapit na.
the words his

it"? 62. He just didn't say it, but rather made me the target of what he said.

63. Udde wara alle so awan, antu
    but exist man at none, this.is

inay! 64. Ifungal ku kad   kelamang,
that   root/base I perhaps just.only,

allaye akwan ku-n yo massapit yaw.
man.p do   I-cmp the say   this

65. Ifungal ku kad   kelang allay.
    root/base I perhaps just.only man

66. Se i Buton kadde   tatabban nak
    for pm Buton perhaps discussed he.me

gakkurug. 67. Passig pelang
truly   entirely just.only

nelangalangngi allay, makkiyad sin
glanced.around man   until   when

naragadiyan tam. 68. E   ipakoli-k ira yaw
plowing.time ours   and forgive-1 pl this

Buton, e   awan nad   rakkat na ira yaw
Buton and none should bad   its pl this

allay.
man

63. But when he did not come, that was it! 64. I attribute it to that, to what I am saying. 65. I attribute it to that, man. 66. Because Buton actually did discuss it with me. 67. But he just glanced around disinterestedly man; it was at plowing time. 68. And I forgive these things, Buton, and there should be no remaining malice about this, man.

69. Wara sin maragadi kun dawe,
    exist when to.plow say you.pl.p

inang etam   nangita si sassapan   tam.
went we.inc looked obj wood.to.trim ours

69. When you said it was plowing time, we went looking for some wood to trim for plowing. 70. And we wandered

70. E   naletotaw etam   si angan, e   aimlessly on the way
    and wandered we.inc in going and   and came out at
                                               Kapitan and brought
nepadat etam   sey Kapitan, e   nakatarak   our wood from there
ended.up we.inc at Kapitan and able.truck   by truck.

etam   sinoy si kayu.
we.inc then   obj wood

    71. E   gafuse amme tam   71. And because we
        and result not   we.inc   did not finish our
                                          wood trimming then,
natupak-in   sinassapan tam sinoy,   we contracted with
completed-cmp trimming.it ours then   Paregaru to meet him
                                         there again to
nantataratu etam   anda Paregaru si   finish the trimming.
contracted we.inc and Paregaru obj   72. But on the day
                                         after we made the
maddadarambal etam   na kappay sinay, ta contract, I asked
meet   we.inc fut also   there so you if we were going
                                         there again. 73. But
itupak   tam   nad   ino sassap na.   you said then, man,
complete we.inc should the trimming his "If you want to go,
                                         go ahead," you said,
72. Udde sin kadaramatan na inoy a antu man. 74. And you
    but when next.day   of that rl this wheeled around and
                                         left. 75. And I
ino taratu   tam, e   nepakifut ku sikwam nu said, "That's his
the contract ours and asked   I to.you if   custom. 76. He has
                                         no consideration
umang etam   kappay sinoy. 73. Udde massapit because he is still
go   we.inc also   there   but say a child," I just
                                         said. 77. I told it
ka allay sinoye, "Nu umang kayu, mang to Paregaru.
you man   then.p if go   you.pl, go

kayu," nekun nu allay. 74. E
you.pl said you man   and

talekkud   nu-n   a inanaw. 75. E
turn.the.back you-cmp rl left   and

nekun ku si "Gagange-na. 76. Awan a
said I obj custom-his   none rl

aggatotakkan na se   a'anakira kepay,"
consideration his because child.pl still

nekun ku pelamang. 77. Netuldu-k ki
said I just.only   informed-I pm

Paregaru.
Paregaru

78. Ara kunna sinoy, dingngaggang ku so
    now like that   heard   I at

tolay-ira. 79. "Iyaw awan a surbi na inay,
person-pl   this none rl use its there

se   kunna kappe kena si awan a
because like also just obj none rl

korakorwan si tolay, e nu anya na ino
other   of person and if who fut the

kada'nan na na yo tatarabban tam ya, e
dropped it fut the discussion ours p   and

kakallak na si uliwan" nekun ku si gakkurug
pitiful him in fact   said I in truth

allay, "e amme tam   ira lang uditan allay
man   and not we.inc pl only check man

ammin, se   antu kappe na allay, se
all   because this also fut man   because

sanna na ino mammulta sikwata allay?"
who   fut the judges   we.2   man

80. Aran   tam   ira inay ira a banag.
    remove we.inc pl that pl rl thing

78. Now when that
had happened, I
heard things from
people. 79. And I
truly said, man,
"This is useless,
because it's as if
there are no other
people involved, and
whoever caused this
problem we are
discussing is really
to be pitied, and we
can't bring up
everything, because
who would judge
between us man?"
80. We should get
rid of this kind of
thing.

81. Antu gafu na, ino nad busang
    this source its the should little

a kamali tame, pakoman tam. 82. Massiki
rl mistake ours.p forgive we.inc   even

tan nu ana etam kepe si lammuk, talaga
that if be we.inc still in dark   maybe

awan sikwami iyaw a makkakarolak   onnu
none ours   this rl recipr.siblings or

tawayan si gakkurug. 83. Awan sikwami.
clan   in truth   none ours.exc

81. For this
reason, if we make a
little mistake, we
should forgive it.
82. Even if we were
still in the dark,
perhaps there would
really be none of
this among our
brotherhood or clan.
83. There would be
none among us.

84. Iyo na nu wara kad   busang
    this fut if exist perhaps small

ye nadammat, tata-in ke si gakkurug iyo
rl.p heavy   one-cmp just in truth   this

84. Now if there
is some of this
heaviness or
disharmony, it's one
thing I really don't
understand, because

amme-k ma'awatan, se   bakkan kad   si
not-I understand because not   perhaps obj

antu ino adalan tam.   85. Nu wara
this the studied we.inc   if exist

pakkamaliyan ino tata sikwatam,
cause.mistake the one of.us.inc

makkapakapakoli etam,   ta awan nad
recipr.forgive we.inc so none should

pakapakaliwatan tam.
cause.blame   us

it is not consistent
with what we have
studied. 85. If one
of us makes a
mistake, we should
forgive each other,
so that we would not
be blameworthy.

86. Nangwa-k si   kansyon. 87. Nang ku
    made-I   obj song   went I

nepadda kwara Sanggoon anni Mayik.
showed pm.pl Sanggoon and   Mayik

88. Inaprobaran da.
    approved   they

86. I wrote a
song. 87. I went and
showed it to
Sanggoon and Mayik.
88. They approved
it.

89. Antu inoy o   nassapitan nu si
    this that the said   you obj

"Amme na yan alle." 90. E   pinersonal
not it that man   and personalled

akun ke   a ininsolto sinoye. 91. Amme-k
I   just rl insulted then.p   not-I

pelang   naddamit sinoy. 92. Makkiyad sinoy
just.only spoke   then   since   then

amme ku-n nangwa si kansyon. 93. Ituldu-m
not I-cmp made   obj song   tell-you

ki Mayik nu wara-in   na'da-k sikwana-in si
pm Mayik if exist-cmp gave-I to.him-cmp obj

kansyon. 94. Ma'atal akun.
song   ashamed I

89. That's when
you said, "That's no
good, man." 90. And
I was personally
insulted by that.
91. I didn't speak
then. 92. From that
time on I haven't
written any songs.
93. Just ask Mayik
if I have given him
any more songs.
94. I was ashamed.

95. Antu inoy nasulisug ak sinoy,
    this the tempted   I then

95. I found
that very trying,
because "Here are

se   "ana ira kanu   ino sapit o   these things that
because exist pl reported the word the   child has said," I
                                               said then.

abbing inaya," kun ku ira sinoy.
child that.p said I pl then

96. Naprobaran da. 97. "Dama na yan,"   96. They approved
    approved   they   okay it that   it. 97. "That's
                                               okay," they said.
kun da   kena.
said they just

98. Udde "Amme na yan. 99. Ka''atatal   98. But "That's no
    but reject it that   shameful   good. 99. It's
                                               shameful to those
so dilod   ira," nekun nu.   downstream," you
to downstream pl   said you   said.

100. Inamme-k.   100. I hated that!
     rejected-I

101. Itan daw   ino pakkakampattan ku   101. Just look how
     look you.pl the cause.kept   I   I have truly held a
                                               grudge against you.
ira a pallussawan sikwam si gakkurug.   102. I have not yet
pl rl cause.hate you   in truth   written any more
                                               songs.
102. Awan kepay inangwa-k si kansyon yaw.
     none yet   made-I   obj song   this

103. Waso in-tam   pa'adalan, ay,   103. When we went
     upon went-we.inc study.place oh   to study, oh, excuse
                                               me.
bakkan abbu.
not   please

104. Iyaw, ipakoli-k lamang,   104. This I just
     this, forgive-I only   forgive, so that
                                               Mayik will hear that
takesi   dingngaggan i Mayik, ta, nu   if I was the one at
in.order.that hear.it   pm Mayik so if   fault, you can beat
                                               me up as much as you

```
ikkanak o  nalliwat, dama rak    a        like, so that I will
I          the did.fault okay they.me rl  not slander.
```

```
sultukan nu kayarak    a  sultukan,
punch    if as.much.as rl punch
```

```
takesi         amme-k pe  akwan no
in.order.that  not-I  just do    the
```

```
mamaraparal.
slander
```

```
    105. Wara sin madal etam    anda          105. At our study,
         exist when study we.inc and     when we were
                                          discussing about
matatarabbag etam    mappe'afu so da bunga,   fruit bearing, that
discuss      we.inc about        at pl fruit  was the source of
                                          it, namely, that if
antu yan no fungallan man   yan, a  nu    they did not approve
this that the root          again that rl if  of the fruit of my
                                          teaching, then even
amme ra   aprobaran a  bunga-k ino tuldwan    if my faith would be
not  they approve   rl fruit-my the teach ruined, I would
                                          disrupt this chapel.
ku a  tolay, massiki madaral iyo angngurug    106. There was one
I  rl person even    destroy the faith    who spoke; it was
                                          Baskelo, in fact.
ku, kungkulan ku yo   kapilya. 106. Ana   107. "Just don't
my  confuse   I  this chapel        be    speak," I said.
                                          108. "Just don't
kanu      ino nassapitan na, kallaye i    speak there."
reported  the said       he man.p   pm
```

```
Baskelo ingke. 107. "Amme-m pelang
Baskelo really       not-you just.only
```

```
aggedamadamit," nekun ku. 108. "Amme-m
speaking        said  I        not-you
```

```
pelang     maddamit sinay."
just.only  speak    there
```

```
    109. Wasin ikkami a  madal, sinalangad     109. When we were
         upon  we.exc rl study  took.issue studying, Kolakkan
                                          took issue with me,
nak   i    Kolakkan sitan yi, se          because Yawindo had
she.me pm  Kolakkan then  p   because     a question. 110. And
                                          that was the start
makwestion da   Yawindo. 110. Antu-in in      of much tension in
asked       they Yawindo        this-cmp the  our studies.
```

oddu parikut na-in in aggadal mi.
much tension it-cmp the study ours

111. Solbaran ku nad-in   aggadal
     solve   I   should-cmp study

mi so uray-k pay. 112. Udde nallangngan
ours at mind-my just   but scolded

nak   i Kolakkan, se   sinakaw
she.me pm Kolakkan because stole

tam-un   ino aw i Dios. 113. "Amme na
we.inc-cmp the day pm God   not it

nad   kunna yan," kun i Kolakkan.
should like that said pm Kolakkan

114. "Despensaran dak   se   pare'garu
     excuse   you.me because crooked

ira yo assapitan ku ya. 115. Anggam ku
pl the saying   my p   like I

nad lang si awan a narakkat sikwatam.
should only obj none rl bad   to.us.inc

116. Lawaran   tam   nad   iyo madal,"
     make.good we.inc should this study

nekun ku.
said I

111. I intended to resolve our study. 112. But Kolakkan scolded me, because we had stolen God's day. 113. "It shouldn't be like that," Kolakkan said. 114. "Pardon me, because what I said was misguided. 115. I desire that there should be no wrong among us. 116. Let's make our study good," I said.

117. Wasin ikkanetam-un nang a madal
     upon we.inc-cmp   went rl study

inoy, mallang a nadammat ira-in in
then like   rl heavy   pl-cmp the

assapitan daw.   118. Tuttud nu nakuy
saying   yours.pl   seat your maybe

iyane. 119. Treining pay inaya.
there.p   Treining just that.p

117. When we all went to study then, it was like your words were heavy. 118. You were sitting there. 119. Treining was over there.

120. Wasin ikkami a madal, arig   ku
     upon we.exc rl study thought I

120. When we were studying, I thought that we were to

si isamarays pay ammin in binasa tam.
obj summarize just all   the read we.inc

summarize all that
we had read.

121. Udde nattuttud akun sitawwi.
     but sat   I.cmp here.p

121. But I was
sitting here.

122. "Tawwara sikwara se   medyu inammu
     better   them   because medium know

122. "It's better
for them (to do it)
because they are
somewhat
knowledgeable," I
said.

ra," kun ku.
they said I

123. Iyaw, amme-k iyimad sikwayu
     this not-I hide   from.you.pl

123. I'm not
concealing any of
this from you,
because God is
watching me. 124. I
thought that we were
to summarize all
that we had studied.
125. Not so.

yaw, se   i Dios aggatulangngan nak.
this because pm God watching   he.me

124. Arig   ku si isamarays tam   ammin
     thought I obj summarize we.inc all

a nadalan tam.   125. Awan.
rl studied we.inc   none

126. "Sigi,   makkansyon etam-un,"
     go.ahead sing   we.inc-cmp

126. "Okay, let's
sing," you said.

kun nu-n.
said you-cmp

127. "Ma, awan-in allay?" kun ku.
     why none-cmp man   said I

127. "What, no
more, man?" I said.

128. "Makkansyon etam-un."
     sing   we.inc-cmp

128. "Let's sing."

129. Ira inay allay ino amme tam   ira
     pl that man   the not we.inc pl

129. Those are the
things we should not
do, man. 130. If
that is your
mindset, (you should
just say) "What else
are you others
thinking of, that we
should do?"

nad a pakakwan. 130. Nu antu-in so
should rl cause.do   if this-cmp at

uray-m,   "Sanna kepay ino ammu yu   pay
mind-your what still the know you.pl just

o korwan, ta akwan tam pay?"
the others so do we.inc just

131. Sinoye, inita yu mat nu
then.p saw you.pl really if

wara sapitan ku? 132. Awan, nu bakkan ka
exist said I none if not you

imman kelud o mangidayadaying so
cmp.again just.sure the urging.strongly to

elder onnu pangulu sito kapilya a
elder or leader this chapel rl

disiplina. 133. Ansan ta naddisiplina so
discipline how we.2 discipline to

elder onnu lakay sito kapilya? 134. One,
elder or old.man this chapel yes.p

sanna ino netuldu-m sikwak? 135. Awan a
what the told-you to.me none rl

ammu-k si sapitan daw sikwak yan.
know-I obj said you.pl to.me that

131. Back then, did any one of you witness me saying anything? 132. Not at all, but rather you actually urged strongly again that we talk about disciplining elders or leaders of the church. 133. "How do we discipline elders or leaders of this chapel?" 134. Yes, and what did you tell me? 135. I don't know of anyone telling me about that.

136. Wara ino daffug daw a
exist the buffalo yours rl

aggalubbak pelang sinoye, na'allang i
untethered just.only then.p scolded pm

Toyun. 137. "Sakay iyo balay.
Toyun dirty this house

138. Lullungngan da yo kalawatan," kun
muddied they this yard said

i Toyun. 139. "Kadde," kun nu.
pm Toyun so.what said you

140. Malow-in kuyung ku a naddingngag.
pain-cmp stomach my rl heard

136. When your buffalo was just running loose there, Toyun scolded you. 137. "This house is dirty! 138. They're muddying up the yard," said Toyun. 139. "So what," you said. 140. Hearing that, my stomach hurt.

141. Wasin i Tukkaklak pelang-in
upon pm Tukkaklak just.only-cmp

141. Then when Tukkaklak went over there, you arrived

manaladandan sinoye, ginamwang ka a
follow   there.p arrived   you rl

aggagafut ka si lufid. 142. "To   angan
holding   you obj rope   where go

nu?" kun ku. 143. "Do'man ku nad   ino
you said I   catch   I should the

daffug mi   ya. 144. Anto ginan na allay?
buffalo ours p   where reside it man

145. Se   amme lullungan yan daffug
     because not mess.up   that buffalo

yan kalawatan da,   se   i'bu ammin
that yard   theirs because urine all

yan gukab."   146. Ay, malaw   inay a
that under.house   oh painful that rl

sapit. 147. Allakkan dak.
word   pity   you.me

carrying a rope.
142. "Where are you
going?" I said.
143. "I should catch
our buffalo.
144. Where is it,
man? 145. That
buffalo can't really
mess up their yard,
because it's just
urine under their
house." 146. Oh,
those words hurt.
147. Take pity on
me.

148. E   ira yaw allay si gakkurug ino
     and pl this man in truth   the

kalowan   ino nakam ku si gakkurug.
cause.hurt the mind my in truth

149. Ira inoy allay ino pakkakampattan so
     pl that man - the cause.kept   in

nakam ku allay.
mind my man

148. And truly,
man, these things
are what really hurt
my heart. 149. Those
are the things I've
harbored in my
heart, man.

150. Udde one, wara ikkallay ang ku
     but yes.p exist you.man go I

sinassapit allay? 151. Awan. 152. Gampade,
mediator   man   none   however,

antu kalowan   ino nakam ku, 153. se inay
this cause.hurt the mind my   for that

a tarabafu a amme ta   pakkinnawatan,
rl work   rl not we.2 cause.understand

nattul   ka sito kapilya. 154. Tata
affronted you this chapel   one

150. But anyway,
did I go and talk
about this man?
151. Not at all.
152. However, that
is what grieved my
heart. 153. Because
of those things
about which we had a
misunderstanding,
you were miffed at
this chapel.
154. That was
another thing that
hurt my heart.

im-man   a nallowan ino nakam ku.
cmp-again rl hurt   the mind my

155. Pakawanan nak   nu wara narakkat
     forgive   you.I if exist bad

a sapit ku sikwam. 156. Pakawanan nak pay
rl word my to.you   forgive   he.I just

i afu Dios nu wara ira nakkamaliyan ku
pm lord God if exist pl mistake   my

onnu nassubarang ku allay sikwam.
or   excess   my man   to.you

157. Mampay so ammapakawan ku sikwam nu
     also   at forgiveness my to.you if

fustu inay a diningngag nu a pabasul ku
okay that rl heard   you rl blamed I

sikwam. 158. Mampay sikwayu ammin, agyaman
to.you   also   to.you.pl all,   thank

ak se   ayaw etam   ammin a nara'lang
I because here we.inc all   rl facing

sitaw. 159. E   awan-in sikwak iyan a
here   and none-cmp in.me that rl

banag.
thing

160. Ikumpesar ku ki afu Dios ino
     confess   I pm lord God the

panampakawan ku sitan a idanug   ku ira
cause.forgive my that rl reported I pl

ammin to   naraletungan tam   ammin,
all   this gathering   us.inc all

kamali-m   onnu annanganna a amme ta
mistake-your or   whatever   rl not we.2

pakkinnawatan. 161. Antu-in inoy yo ana
understand   this-cmp that the be

sikwak yaw. 162. Awan-in sikwak yan.
to.me this   none-cmp to.me that

155. Forgive me if
I said something bad
to you. 156. And may
God forgive me if I
erred or sinned
against you, man.
157. And I forgive
you likewise, if you
found my admission
of guilt acceptable.
158. And as for all
of you, I'm thankful
that we are all here
face to face.
159. And those
things are all gone
from me now.

160. I confess to
God that for which I
need forgiveness,
which I make known
to our whole
gathering about your
mistake or whatever
it was that the two
of us had a
misunderstanding
about. 161. That's
all of this that is
in me. 162. There is
no more of it in me
now.

163. Ara sigi   sapitan nu pay nu
     okay go.ahead say   you just if

anya pay anggam nu sassapitan.
what just want you say

164. Sapitan nu pay onnu sobaran nu pay
     say   you just or   add   you just

ino anggam nu sapitan sikwak. 165. Antu-in
the want   you say   to.me   this-cmp

inoy.
that

162. Okay, go
ahead, just say
whatever you want to
say. 164. Just say
or add on whatever
it is you want to
say to me.
165. That's all.

Sanggoon:

166. Antu ino nakasalaman nu a
     this the error   you rl

kalolowan o   nakam i litag nu Andits
cause.hurt the mind pm uncle your Andits

sikwam alle.
to.you man

166. This was your
mistake, which
caused your uncle's
heart to be hurt,
man.

Buton:

167. Sanna kad   ino kaliwatan ku na,
     what perhaps the fault   my fut

litaggi? 168. Tuldwan nak.   169. Sanna
uncle.p   teach   you.me   what

ikkallay iyatal daw   na mattuldu sikwak
you.man ashamed you.pl fut teach   to.me

timma wara-in   man ke   korokorwan si
as.if exist-cmp again just other   of

tolay?
person

167. What, in
fact, was my sin,
uncle? 168. Tell me.
169. Man, why would
you be ashamed to
teach me, as though
I am from another
clan?

Andits:

170. Antu ino kun   ku so da'bu inoy, a
     this the said I at while then rl

nu kamali na tata, kamali ta adwa.
if mistake of one   mistake we two

170. This is what
I said a while ago,
that if one of us
erred, both of us
erred.

Buton:

171. On kamali ta lud.
     yes mistake we.2 sure

171. Yes, both of us really erred.

Sanggoon:

172. Anda iyan ke, awan a ida'nag ku
     and that just none rl drop   I

si "liwat nu   Andits," onnu awan ke
obj fault yours Andits   or   none just

sapitan ku si liwat i Buton.
say   I obj fault pm Buton

172. And about that, I'm not going to say that it's your fault, Andits, or that it is Buton's fault.

173. Antu ino kun ku so da'bu inoy a
     this the said I at while then rl

wara allay so mangurug eta, e madyat
exist man at believe we.2 and hard

nad   a ibbattan ta ino gagangay ta a
should rl stop   we.2 the custom ours rl

tolay, udde malliwat eta talaga.
person but do.fault we.2 perhaps

174. Siguro, amme na ke   nakkamali i
     maybe   not he just did.mistake pm

Buton, udde ino ka''atallan onnu
Buton but the respect   or

ke'atatallan nu.
deference   your

173. This is what I said a while ago, that when we believe, it is hard for us to stop our typically human ways, and sometimes we may sin.
174. Perhaps Buton did not err, but (what about) your respect or deference.

175. E kunnera pelang inoy,
     and like.that just.only then

gampade, "maku kunna," kun na nad nu
however why like.it said he should of

inammu na a attalan. 176. Kunna kappay
know   he rl respect   like.it also

angngidamit nu   ki Buton, so akkawayi
saying   yours pm Buton at relatives

175. And things were like that; however, he should have said "Hey, something's wrong here," if he had shown proper respect.
176. Likewise concerning what you said about Buton to the relatives or

onnu so akkakaluma pelamang. 177. Amme-k
or   at neighbors just.only   not-I

inammu yan, se   amme-k lud mapuntusan
know   that because not-I sure aware

nu sannanganna yan amme-yu
if what.depict that not-you.pl

pakkinnawatan.
understand

neighbors. 177. I
don't know about
that, because I was
not aware of what it
was that your
misunderstanding was
about.

178. Antu ino kun ku so da'bu inoy, a
     this the said I at while then rl

tantaro lang nu ino ugali ira.   179. E
maybe   only if the custom theirs   and

mepangngat ikkallaye a balawan dakayu
fitting   you.man   rl rebuke I.you.pl

se   manak daw   ira lud. 180. E
because did   you.pl pl sure   and

anggam nu mappe nu ira inoy a banag-e
like   you also if pl that rl thing-p

daggera nu inoye, appan ta   ira ino
add.pl if that.p take.we.2 pl the

gagangay si'in   e daggera. 181. Anggam
custom   long.ago and add.pl   like

na nad   si naggaddang ino ammin ira a
he should obj straight   the all   pl rl

mepa'ita ta, ta ira ammin inoy o   tata a
show   we.2 so pl all   that the one rl

mangalalim onnu metata'nap so dayaw o
please   or   adds.to   at admire the

tolay a nannakam.
people rl kindly

178. This is what
I said a while ago,
that perhaps it can
be attributed to
their customs or
habits. 179. And
it's fitting that I
rebuke you both,
because of our
relationship.
180. And do you want
that kind of thing
to increase, for if
we practice our old
customs they will
increase. 181. It's
preferable that we
show only right
behavior, so that we
will be admirable
people of good
character.

Yawindo:

182. Gakkurug.   182. That's true.
     true

Andits:

183. Gakkurug. 184. Arangngan ku
     true   request I

sikwayu, massiki tan abbing, nu massapit
to.you.pl even   that child if say

ak si falsu, allangngan dak, sito lawum.
I obj false scold   you.me here inside

185. Massiki sintaw.
     even   where

183. That's true.
184. I request of
you, even children,
that if I speak
falsely, scold me,
right here inside.
185. Wherever.

186. Nu mabbungut ak, pa'lungan dak.
     if get.angry I   beat   you.me

187. Kunsa'ay se   amme-k mangngurug so
     why   because not-I believe   at

nalawara sapit?
good   word

186. If I'm angry,
beat me. 187. Why
would I not obey
good words?

188. Antu yaw yo daretsu a sapitan
     this this the direct rl speech

ku. 189. Massiki abbing, nu kamali sapitan
my   even   child if mistake speech

ku, allangngan dak.   190. Se   nu amme-k
my scold   you.me   because if not-I

mangngurug, Satanas ak-un, nu amme-k
believe   Satan   I-cmp if not-I

mangngurug so nalawad.
believe   at good

188. This is what
I say directly.
189. Even children,
if I speak
mistakenly, scold
me. 190. For if I
don't believe, I am
Satan, if I don't
believe the good.

Sanggoon:

191. Antu yaw ino dama-k pelang
     this this the able-I just.only

kappay a masapit. 192. Iyaw appan tam
also   rl say   this take we.inc

si angngurug a attatarabbag, a bakkan a
obj faith   rl discussion   rl not   rl

191. This is what
I am able to say
further. 192. This
discussion is
according to faith,
not according to our
Ga'dang customs.
193. Since I am the
one you have

ino gagangay a ginaga'dang tam   a
the custom   rl Ga'dang   ours.inc rl

appointed to be like
your father, here is
father right here
who is the father of
us all, but since I
am the one who is
like the president
of our chapel, well,
I am the one who
will speak much
(i.e., judge the
case).

attatarabbag. 193. Gafuse ikkanak pay o
discussion   because I   just the

ne'ekwa yu   a kunnangke ama   yu,
placed you.pl rl as.if   father yours

ayaw i ama   toya a ama   tam ammin,
here pm father here rl father ours all

udde gumafuse ikkanak pay o   kunnangke
but   because I   just the as.if

presidente yu   sitaw a kapilya tam,
president yours here rl chapel ours

allaye ikkanak o   kunnangke maka'oddu a
man.p I   the as.if   make.much rl

maddamit.
speaking

            194. E   kunna yaw yo masapit ku.
                 and like this the say   I

            194. And this is
            what I say.
            195. Anyway, I'll
            just do this, even
            though it's not the
            case that I am the
            only one who can
            read the words of
            God in the Bible.
            196. And I know that
            you have surely read
            them, or if not, we
            all studied there
            where it says,
            "There should be no
            fighting. 197. We
            should teach each
            other if there are
            those among us
            siblings who err.
            198. We should go
            and discuss that
            mistake, or call the
            leaders of the
            chapel." 199. You
            should not be afraid
            to ask help from the
            elders when you need
            it, saying, "Perhaps
            they will discipline

195. Aliwan nu pande-k   pelang   yaw, e
     anyway if making-my just.only this and

aliwan nu ikkanak pelang   o   makabasa
anyway if I   just.only the able.read

to sapit na Dios a to Biblia. 196. E
the word of God rl the Bible   and

ammu-k, sempre nabasa yu   na yan, onnu
know-I surely read   you.pl fut that or

bakkan neyadalin   sikwatam-un inay a kunna
not   studied.cmp we.inc-cmp that rl say

si "Awan nad   makkakwa.
obj none should fight

197. Makkakatuldu   etam   nu wara
     reciprocal.teach we.inc if exist

pakkamalyan ino ikkanetam a makkakarolak.
mistake   the we.inc   rl siblings

198. In-tam-ungke tatabban inay a
     go-we-emph   discuss that rl

nakkamali, onnu maye-ta   so lakay   na
mistake   or   call-we.2 to old.man of

kapilya". 199. Amme yu   nad   mababbang
chapel   not you.pl should worry

a makimawid si duffun so lallakayira nu
rl ask   obj help   to old.men   if

inoye ka'awan daw,   tantaro lang nu
that need   you.pl perhaps only if

sipangngan dak   na lang nu ikimawiggu
slap.face they.I fut only if ask.about

yo   problema-k kun daw. 200. Awan.
this problem-my say you   none

me if I ask about my
problem." 200. Not
at all.

---

201. E   nu kun i Buton a "Sanggoon,
     and if say pm Buton rl Sanggoon

inta   abbu   ikkallay so akwi   litag,
go.we.2 please man   to place.of uncle

ta bulunan   nak, se   ana ino amme
so accompany you.me because be the not

mi   mallang a pakka'awatan allaye;
we.ex like   rl understand   man.p

nalawad o ana ka pay a aggadingngag,"
good   the be you just rl listening

nu kun na ikkallaye, sannera dikkallay o
if say he you.man.p what   you.man   the

nammay?
rejected

201. And if Buton
would say,
"Sanggoon, man,
let's go to uncle's
place, and you come
with me, because we
have a
misunderstanding,
man; it would be
good if you were
there to listen,"
man, why in the
world would that be
rejected?

---

202. E   namat nanu umang-ak-e samer
     and really when go-I-p   sum.up

ino ang ku sapitan, udde aggadingngag ak
the go I say   but hearing   I

pelang   nad   sikwayu, e nu wara
just.only should to.you.pl and if exist

dama-k a iyasab na, asafan takayu   na.
able-I rl help   fut help   I.you.pl fut

202. And if I
really go just to
sum up, but I hear
you talk, and if I
am able to be of
help, I'll just help
or advise you.
203. Or if it's not
me that you call,
then Treining, or
even Andits.

203. E   nu bakkan ak o   iyawit daw,   e
     and if not   I   the call   you.pl then

Treining, mampe   ki Andits.
Treining likewise pm Andits

204. Allaye wara allay so napatu ino   204. But as for
     man.p exist man   at hot   the   Buton, man, he has a
                                               hot head, because
ulu i Buton ya'e, se   ana inay high   maybe he has high
head pm Buton emph because be that high   blood pressure, man!
                                               205. I could not
blood nakuy allay ya'e'e. 205. Amme-k ira   endure it and I
blood maybe man   emph   not-I pl   might spank him if
                                               he speaks in his
na lang nakattam ta siniwa'wattan ku na nu   usual abrupt way.
fut only endured so spanked   I he if   206. This is what I
                                               have accepted or
pakakwan na pelang   o   assapitan na inay   tolerated about him.
force   he just.only the saying   he then

a passig pelang   pinapa'lat a inoy!
rl full   just.only sudden   rl then

206. Antu lang nappa'affunan ku sikwana.
     this only tolerated   I to.him

207. Nu kun pena i Andits, allaye   207. When Andits
     if said just pm Andits man.p   said it, man, that
                                             should have been
kunnenoy o   tubbun na ino adal tam inoy   added on to our
like.that the add.on fut the study ours then study then, so that
                                             (the problem) would
ta amme na nad   umoddu. 208. Kunna   not increase.
so not it should get.much   like.it   208. It's like what
                                             Bayombong said a
mappay o   kun i Bayombong so da'bu inoy,   while ago, that we
also   the said pm Bayombong at while then   are shameful if we
                                             do not have our
a ka''atatal etam   nu amme tam ma'inggud   faith in order.
rl shameful   we.inc if not we tidy   209. It's not just
                                             Buton or Andits who
o   angngurug tam. 209. Bakkan pelang   i   is laughable in that
the faith   ours   not   just.only pm case, but rather all
                                             of us believers in
Buton, onnu i Andits, ino kakkatawa sinay, this chapel.
Buton of pm Andits   the laughable there

nu bakkan etam   ammin a mangngurug sitaw
if not   we.inc all   rl believe   here

a kapilya.
rl chapel

210. Kunnantu, se   sito fuwab
     therefore because this afternoon

e   nadingngag pay ino kalussaw ira i
then heard   just the hate   pl pm

Andits pay sikwam Buton, e   nu masapit ira
Andits just to.you Buton and if say   pl

pay-in i Andits o   kalusso-m ira pay
just-cmp pm Andits the hate-you pl just

sikwana, sigi,   sanna ino number one a
to.him go.ahead what the number one rl

in-tam   inada'adal? 211. Reforma,
go-we.inc study   reform

mangangkakwa. 212. Reforma, mangangkakwa.
change   reform   change

213. E   makkiyad sitaw-in ya, ino ammu
     and until   here-cmp p   the know

yu   a makadaral so angngurug tam,
you.pl rl able.ruin at faith   ours.inc

amme tam-un nad   a pakakwan-in allay.
not we-cmp should rl fight-cmp   man

210. Therefore, because this afternoon you heard Andits's grievances to you, Buton, and you said your grievances, Andits, okay, what is the primary thing we should learn? 211. Reform, change. 212. Reform, change. 213. And from this time on, whatever you know of that ruins our faith, we should not do it, man.

214. Agyan-in tata si fuwab   a
     was-cmp one of afternoon rl

nappakabebutan ku sikwam Buton, e   nekun
asked   I to.you Buton and said

nu sikwak si ino angkwa so angkwa kun nu,
you to.me obj the thing of thing said you

e   amme-k ira pelang   na'awatan inoy.
and not-I pl just.only understood that

215. Se ammu-yu   lud o assapitan i
     for know-you.pl sure the speech pm

Buton, a passig pelang   angkwa so angkwa
Buton rl full   just.only thing of thing

214. There was one afternoon when I questioned you, Buton, and you said "the thingummy, you know", and I just didn't understand that. 215. For you know the speech of Buton, which is often full of "you know, you know."

kunna kun na nu   korwan.
like says he when other

216. Mampe   ki Andits, nu sanna ira
     likewise pm Andits if what pl

pelang   pay nekalussaw na so "ayay amme
just.only just hated   he of hey   reject

na yo kakkatawa". 217. E   siguro, so
it this laughable   and maybe at

abbafa pay a pannaka'awat,   allaye
short just rl able.understand man.p

kalussaw na ikkallaye, se   kunnangke
hate   he you.man.p because as.if

insolto mappe sikwana, se   tuddung
insult really to.him because of.course

manuwang   na pelamang allay e   nainsolto
son.in.law his just.only man   and insulted

a lakay   ikkallaye.
rl old.man you.man.p

216. And as for
Andits, what he just
hated was this being
made to seem
ridiculous. 217. And
perhaps, because he
did not completely
understand, he hated
it, man, because it
was as if he was
insulted, because of
course it was just
his son-in-law, man,
who insulted the old
man, man!

Andits:

218. Ma'inay,   magi'na-k-ungke
     don't-know felt-I-really

gakkurug yo   nakam ku se   lakay-ak-un
true   this mind my because old.man-I-cmp

si gakkurug allay.
in truth   man

218. I don't know,
I really felt that
in my heart, because
I really am an old
man, man.

Sanggoon:

219. Para so ikkanak allay, para inay
     for to me   man   for that

ino ka'iyutan   ku inay allay, mangwa ka
the cause.irked me that man   do   you

pay nu umapal ka ikkallaye kun ku
just if envy you you.man.p said I

ma'nayan. 220. Udde amme-k paliwatan i
really   but not-I blame   pm

219. As for me,
man, that is what
irked me, man,
because "Just go
ahead and be
jealous, if that's
what you want to do,
man," I really said.
220. But I don't
blame Andits for
that, because when
one gets old,

Andits sinay, se   waso   doesn't that cause
Andits that   because upon   senility? 221. It
                                                          causes senility.

mallakay-in   pay, pakkabawan,
becoming.old.man-cmp just cause.senility

bakkan? 221. Pakkabaw.
not   cause.senility

222. E   ino daffug ira kanu   inoy   222. And that
     and the buffalo pl reported that   buffalo that we
                                                     spoke of, perhaps if
a nassapit, sabagay, nu appan ta   ino   we follow the ways
rl said   anyway if take we.2 the   of people, which
                                                     were told us by our
sapit a binaba'lag, anda waso masapit ira   parents, then who
word rl flesh   and upon words   pl   would be the first
                                                     to be affected?
a mapparanak, e   sanna ino mapalungu a   223. Bakatnay, we
rl parents   and what the first   rl   should say, if she
                                                     hears of that
mafektaran? 223. I Bakatnay kun ta   nad   scolding. 224. But
affected   pm Bakatnay say we.2 should   not so.

nu nadingngag na ira inay a allang.
if heard   she pl that rl scold

224. Udde awan.
     but none

225. E   waraso da   Andits anni Galat   225. And when
     and upon   them Andits and Galat   Andits and Galat
                                                    heard of it, man,
ino nakadingngag allaye, e   ira lang-in   it's like they were
the able.hear   man.p   then they only-cmp   the ones affected,
                                                    because he is really
ino kunnangke nafektaran allay, se   their child, and
the as.if   affected   man   because   Andits may have
                                                    thought that it's as
anak dera   lud, anda dandamman kad   i   if we can't teach
child theirs sure and think   perhaps pm   our children, and
                                                    people might say,
Andits si mallang a amme ta   mappay   "If their children
Andits obj like   rl not we.2 just   can't look after
                                                    their buffalo, what
makatuldu so da a'anak   e   massapit   is it really that
able.teach to pl children and say   they taught them
                                                    there?" 226. They
kad   na lang da   tolaye "Nu amme   may not just blame
perhaps fut only they person.p if not   Andits and Galat.
                                                    227. However, they

lang-in ma'imut ino anak dera   so
only-cmp care.for the child theirs at

daffug dera   ya, sanna ira ma'lud na'dan
buffalo theirs p   what pl sure   gave

dera sinay?" 226. Ammay-in pelang-in
them there   not-cmp just.only-cmp

appan da   Andits anni Galat.
take   they Andits and Galat.

227. Gampama'de amme ra   kena maka'imut
     however   not they just able.control

ino a'anak dera   a   mappasapasapat ira
the child theirs rl involved   they

lang a dumakkut sito bumaryo. 228. Kunna
only rl dirtying this village   like

nakuy ino nakan da,   e   antu ino yo
perhaps the mind theirs and this the this

atallan da.
ashamed they

cannot control their
children who are
involved in dirtying
this village.
228. They might
think that, and that
is what (Andits) is
ashamed about.

229. E   gampade wara pay o   Buton
     and however exist just the Buton

allay, e   nakkiyad pelang   sinoy nu wara
man   and since   just.only then if exist

madingngag na, kumaral ira-n kelang
hear   he the.more pl-cmp just.only

mallalattu onnu mamaruntut,   e   ira
to.jump   or   angry.reaction and pl

ikkallay inoye ino amme ta pakkinnawatan
you.man that.p the not we.2 understand

a matatama.
rl father.son

229. However, as
for Buton, man, from
that time whenever
he heard something,
he just all the more
reacted suddenly and
angrily, and that's
what caused the
misunderstanding
between the father
and son.

230. Gampama'de ino sapit na Bible,
     however   the word of Bible

awan nad   a ilefalefang, madakkut,
none should rl cover.up   dirt

230. However,
according to the
Bible, there should
be no covering up of
dirt or wrong, but
we should manifest

nalawad a sapit si iparang tam.
good   rl words in show   we.inc

231. Iya'lang   tam   ke nad   so
     bring.before we.inc just should at

kasittole   ta,   ka''atatal onnu amme na
fellow.person our.2 shameful   or   not it

ka''atatal, sapitan nu. 232. Se   i
shameful,   say.it you   because pm

Dios, amme na ka'imaddan.   233. Se
God   not he be.hidden.from   because

massiki kun ta si "amme-k sinapit" kun
even   say we.2 obj not-I   said.it say

nu, i Dios, dingngag na. 234. E   anda
you pm God hears   he   then and

masansongan nu ino baggi-m   so kaparefu-m
fool   you the body-yours at same-yours

a tolay, udde ki Dios, amme-m
rl person but pm God   not-you

malefangngan.
hide.from.view

good speech. 231. We
should bring it
before our fellow
people and say it,
shameful or not.
232. Because nothing
can be hidden from
God. 233. For even
if we say that we
never said it, God
heard. 234. And you
can deceive your
fellow man, but you
can't hide from God.

235. E   nu gangngariyan si makkamali
     and if for.example obj err

etam   se   tolay etam pelang   lud,
we.inc because people we.inc just.only sure

inoy-in kun ku inoy a amme tam
that-cmp said I that rl not we.inc

me'attam onnu ma'atal etam   gafuse ino
endure   or   ashamed we.inc because the

pakkamaliyan tam e lakay   onnu diyadal
error   ours p old.man or   youth

onnu manuwang ta   onnu katuwangan ta,
or   son.in.law our.2 or   parent.in.law our

e   may-eta ikkallay si bulun   ta
then call-we.2 you.man obj companion our.2

e   in-ta   makitatabbag ta amme ta
and go-we.2 discuss   so not we.2

235. And if, for
example, we err, for
we are people after
all, then it's like
I said a while ago,
that we should not
just tolerate it or
be ashamed because
of our mistake; old
man or youth,
son-in-law or
parent-in-law, we
should get a
companion and go and
discuss it, not just
try to forget it,
because if we allow
it to go on, that
problem just gets
bigger or increases.

```
palalyawan se        nu purayan ta  inay,
try.forget because if permit  we.2 that

dumokal onnu umoddu  inoy a  problema.
get.big or    get.much that rl problem
```

```
     236. Aggataronan takayu   mallay umang
          was.waiting I.you.pl man    come

makitatabbag a  makimawid. 237. Sapitan
discuss     rl request          say

dawe     nu sanna ino inang nepadda sikwak
you.pl.p if what the came show     to.me

e   amme-k nepabbebeng. 238. Awan a  kun
and not-I concerned           none rl say

daw    yan. 239. Amme takayu    nepabburung
you.pl that      not I.you.pl concerned.for

se     awan pe  kimawid daw   sikwak
because none just request you.pl to.me

allay, e   amme-k inammu yan a  amme yu
man    and not-I knew   that rl not you.pl

pakkinnawatan a  adwa.
understand    rl two
```

236. I waited for you, man, to come and ask to discuss it. 237. You tell me if anyone came to inform me and I was unconcerned. 238. You can't say that. 239. I did not concern myself about it because you did not come and ask me, man, and I did not know about that misunderstanding between the two of you.

```
     240. E   nu minomorek takayu   a
          and if initiative I.you.pl rl

pattarabban na sinoy, ana na  makkun
discuss     rl that   be fut who.says

sikwayu    allay si  "ina'ling na allaye
to.you.pl man    obj faced     he man.p

se     kolak  nangke," kun pe   na i
because sibling really   say just fut pm

Andits. 241. Onnu kun pe   na i  Buton si
Andits       or  say just fut pm Buton obj

"on se      kaparefu na  kasillakay, e
yes because same     his old.man     and

antu ino netayang  na se      atallan na,"
this the approached his because respect he
```

240. And if I approached you to discuss that, there would be someone who would say, "He approached him, man, because he is really his sibling," Andits might say. 241. Or Buton might say, "Yes, because he is an old man like (Andits), and that is who he approached because he respects him," you might say.

kun daw-in   na.
say you.pl-cmp fut

242. Antu ino pinurayan takayun
     this the permitted I.you.pl

pelang   kiyad si amme yu   nad   umang
just.only until to not you.pl should come

makimawid allay. 243. Se   amme-k pay
request   man   because not-I just

anggam o manata'wig nad   nu dama na,
like   the favoritism should if able it

se   amme anggam i Dios ino kunna inoy.
because not like   pm God the like that

242. This is why I just waited until one of you would come and ask me, man. 243. For I don't like favoritism if it can be avoided, for God does not like that.

Andits:

244. Pidya   etam-un   ke'in   a
     how.many we.inc-cmp just.cmp rl

Ga'dang? 245. Busang etam ke'in.
Ga'dang   few   we.inc just.cmp

246. Busang etam ke'in.   247. Amme-k
     few   we.inc just.cmp   not-I

nad   anggam si wara mabbabangkirit
should like   obj exist strife

sikwatam, nu amme tam   lud ingguran ino
to.us.inc if not we.inc sure order   the

nakam tam. 248. Itakkud   tam   ino
mind ours   throw.away we.inc the

gagangay tam inoy a massisiblat onnu
custom   ours that rl vindictive or

apalapal onnu naral. 249. Itakkub
jealous or   evil   throw.away

tam-un.   250. Aryan tam   ira a
we.inc-cmp   remove we.inc pl rl

intremente a bungut, se   sanna ino
instrument rl anger because what the

surbi na ino bungut?
use   its the anger

244. How many of us Ga'dangs are there now? 245. We are few now! 246. We are few now! 247. I don't want there to be strife among us, but rather we should put our minds in proper order. 248. Let's throw out our customs of vindictiveness or jealousy or evil. 249. Let's throw them out! 250. Let's get rid of that anger thing, for what's the use of anger?

251. Nanu inattak nak-e,   sanna kappay
     if   clubbed you.I-p what   also

na ino milow sikwak? 252. Sempere awan ak
fut the mourn for.me   surely none I

kappe lang pay na.
also only just fut

253. Antu inay a nu wara
     this that rl if exist

pakkamaliyan   daw, onnu kamali-k, laye
cause.mistake.it yours or   mistake-my man.p

allakkan dak   pe na. 254. Nu wara
scold   you.me just fut   if exist

kamali-k, ang ka sapitan sikwak. 255. Antu
mistake-my go you say.it to.me   this

mat   maral-e   me-k siguran sapitan
really slander-p not-I sure   say.it

abbu   inay. 256. Udde nu da rakkat anna
please that   but if pl bad   and

bungut, tanamman dak a aggatulang.
anger   bury   you.I rl staring

257. Patayan dak. 258. Sanna ino surbi
     kill   you.I   what the use

ikkallay? 259. E   iyara'arang ku si
you.man   and request   I obj

mallawad etam   nad   a Ga'dang, gampade
make.good we.inc should rl Ga'dang however

kalussaw ak-un mangke lang sikwayu, aran
hate   I-cmp really only to.you.pl remove

dak-un   lang-in, takesi kunna, awan a
you.I-cmp only-cmp so   that   none rl

panuntulan daw   si tarabafu-k a
lead   you.pl obj work-my   rl

narakkat. 260. Kunna inoy itulung ku lang
bad   like that help   I only

sikwayu. 261. Bakkan a tolay ak kepelang
to.you.pl   not   rl person I just.only

251. If I am
beaten, who will
mourn for me then?
252. I just won't be
around then.

253. That is why,
if you err, or if I
err, man, just scold
me. 254. If I err,
come and tell me.
255. I won't say
that it is slander.
256. But if I'm bad
or angry, bury me
alive! 257. Kill me!
258. What good am I,
man? 259. And I
request that we
Ga'dangs behave
well; however, if I
really hate you,
just remove me, in
order that there
will be none to lead
you into bad things.
260. That's how I
can help you.
261. I'm not even a
person if I hate
others. 262. It's
you children who
should do what is
good.

nu ikalusso-ya. 262. Ikkayu mat   nad   a
if hate-p   you.pl really should rl

anak a mangwa si napya.
child rl do   obj good

Baggit:

263. Antu lud, inanggwet   ku ammin ino
     this sure brought.out I all   the

mepanggip sitan ira a banag. 264. Udde
about   that pl rl thing   but

waraso sinapit mi   ira-n inoy,
upon   said   we.exc pl-cmp that

nalluwat-in e   nabalin-in.
washed-cmp and cone-cmp

263. That's for
sure, I have brought
out everything
about that.
264. Having said
what has been said,
it is washed away
and finished.

Yawindo:

265. Mabisin-in ak-un.
     hungry-cmp I-cmp

265. I'm hungry.

Sanggoon:

266. Antu ino masapit ku ke.
     this the say   I just

267. Gagangay, e nang etam pe   sitaw a
     customary and came we.inc just here rl

mangngurug. 268. Massiki ikka Buton, abbing
believe   even   you Buton child

ka kepay si uray-m.   269. Ma'awatan si
you still in mind-your   understood obj

abbing ka, se   abbing ka kepay lud.
child you because child you still sure

270. I Andits, lakay-in.   271. Amme-m
     pm Andits old.man-cmp   not-you

tonan si i Andits, umara'ni sikwam se
wait obj pm Andits approach you   because

i Andits abbing. 272. Lakay   si angngita
pm Andits child   old.man in sight

266. I'll just say
this. 267. It's
customary, and
(that's why) we who
believe have come
here. 268. As for
you, Buton, you're
still a child in
your mind. 269. It's
understood that you
are a child, because
you really are still
a child.
270. Andits, he is
an old man.
271. Don't you wait
for Andits to
approach you, for
Andits is a child.
272. We can see he
is an old man, but
as for his stand, I
don't know about
him, because he

tam, udde si tata'dag, amme-k inammu
ours but in stand   not-I know

sikwana, se   lakay   lud, nabbalin
of.him because old.man sure finished

me'anak. 273. Se   nu si angngurug,
born   because if in faith

abbing kepay. 274. E   ma'awag si ikka a
child still   and needed obj you rl

lakay si angngurug ino umara'ni,
old.man in faith   the approach

gangngariyan si nu wara duma'nga a
for.example obj if exist drop   rl

buruburung. 275. Kunnatan nu wara amme-m
worry   even   if exist not-you

pakkinawatan allay-e, ing ka e'e.
understand   man-p   go you p

276. Amme-k sapitan si "I Baggit, umang
     not-I say   obj pm Baggit go

sikwam," se tantaro nu amme kepay ma'addang
to.you for perhaps if not yet   reached

ino kata'naggan   no lintig na Dios.
the most.difficult the law   of God

277. E   ikkanak kallay-e, kunnanatan
     and I   man-p   although

nu liwat i Baggit, massiki liwat na, umang
if fault pm Baggit even   fault his go

ak pelang   sikwana'e, kesi
I just.only   to.him.p   so.that

palapalawan   mi   pelang   adwa nu
explain.recipr we.exc just.only two if

sanna ino amme-mi pakkinnawatan mi adwa.
what the not-we understand   we two

278. E   nu amme-na dingngaggan, antu
     and if not-he listens   this

really is an old
man, but recently
born. 273. Because
as for his faith, he
is still a child.
274. And it's
necessary that you,
being mature in
faith, be the one to
approach, if, for
example, there is
some source of
concern. 275. Even
if there is
something you do not
understand, man, you
just go. 276. I
don't say that
Baggit should come
to you, because he
may not yet have
grasped the most
profound laws of
God.

277. And as for
me, man, even though
it were Baggit's
fault, even if his
fault, I would just
go to him, so that
the two of us might
explain to each
other whatever it is
that we have a
misunderstanding
about.

278. And if he
does not listen,
this is what the

ino sapit na Bible, a adalan tam-ya, a nu
the word of Bible rl study we.inc-p rl if

amme na kuruwan, mayag ka lang-in si
not he believe call you only-cmp obj

korwan, kun na kappay. 279. E nu amme na
other say it also   and if not he

kappay kuruwan, mayag ka-n si elder, ta
also believe call you-cmp obj elder so

nu amme na kappay kuruwan, sanna kappay ino
if not he also   believe what also   the

akwan ta? 280. Umang so kun i Buton inoy,
do   we.2   goes to said pm Buton that

a pallalasinan-in, ta i Dios pelang-in
rl put.out-cmp   so pm God just.only-cmp

ino makammu. 281. Ta aran tam   ino
the know   so remove we.inc the

gagangay tam-un a Ga'dang.
custom   our-cmp rl Ga'dang

Bible refers to,
what we have
studied, that if he
does not believe or
obey, just call
another person, it
says. 279. And if he
still does not obey,
call an elder, and
so if he still does
not obey, then what
will we do?
280. It's like what
Buton said, we'll
put them out, and
they will then be
God's
responsibility.
281. So then let's
get rid of our
Ga'dang tradition
(of retribution).

282. E anda iyo paraparal ke,
       and and this slander just

se   antu yan o number one ingke a
because this that the number one really rl

antu ingke ammu-k ya. 283. Se   massiki
the really know-I p   because even

ikkanak, oddu pe dingngaggan ku
I   much just heard   I

sikwayu   ammin. 284. Awan ke sapitan ku
from.you.pl all   none just say   I

si "I Galat", kun ku pelamang.
obj pm Galat   say I just.only

285. Ikkanetam ammin to Iglesia a iyaw-e.
     we.inc   all   this church rl here-p

286. Oddu dingngaggan ku a paraparal
     much heard   I rl slander

sikwak. 287. Total ino sapit na tolay a
to.me   total the word of person rl

282. And now about
this slander, for
that is really the
number one (problem)
that I know about.
283. For I myself
even heard a lot
from all of you.
284. I'm not going
to say that it was
just Galat. 285. It
was all of this in
this church. 286. I
heard a lot of
slander toward me.
287. To sum up, the
speech of a vacuous
person, serves no
purpose. 288. It
will just pass by.
289. For if you
start a fire, man,
it increases.
290. There is none
that does not.
291. Our studying
serves no purpose in

bayakakaw, awan a surbi na. 288. Malla'wut
vacuous   none rl use   its   pass

pe   na lang inay. 289. Se nu pa'afuyan
just fut only that   for if set.fire

nu, alle, umoddu-e. 290. Awan a amme na.
you man increase-p   none rl not it

291. Awan surbi na ino adal tam
        none use   its the study ours.inc

sinoy. 292. E   passan tam   pelang
then   and complete we.inc just.only

mararintungu a mattatarukki.
fueling   rl arguing

293. Danadanoy, antu-in pelang   a dalan
        later   this-cmp just.only rl path

tam   o   marrarariri. 294. Sapit na Dios,
our.inc the strife   word of God

awan a riri.
none rl strife

that case. 292. And
we are just always
fueling arguments.
293. After a while,
strife will be our
way of life.
294. God's word says
no strife.

295. Se   ino paraparal ya a
       because the slander p rl

maggabwat si dila   pakasikkulan, a kunna
springs   from tongue cause.fire   rl like

ino inadal tam. 296. Kunna pay o fego,
the studied we.inc   like just the match

taggat ke, udde nu sigiyan nu, sikkulan na
one   just but if start.it you burns   it

ammin a padanadanak. 297. Kunna inoy ino
all   rl grassland   like that the

ke'ampariyan na dila. 298. Kunna ira inoy
example   of tongue   like pl that

o   kedalanan na ira ino binungubungut.
the way   its pl the anger

295. For the
slander that comes
from the tongue
starts a fire, as we
learned in our
study. 296. It's
like a match; it's
just one, but if you
strike it, it can
burn a whole
grassland. 297. That
is an example of the
tongue. 298. That is
the way that anger
goes.

299. E   ino kun ku ki Baggit inoy,
       and the said I pm Baggit then

299. And what I
said to Baggit then,
likewise to Buton,

mampe   ki Buton, a me   na se
likewise pm Buton rl not it because

pinapa'lat yo dadamit ku mat   lud.
sudden   the speech my really sure

300. Nu damana nad, reforma.
     if able   ought reform

301. Mareforma. 302. Kakkapan tam
     reform   try   we.inc

tangngallan ino bifig tam,   nakam tam,
control   the lips ours.inc mind ours

aggangwa tam.
doings   ours

it was not (good)
because I really
spoke abruptly.
300. If possible, we
should reform.
301. Reform!
302. Let's try to
control our lips,
minds, and actions.

303. Mampe   ki Baggit, massapit
     likewise pm Baggit say

kadde, me na se   wara kad
okay   not it because exist perhaps

dingngaggan ku ya'e allay, me-k makattam si
heard   I p   man   not-I endure   in

gakkurug. 304. Kakkapan tam.
truth   try   we.inc

303. Likewise
Baggit, he talked,
and it was bad
because I really
heard of it, man,
and really could not
put up with it.
304. Let's try.

305. Me-k anggam sapitan si "Nanu
     not-I like   say   obj when

linggu, narriforma kayu-n," udde
Sunday reformed   you.pl-cmp but

mangarananan etam   si aggabusang. 306. Kun
remove   we.inc by little   said

i Elena, a nadalan mi   so dilod
pm Elena rl studied we.exc at downstream

ya, "Garsifan a aggabusang". 307. Me-k
p   scissor.it rl little   not-I

anggam a sapitan a ino tansit   nu,
like   rl say   rl the hostility your

ga'bungan nu, nu me na lud ararananan nu
cut.off   you if not it sure remove   you

305. I don't want
to say, "By Sunday,
you be reformed,"
but let's remove
(the bad) little by
little. 306. As
Elena said in our
study downstream,
"Cut off little by
little." 307. I
don't want to say
that you must just
cut off your
malevolence, but
rather remove it
little by little.
308. Then tomorrow,
cut some off.
309. Then the
following day, cut
off some more again

si aggabusang. 308. Nanu daramat, garsib
by little   when tomorrow scissor

nu. 309. Nanu daramat imman, ino
you   when tomorrow again   the

gagange-m a narakkat, ginarsib nu man
custom-your rl bad   scissor you again

ke inay. 310. E nanu ngkwa, awan-in!
just that   and when what none-cmp

311. Se nu passan tam   pelang   inoy
     for if leave we.inc just.only that

mattatarukki anda mamaraparal, allay.
arguing   and slander   man

of your bad habits.
310. And later on,
it's all gone.
311. For if we just
allow that arguing
and slander to
continue, oh, man!

312. E kakkapan tam   mallakad si
     and try   we.inc walk   in

na'inggud. 313. Tantaro me tam   inammu nu
straight   maybe   not we.inc know   if

na'ansa na ino gamwang i Kristo.
when   fut the coming pm Christ

314. Anggam daw   kad   o mabattang?
     want   you.pl perhaps the left

312. And let's try
to behave in an
orderly way.
313. For we may not
know when Christ
will return. 314. Do
you want to be left
behind?

Andits:

315. La'ay!
     man

315. Man!

Sanggoon:

316. Nassalaservi kayu   si tarun,
     served   you.pl for one.year

tallurun,   limarun,   gampama'de nanu
three.years five.years however   when

gumwang i Kristo, ana na ra Andits, anni
come   pm Christ be fut pl Andits and

Buton a "Allay, anto mat   da Baggit,
Buton rl man   where really pl Baggit

316. You worked
for one, three, or
five years; however,
when Christ comes,
there will be Andits
and Buton saying,
"Man, where are
Baggit, Yawindo, and
Mayik?" you will say
when they ascend to
the sky when Christ
comes; however, when

Yawindo anda Mayik inoy?" kun daw   nanu
Yawindo and Mayik there say you.pl when

metullu ira-n   na sey langit nanu gumwang
ascend they-cmp fut at sky   when come

i Kristu, gampama'de ana etam   na sinay
pm Christ however   be we.inc fut there

kepay a madatangngan a mattatarukki,
still rl arrived   rl arguing

makkakwa. 317. Allaye!
fighting   man.p

that arrives we will
still be there
arguing and
fighting. 317. Oh
man!

318. E wara lud lang o bawu ira
and exist sure only the new pl

nangngurug a akwan da   ingke si napya
believed   rl do   they really obj good

ino panggamman na Dios, allaye, ira lud
the pleases   of God man.p   they sure

lang o netullu allay, amma   sikwatam
only the ascend man   rather.than we.inc

a napalungu a nangngurug.
rl first   rl believed

318. And there may
be those who have
just believed, who
do what pleases God
well; man, they will
be the ones who
ascend, man, rather
than we who believed
first.

319. Mampe   sikwam Buton, massiki
likewise you   Buton even

mangurug etam a kun tam,   appan ta
believe we.inc rl say we.inc take we.2

kappay lang o gagange tam, nu ansanna
also   only the custom our if how

tuldu   na Dios sito biblia gafuso da
teaching of God this bible about pl

addayaw so da mapparanak. 320. Massiki
honoring to pl parents   even

amme-m katuwangan, nu palungu amma sikwam,
not-you in.law   if first   more you

ma'awag si dayawan nu, gafuse palungu amma
needed obj honor you because first   more

319. As for you,
Buton, even if we
have believed as we
say, let's also
observe our custom,
like the teaching of
God in the Bible
about honoring one's
parents. 320. Even
if you dislike your
in-law, if he
preceded you, it's
necessary that you
honor him, because
he preceded you.
321. Not because
Yawindo finished
seventh grade and I,
high school. 322. I
don't believe in
that kind of talk,

sikwam. 321. Me na gafuse i Yawindo,
you   not it because pm Yawindo

mekapitu pelamang e   ikkanak high school.
seventh just.only and I   high school

322. Amme-k kurukuruwan no sapitan na ya,
     not-I believe   the saying it p

la'ay. 323. Kuruwan nu se   palungu
man   believe you because first

kappelang amma sikwam. 324. Malaksid nu
also.only more you   except if

wara sapitan na si falsu, allay, massiki
exist say   he obj false man   even

nu i ama,   nu wara sapitan na si kamali,
if pm father if exist say   he obj mistake

kontara so sapit na Dios, me-k kuruwan
contrary to word of God   not-I believe

allaye. 325. Udde nu wara sapitan na si
man.p   but if exist say   he obj

fustu, maningngag etam. 326. Amme tam
correct listen   we.inc   not we.inc

andalan ino sapit na Dios, se   inay,
upstage the word of God   because that

tata a pakada'nan ta si angngurug.
one rl cause.drop we.2 obj faith

---

man. 323. You obey
him because he
preceded you.
324. Except if he
speaks incorrectly,
man, even if it's my
father, if he speaks
mistakenly, contrary
to the word of God,
I don't obey it,
man. 325. But if he
speaks correctly,
let's listen.
326. Let's not try
to upstage the word
of God, because that
is one cause of the
downfall of our
faith.

---

327. E   nalawar-in se
       and good-cmp   because

napalawan-in, e ammu-m-un   pay Buton
removed-cmp and know-you-cmp just Buton

ino kalussaw ira i litag nu   sikwam.
the hate   pl pm uncle your to.you

327. It's good
that this has been
taken care of, and
you know, Buton, the
grudges that your
uncle had toward
you.

---

328. E   ikka pay Andits, ammu-m-un
       and you just Andits know-you-cmp

pay ino galad pay i Buton. 329. Ira inay,
just the way just pm Buton   pl that

328. And you,
Andits, you know the
way of Buton.
329. That's how it
is, and this should
not be allowed to

a bakkan nad   a makadaral so nakam daw   agitate the two of
rl not   should rl able.ruin to mind your   you.

adwa.
two

Andits:

330. Awan-in   yan sikwak alle.   330. As for me,
none-cmp that to.me man   that takes care of
                                              it, man.

Laka:

331. Kallay. 332. Tubburan ku si   331. Man.
     man   add.on I obj   332. I'll add just a
                                              little.
bisang, lamang.
little only

333. Iyaw a amme yu   pakkinnawatan   333. This
     this rl not you.pl understand   misunderstanding of
                                              yours or confusion
onnu akwatam ammin kungkul lang-in, bakkan   of all of us, this
or ours.inc all   confuse only-cmp not   lack of unity is why
                                              we came here to
allay a napatata sito in-tam   adalan   contemplate; for I
man   rl cause.one here go-we.inc study   heard you forgive
                                              each other, if it is
se   iyo anningngag ku so appakapakoli   sincere. 334. And it
because this heard   I at recipr.forgive   should be that you
                                              are now of one mind
yu,   nu amme na nallallamud. 334. E   about the
you.pl if not it mixed   and   misunderstanding
                                              between you siblings
naggannad nu napatata si ino amme yu   or father and son,
should.be if caused.one obj the not you.pl   and you just
                                              arranged for us to
pakkinnawatan makkakarolak onnu matatama,   come discuss it.
understand   siblings   or father.son   335. I do not know
                                              how to teach, for
e nangapangwa kayu pelamang si   even if you teach,
and caused   you.pl just.only obj   what if your faith
                                              falters, so surely
in-tam   pattatarabban. 335. Amme-k ammu a   you say that you
go-we.inc discuss   not-I know rl have many mistakes,
                                              and you'll cite that
mattuldu, se   massiki nu tuldwan nu, nu   as your reason for
teach   because even if teach   you if   not teaching.
                                              336. In our studying

aggedada'nan na ino angngurug nu, udde nu
dropping   fut the faith   your but if

"oh! oddu a kamali-k," e   sapitan ku ta
oh   much rl mistake-my then say   I so

amme-k-un a akwan," sempre kun nu na
not-I-cmp rl do   surely say you fut

inoy. 336. So aggiskwela so angngurug
that   at learning at faith

tam   ki Dios, inay a nakkamaliyan.
our.inc pm God   that rl mistake

about our faith in
God, that is a
mistake.

337. Udde waraso nallallamud iyo
     but upon mixed.up   this

diferensya yu   a makkakolak anna
difference yours rl siblings and

matatama, waraso kunna yoya, ammin a ayo
father.son upon   like this.p all rl be

taw a makkakaluma, akwatam ammin yan a
here rl neighbors   ours   all   that rl

kakkatawa, se   kakkatawa retam   e.
laughable because laughable they.us.inc p

337. But when you
siblings and father
and son got mixed up
in this difference of
opinion, when it was
like that, the ridicule
belongs to all
of us neighbors
here, for they will
ridicule us.

338. Nu wara kunna yaw, nanu wara
     if exist like this when exist

dingngag nu si sapit i Buton, ikka Dayaw
hear   you obj word pm Buton you Dayaw

si, allay amme-k anggam allay.
p   man   not-I like   man

339. Assapitan da litag inay. 340. Amme-k
     saying   pl uncle that   reject-I

inay alle.
that man

338. If there is
something like this,
if you, Sanggoon,
might hear something
that Buton said,
man, I just don't
like that. 339. That
is speaking to an
uncle. 340. I
dislike that, man.

341. Nu kunna, gampade dingngaggan ku
     if like.it however hear.it   I

341. If it's like
that, however I hear
it from Andits, and

na ki Andits e, nu gakkurug ira kunna   ira
fut pm Andits p if true   pl like.it pl

kepay na, gampade mewaragaw   ira inoy,
yet   fut however told/spread pl that

le'e'e gampade naddang ira yo
man.p however arrived pl this

naddingngaggan ino kabangibang tam   ira
heard   the vicinity   our.inc pl

ya, e   kanayun a kunna yaw, allaye, inoy
p   and always rl like this man-p   that

in-daw   kad   itan ino Bible ira ya,
go-you.pl perhaps look the Bible pl p

"makkapalapeletuwera kappelang maku?" kun
gather.to.resolve   still.only why   say

da   kad.   342. Naral.
they perhaps   ruin

if those things are true, but are spread around, man, and if others hear about it in our vicinity, man, that it is always like this, man, that might prompt them to say, "Just go look at those Bible believers; they are still disputing, if you please!" 342. Disrepute!

---

343. Amme na kun ino kun ku inoy, a
     not it like the say I that rl

nu wara iyasu i Andits, amme-m kepay
if exist case pm Andits not-you still

tonan si gakkurug, me-m   kun. 344. Gabwat
wait in truth   not-you do   get.up

kun nu. 345. Umang ka se   ino sinapit
do you   go   you because the said

i Andits a "kunna yaw allay ino amme-k
pm Andits rl like this man   the not-I

anggam," kun na. 346. Takesi kunna
like   said he   so.that like

mali'nawan a masinggud.
cleaned   rl ordered

343. Don't do it, as I said before, if you have a case with Andits, don't just wait around, really, don't do it. 344. Get up. 345. Go and talk about it, about what Andits said, "I don't like this, man!" 346. And thus it will be cleaned away and put in order.

Yawindo:

347. Mali'nawan, amma so
     cleaned   more than

makkarupampang.
dried.on/hardened

347. It will be cleaned up, rather than dried up and hardened.

Laka:

348. On, antu inay ino anggam ku.
     yes this that the like I
Sanggoon

348. Yes, that is what I like.

349. Amme-m indaggan a sumallap i
     not-you wait   rl setting pm

sinag so bungut nu kunna   mallay.
sun   on anger if like.it man

349. He's saying that we should not tolerate our anger past the setting of the sun, man.

Laka:

350. On, se   nanu kun kanu   i
     yes because when said reported pm

Buton a kun yo tolay ira, nu kun i
Buton rl said this people pl   if say pm

Andits, "Inya na ino ang ku ibanag sinay?"
Andits who fut the go I   inform that

amme-m kun gafuse "tolayira" kun nu kepay
not-you do because people   say you still

alle. 351. Ang ka ki Buton, nu pani'nikan
man   go you pm Buton if confirm

nu inay onnu me na a pakawanan na inay
you that or   not it rl forgive   fut that

a sapit na tolay, mampe   ki Andits.
rl word of person likewise pm Andits

352. Takesi kunna, mali'nawan ingke si
     so.that like.it cleaned   really in

fustu. 353. Se   ino kun tam   ira a
correct   because the say we.inc pl rl

makka'a'appetam kepe si dinandam si
give.and.take   still in thought in

gakkurug, a passiyan tam   kepay ino
truth   rl complete we.inc still the

dingngaggan kun na ki angkwa kun tam,
heard   said he pm what   say we.inc

ay antu inoy o   kada'anan kepay a
well this that the old   still rl

350. Yes, because if Buton says that the people said it, if Andits said, "Who should I go tell this to?" don't say because of people, man. 351. You go to Buton, to confirm whether or not people really said that; likewise, to Andits. 352. And thus it will be properly cleaned up. 353. For in our thinking and dialogue, if we just always say, "I heard that he said such and such," well, that is our old way of thinking.

dinandam tam   inoy.
thought our.inc that

Yawindo:

354. Kunna mat   yan ino tuldu   a   354. Now that is
     like really that the teaching rl   good teaching, man.

nalawad allaye.
good   man.p

Andits:

355. Amme-k ira nad   anggam a   355. I didn't want
     not-I pl should like rl   it to come to this.
                                              356. But what can
addangan na yaw. 356. Udde, na   akwan nu,   you do, for he is
arrived fut this   but   what do   you   still a child.
                                              357. And I called
se   antu abbing? 357. E   nepa'ayag ku   him, man, but he
because this child   and called   I   went downstream and
                                              did not come.
mallay, udde inanaw sey dilod   e   amme   358. This should be
man   but left   at downstream and not   finished now.

na inang. 358. Nabalin nad   yan.
he came   finished should this

Laka:

359. Napapya. 360. Kunna yaw ino   359. Good.
     good   like this the   360. This is what I
                                               like. 361. It's good
anggam ku. 361. Napapya nu i Andits e   if Andits hears
like   I   good   if pm Andits then   something from
                                               Buton, and just
wara dingngag na ki Buton, kinupikup na   covers it and keeps
exist heard   he pm Buton cover.over he   it in.

yan, imfunan na.
that keep   he

Andits:

362. On.   362. Yes.
     yes
Laka

363. Udde nu amme ta   makupikup, riri
     but if not we.2 cover   ruin

a matama   inay. 364. Napapya nu dingngag
rl father.son that   good   if hear

pay i Buton ki ama   na, e atalan na,
just pm Buton pm father his and respect he

kinupikup na inay, e   awan a kada'luwan
accepted he that   and none rl smell

na. 365. Nalawar-in inay.
he   good-cmp   that

363. But if we do not cover it, that ruins the father and son relationship. 364. It's good if Buton hears his father and respects him and accepts it and does not make a fuss. 365. That's good.

366. Antu-in pay inoy dama-k
     this-cmp just that able-I

ikontribyusyon sikwayu   nu inay a sinapit
contribute   to.you.pl if that rl said

ku e fustu.
I p correct

366. That's all I am able to contribute, if what I said is okay.

Andits:

367. Allay, fustu.
     man   correct

367. Right on, man.

Yawindo:

368. Alla'ay. 369. Antu-in inoy
     man   this-cmp that

naramamungan sapit-in inoy alle, a
meeting   say-cmp that man   rl

nabukallan na.
flee   fut

368. Man. 369. That's what we came to say, man, so let's take off.

Sanggoon:

370. Allay ing-kayu-n   antu mallutu
     man   go-you.pl-cmp then cook

si kafe   ta pamagwan daw.
obj coffee so wash.hands you.pl

370. Man, you go and cook some coffee, so you can wash your hands.

Bibliography

Akmajian, Adrian; Richard Demers; and Robert Harnish. 1979. *Linguistics: an introduction to language and communication.* Cambridge: MIT Press.

Albert, Ethel M. 1972. "Culture patterning of speech behavior in Burundi." In *Directions in sociolinguistics: the ethnography of communication,* ed. by John Gumperz and Dell Hymes, pp. 72-105. New York: Holt, Rinehart and Winston.

Alston, William. 1964. *Philosophy of language.* Englewood Cliffs, N.J.: Prentice-Hall.

Antworth, Evan L. 1979. *Grammatical sketch of Botolan Sambal. Philippine Journal of Linguistics,* Special Monograph 8. Manila: Linguistic Society of the Philippines.

Armstrong, Este et al. 1976. "On split-brain research and the culture-and-cognition paradox." *Current Anthropology* 17:2:318-26.

Arnheim, Rudolf. 1969. *Visual thinking.* Berkeley: Univ. of California.

Aronovitch, Hilliard. 1979. "Rational motivation." *Philosophy and Phenomenological Research* 40:2:173-93.

Baier, Kurt. 1958. *The moral point of view.* Ithaca, N.Y.: Cornell Univ. Press.

Barfield, Owen. 1960. *The meaning of the word "literal."* Colston Papers, vol. 12. London: Butterworths Scientific Publications.

Barton, R. F. 1967. "Procedure among the Ifugao." In *Law and warfare: studies in the anthropology of conflict,* ed. by Paul Bohannan, pp. 161-81. Austin: Univ. of Texas Press. (Originally published in 1919 as "Ifugao law." *Univ. of California Publications in American Archaeology and Ethnology* 15:1-186.)

Beck, Robert. 1975. *Perspectives in philosophy.* New York: Holt, Rinehart and Winston.

Beekman, John; John Callow; and Michael Kopesec. 1981. *The semantic structure of written communication.* Dallas: SIL.

Bellman, Beryl. 1977. "Ethnohermeneutics: on the interpretation of intended meaning among the Kpelle of Liberia." In *Language and thought: anthropological issues,* ed. by Wm. C. McCormack and S. A. Wurm, pp. 271-82. The Hague: Mouton.

Berry, J. W. and P. R. Dasen. 1974. *Culture and cognition: readings in cross-cultural psychology.* London: Methuen.

Bettinghaus, E. P. 1973. *Persuasive communication.* New York: Holt, Rinehart and Winston.

Bird, Otto. 1981. "Ethics in a permissive society: the controversy regarding the objectivity of moral values." In *The great ideas today*, pp. 160-87. Chicago and London: Encyclopaedia Britannica.

Black, Donald. 1976. *The behavior of law*. New York: Academic Press.

_____ and Maureen Mileski, eds. 1973. *The social organization of law*. New York: Seminar Press.

Bloch, Maurice, ed. 1975. *Political language and oratory in traditional society*. New York: Academic Press.

Bogen, Joseph. 1977. "Some educational implications of hemispheric specialization." In *The human brain*, ed. by M. C. Wittrock, pp. 133-52. Englewood Cliffs, N.J.: Prentice-Hall.

Bohannan, Paul, ed. 1967. *Law and warfare: studies in the anthropology of conflict*. Austin: Univ. of Texas Press.

Braine, Martin D. S. 1978. "On the relation between the natural logic of reasoning and standard logic." *Psychological Review* 85:1:1-21.

Brandt, Richard B. 1955. "The definition of an 'ideal observer' theory in ethics." *Philosophy and Phenomenological Research* 15:3:407-13.

Brichoux, Robert. 1984. "Hortatory strategy in Subanun II." *Studies in Philippine Linguistics* 5:1:80-117.

_____ and Austin Hale. 1977. "Some characteristics of hortatory strategy in Subanun." *Studies in Philippine Linguistics* 1:1:75-92.

Brooks, Cleanth and Robert Penn Warren. 1970. *Modern rhetoric*. New York: Harcourt, Brace and World.

Brown, Gillian and George Yule. 1983. *Discourse analysis*. Cambridge: Cambridge Univ. Press.

Brown, Roger. 1978. "A new paradigm of reference." In *Psychology and biology of language and thought: essays in honor of Eric Lenneberg*, ed. by George A. Miller and Elizabeth Lenneberg, pp. 151-66. New York: Academic Press.

Bruffee, Kenneth. 1972. *A short course in writing*. Cambridge: Winthrop Publishers.

Bub, Daniel and Harry Whitaker. 1980. "Language and verbal processes." In *The brain and psychology*, ed. by M. C. Wittrock, pp. 211-43. New York: Academic Press.

Burghardt, Wolfgang and Klaus Holker, eds. 1979. *Text processing/Textverarbeitung*. Research in Text Theory 3. Berlin: Walter de Gruyter.

Burns, David; Arlene Kagle; Susan Dallinger; Barbara Deane; and Patrice Horn. 1981. "Persuasion." *Self Magazine*, April 1981, pp. 66-96.

Buser, Pierre and Arlette Rougeul-Buser. 1977. *Cerebral correlates of conscious experience*. Amsterdam: North-Holland Publishing Co.

Carroll, John B. 1964a. "Words, meanings and concepts." *Harvard Educational Review* 34:2:178-202.

_____. 1964b. *Language and thought*. Englewood Cliffs, N.J.: Prentice-Hall.

Cassirer, Ernst. 1961. *The logic of the humanities*. Translated by Clarence Smith Howe. New Haven: Yale Univ. Press.

Castañeda, Alfredo and Manuel Ramirez III. 1972. *Culturally democratic learning environments: a cognitive styles approach*. Riverside: Systems and Evaluations in Education.

Chafe, Wallace. 1970. *Meaning and the structure of language*. Chicago: Univ. of Chicago Press.

Chisholm, James S. 1976. "On split-brain research and the culture and cognition paradox." *Current Anthropology* 17:319-20.

Chittick, Roger and Robert Stevick. 1961. *Rhetoric for exposition*. New York: Appleton-Century-Crofts.

Chomsky, Noam. 1969. "Linguistics and philosophy." In *Language and philosophy*, ed. by Sidney Hook, pp. 51-94. New York: NYU Press.

Christopher, Robert C. 1983. *The Japanese mind: the Goliath explained*. New York: Simon and Schuster.

Comaroff, John. 1975. "Talking politics: oratory and authority in a Tswana chiefdom." In *Political language and oratory in traditional society*, ed. by Maurice Bloch, pp. 141-61. New York: Academic Press.

Cooper, Lane. 1960. *The rhetoric of Aristotle*. Englewood Cliffs, N.J.: Prentice-Hall.

Correira, Alfred. 1980. "Computing story trees." *American Journal of Computational Linguistics" 6:135-49*.

Crossley, David and Peter Wilson. 1979. *How to argue*. New York: Random House.

D'Angelo, Frank J. 1977. *Process and thought in composition*. Cambridge: Winthrop.

Damer, T. Edward. 1979. *Attacking faulty reason*. Belmont, California: Wadsworth.

de Beaugrande, Robert. 1980. *Text, discourse, and process*. Norwood: Ablex.
_____ and Wolfgang Dressler. 1981. *Introduction to text linguistics*. New York: Longman.

de Bono, Edward. 1970. *Lateral thinking: creativity step by step*. New York: Harper and Row.

de Saussure, Ferdinand. 1959. *Course in general linguistics*. New York: McGraw-Hill.

DeKosky, Steven; Kenneth Heilman; Dawn Bowers; and Edward Valenstein. 1980. "Recognition and discrimination of emotional faces and pictures." *Brain and Language* 9:206-14.

DeLancey, Scott. 1987. "Transitivity in grammar and cognition." In *Coherence and grounding in discourse*, ed. by Russell S. Tomlin, pp. 53-68. Amsterdam and Philadelphia: John Benjamins.

DeMan, Paul. 1975. *Semiology and rhetoric: allegories of reading*. New Haven: Yale Univ. Press.

Derrett, J. Duncan. 1977. "'Must' and 'ought': problems of translation in Sanskritic Hindu law." In *Language and thought: anthropological issues*, ed. by Wm. C. McCormack and S. A. Wurm, pp. 251-59. The Hague: Mouton.

Derrida, Jacques. 1972. "Structure, sign, and play in the discourse of the human sciences." In *The structuralist controversy: the languages of criticism and the sciences of man*, ed. by Richard Macksey and Eugenio Donato, pp. 247-72. Baltimore: Johns Hopkins.

_____. 1976. *Of grammatology*. Baltimore: Johns Hopkins.

Detweiler, Robert. 1978. *Story, sign, and self: phenomenology and structuralism as literary-critical methods*. Philadelphia: Fortress Press.

Dil, Anwar S., ed. 1980. *Language and cultural description: essays by Charles O. Frake*. Stanford, Calif.: Stanford Univ. Press.

Dimond, S. J. and J. G. Beaumont, eds. 1974. *Hemisphere function in the human brain*. New York: Halsted Press.

Dingwall, William Orr. 1981. *Language and the brain: a bibliography and guide*. New York: Garland.

Doležel, Lubomír. 1977. "Narrative modalities." In *Essays in literary semantics*, ed. by Trevor Eaton, pp. 93-102. Heidelberg: Groos.

_____. 1980. "Truth and authenticity in narrative." *Poetics Today* 1:3:7-25.

Dressler, Wolfgang U., ed. 1978. *Current trends in textlinguistics*. Research in Text Theory 2. Berlin: Walter de Gruyter.

Eccles, Sir John C. 1981. "The self-conscious mind and the meaning and mystery of personal existence." *Teachers College Record* 83:3:403-26.

Eco, Humberto. 1976. "A theory of semiotics." In *Advances in semiotics*, ed. by Thomas A. Sebeok. Bloomington: Indiana Univ. Press.

Edie, James M. 1967. *Phenomenology in America*. Chicago: Quadrangle Books.

Ehninger, Douglas. 1968. "On systems of rhetoric." *Philosophy and Rhetoric* 1:131-44.

_____. 1975. "A synoptic view of systems of western rhetoric, II." *Quarterly Journal of Speech* 61:448-53.

Eikmeyer, Hans-Jurgen and Hannes Rieser, eds. 1981. *Words, worlds, and contexts: new approaches in word semantics*. Research in Text Theory 6. Berlin: Walter de Gruyter.

Engel, S. Morris. 1976. *With good reason*. New York: St. Martin's.

Enkvist, Nils Erik and Viljo Kohonen, eds. 1976. *Reports on text linguistics: approaches to word order*. Abo: Academy of Finland.

Errington, Ross. 1984. "Hortatory mitigation: the case of the camouflaged backbone." *Studies in Philippine Linguistics* 5:1:161-95.

Ferguson, Marilyn. 1976. *The aquarian conspiracy*. Los Angeles: J.P. Tarcher.

_____, ed. 1981. *Right/left hemisphere specialization*. Excerpts from *Brain Mind Bulletin*, 1-5, 1977-81.

Fillmore, Charles; Daniel Kempler; and William S-Y. Wang, eds. 1979. *Individual differences in language ability and language behavior*. New York: Academic Press.

Fink, Paul. 1965. *The challenge of philosophy*. Scranton, Pa.: Chandler.

Firth, Roderick. 1952. "Ethical absolutism and the ideal observer." *Philosophy and Phenomenological Research* 12:3:317-45.

Fisher, Walter R. 1978. "Toward a logic of good reasons." *The Quarterly Journal of Speech* 64:376-84.

Fleming, Ilah. 1978a. "Discourse from the perspective of four strata." In *The Fifth Lacus Forum*, ed. by Wolfgang Wölck and Paul Garvin, pp. 307-17. Columbia, South Carolina: Hornbeam.

_____. 1978b. *Field guide for communication situation, semantic, and morphemic analysis*. Mimeo. Dallas: SIL.

_____. 1979. "Participant identification in C. A. Carib discourse." In *Papers of the 1978 Mid-America Linguistics Conference at Oklahoma*, ed. by Ralph E. Cooley, Mervin. R. Barnes, and John A. Dunn, pp. 92-101. Norman, Oklahoma: Univ. of Oklahoma.

Foster, George. 1973. *Traditional societies and technological change*. New York: Harper and Row.

Fowler, H. Ramsey. 1980. *The Little, Brown handbook*. Boston: Little, Brown and Co.

Frake, Charles O. 1962. The ethnographic study of cognitive systems. In *Anthropology and human behavior*, ed. by T. Gladwin and W. C. Sturtevant, pp. 72-85. Washington, D.C.: Anthropological Society of Washington.

_____. 1963. "Litigation in Lipay: a study in Subanun law." In *The proceedings of the Ninth Pacific Science Congress*, vol. 3. Reprinted in *Language and cultural description: essays by Charles O. Frake*, ed. by Anwar S. Dil, pp. 132-43. Stanford, Calif.: Stanford Univ. Press.

_____. 1972. "Struck by speech: the Yakan concept of litigation." In *Culture and cognition: rules, maps, and plans*, ed. by James Spradley, pp. 279-301. New York: Chandler.

Frankena, William. 1963. *Ethics*. Englewood Cliffs, N.J.: Prentice-Hall.

Frantz, Donald G. 1977. *Grammatical relations in universal grammar*. Grand Forks, North Dakota: SIL.

Fukuda, Takashi. 1983. "A discourse-oriented grammar of Eastern Bontoc." M.A. thesis. Univ. of Texas at Arlington.

Gadamer, Hans-Georg. 1976. *Philosophical hermeneutics*. Berkeley: Univ. of California.

Gazzaniga, Michael. 1977. "Review of the split brain." In *The human brain*, ed. by M. C. Wittrock, pp. 89-96. Englewood Cliffs, N.J.: Prentice-Hall.

_____ and Joseph E. LeDoux. 1978. *The integrated mind*. New York: Plenum Press.

Geschwind, Norman. 1974. "The anatomical basis of hemispheric differentiation." In *Hemisphere function in the human brain,* ed. by S. J. Dimond and J. G. Beaumont, pp. 7-24. New York: Halsted.

_____. 1979. "Specializations of the human brain." *Scientific American* 3:180-99.

Gibbs, James L., Jr. 1973. "Two forms of dispute settlement among the Kpelle of West Africa." In *The social organization of law,* ed. by Donald Black and Maureen Mileski, pp. 368-78. New York: Seminar Press.

Giglioli, Pier Paolo, ed. 1972. *Language and social context.* New York: Penguin.

Givón, Talmy. 1981. "Logic versus pragmatics, with human language as the referee: toward an empirically viable epistemology." Paper given at the University of Texas at Arlington Conference in Linguistics and the Humanities.

_____. 1983. *Topic continuity in discourse: a quantitative cross-language study.* Amsterdam and Philadelphia: John Benjamins.

_____. 1987. "Beyond foreground and background." In *Coherence and grounding in discourse,* ed. by Russell S. Tomlin, pp. 175-88. Amsterdam and Philadelphia: John Benjamins.

Gladwin, Thomas. 1964. "Culture and logical process." In *Explorations in cultural anthropology: essays in honor of George Peter Murdoch,* ed. by Ward H. Goodenough, pp. 167-77. New York: McGraw-Hill.

Goodenough, Ward H. 1981. *Culture, language, and society.* Menlo Park, Calif.: Benjamin-Cummings.

Goody, Jack, ed. 1968. *Literacy in traditional societies.* Cambridge: Cambridge Univ. Press.

_____ and Ian Watt. 1968. "The consequences of literacy." In *Literacy in traditional societies,* ed. by Jack Goody, pp. 27-68. Cambridge: Cambridge Univ. Press.

Gordon, H. and A. Carmon. 1976. "A transfer of dominance in speed of verbal response to visually presented stimuli from right to left hemisphere." *Perceptual and Motor Skills* 42:1091-1100.

Gorovitz, Samuel; Merrill Hintikka; Donald Provence; and Ron Williams. 1979. *Philosophical analysis: an introduction to its language and techniques.* New York: Random House.

Gregory, Michael. 1981. "Hamlet's voice: aspects of text formation and cohesion in a soliloquy." Paper given at University of Texas at Arlington Conference in Linguistics and the Humanities.

_____ and Susanne Carroll. 1978. *Language and situation: language varieties in their social contexts.* London: Routledge and Kegan Paul.

Grimes, Joseph. 1975. *The thread of discourse.* The Hague: Mouton.

_____, ed. 1978. *Papers on discourse.* SIL Publications in Linguistics 51. Dallas: SIL and Univ. of Texas at Arlington.

Gumperz, John and Dell Hymes, eds. 1972. *Directions in sociolinguistics: the ethnography of communication.* New York: Holt, Rinehart and Winston.

Hairston, Maxine. 1974. *A contemporary rhetoric.* Boston: Houghton Mifflin.

Hale, Austin, ed. 1973. *Clause, sentence, and discourse patterns in selected languages of Nepal.* SIL Publications in Linguistics 40. 4 vols. Norman, Oklahoma: SIL of the Univ. of Oklahoma.

_____. 1984. "A discourse pecking order." In *Theory and application in processing texts in non-Indoeuropean languages* [Papiere zur Textlinguistik/Papers in Textlinguistics 43], ed. by R.E. Longacre, pp. 1-24. Hamburg: Helmut Buske.

Hall, William. 1983. "Some aspects of formal speech among the Western Subanon of Mindanao." Ph.D. dissertation. Philadelphia: Univ. of Pennsylvania.

Halliday, M.A.K. and Ruqaiya Hasan. 1976. *Cohesion in English.* London: Longman.

Hardy, William. 1978. *Language, thought, and experience.* Baltimore: University Park Press.

Hardyck, Curtis; Hilary Naylor; and Rebecca Smith. 1979. "How shall a thingummy be called?" In *Individual differences in language ability and language behavior,* ed. by Charles Fillmore, Daniel Kempler, and William S-Y. Wang, pp. 261-75. New York: Academic Press.

Harm, Harry. 1983. "Logic line in Jude: the search for syllogisms in a hortatory text." Ms.

Harman, Gilbert. 1969. "Linguistic competence and empiricism." In *Language and philosophy,* ed. by Sidney Hook. New York: NYU Press.

Hartmann, R. R. K. 1980. *Contrastive textology: comparative discourse analysis in applied linguistics.* Heidelberg: Groos.

Havelock, E. A. 1976. *Origins of western literacy.* Toronto: Ontario Institute for Studies in Education.

Hayakawa, S. I. 1964. *Language in thought and action.* New York: Harcourt, Brace and World.

Hecaen, H. and P. Marcie. 1974. "Disorders of written language following right hemisphere lesions: spatial dysgraphia." In *Hemisphere function in the human brain,* ed. by S. J.Dimond and J. G. Beaumont, pp. 345-66.New York: Halsted.

Hermelin, B. and N. O'Connor. 1971. "Right and left handed reading of braille." *Nature* 231:170.

Hidalgo, Cesar A. and Araceli C. Hidalgo. 1971. *A tagmemic grammar of Ivatan. Philippine Journal of Linguistics,* Special Monograph 2.

Hill, Christopher. 1982. "Why cartesian intuitions are compatible with the identity thesis." *Philosophy and Phenomenological Research* 42:2:254-65.

Hirsch, E. D., Jr. 1967. *Validity in interpretation.* New Haven: Yale Univ. Press.

_____. 1976. *The aims of interpretation.* Chicago: Univ. of Chicago Press.

Hoey, Michael. 1983. *On the surface of discourse.* London: George Allen and Unwin.

Holman, C. Hugh. 1972. *A handbook to literature.* Indianapolis: Bobbs-Merrill.

Hook, Sidney, ed. 1969. *Language and philosophy.* New York: NYU Press.

Hoppal, M. 1979. "On belief systems." In *Research in Text Theory 3,* ed. by Wolfgang Burghardt and Klaus Holker, pp. 236-52. Berlin: Walter de Gruyter.

Hopper, Paul J. 1979. "Aspect and foregrounding in discourse." In *Syntax and Semantics 12,* ed. by Talmy Givón, pp. 213-41. New York: Academic Press.

_____ and Sandra Thompson. 1980. "Transitivity in grammar and discourse." *Language* 56:251-99.

Hovland, Carl; Irving Janis; and Harold Kelley. 1953. *Communication and persuasion.* New Haven: Yale Univ. Press.

Hudson, W. D. 1970. *Reason and right.* California: Freeman, Cooper and Co.

Hughes, Richard E. and P. Albert Duhamel. 1966. *Principles of rhetoric.* Englewood Cliffs, N.J.: Prentice-Hall.

Hurlbut, Hope M. 1984. "Do as I say: a study of selected features of hortatory discourse in Eastern Kadazan." *Studies in Philippine Linguistics* 5:1:118-60.

Husserl, Edmund. 1958. *Ideas: general introduction to pure phenomenology.* Translated by W. R. Boyce-Gibson. New York: Humanities.

_____. 1970. *Logical investigations.* 2 vols. Translated by J. N. Findlay. New York: Humanities.

Huttar, G. L. 1977. "World views, intelligence, and cross-cultural communication." *Ethnic Studies* 1:3:24-34.

Hwang, Shin Ja Joo. 1981. "Aspects of Korean narration." Ph.D. dissertation. Univ. of Texas at Arlington.

Hymes, Dell. 1974. *Foundations in sociolinguistics.* Philadelphia: Univ. of Pennsylvania.

Ihde, Don. 1977. *Experimental phenomenology.* New York: G.P. Putnam's Sons.

Jakobson, Roman. 1980. *Brain and language.* Columbus: Slavica Publishers.

Johnson, Mark. 1981. *Philosophical perspectives on metaphor.* Minneapolis: Univ. of Minnesota.

Jones, Larry B. 1983. *Pragmatic aspects of English text structure.* SIL Publications in Linguistics 67. Dallas: SIL and Univ. of Texas at Arlington.

_____ and Linda K. Jones. 1979. "Multiple levels of information in discourse." In *Discourse studies in Mesoamerican languages,* ed. by Linda Jones, pp. 3-27. SIL Publications in Linguistics 58. Dallas: SIL and Univ. of Texas at Arlington.

Jones, Linda K. 1977. *Theme in English expository discourse*. Lake Bluff, Illinois: Jupiter Press.

_____, ed. 1979. *Discourse studies in Mesoamerican languages*. SIL Publications in Linguistics 58. Dallas: SIL and Univ. of Texas at Arlington.

Kawashima, Takeyoshi. 1973. "Dispute settlement in Japan." In *The social organization of law*, ed. by Donald Black and Maureen Mileski, pp. 58-74. New York: Seminar Press.

Keat, Russell and John Urry. 1975. *Social theory as science*. London and Boston: Routledge and Kegan Paul.

Keenan, Elinor. 1975. "A sliding sense of obligatoriness: the polystructure of Malagasy oratory." In *Political language and oratory in traditional society*, ed. by Maurice Bloch, pp. 93-112. New York: Academic Press.

Kelly, Daniel P. 1982. *Destroying the barriers: receptor oriented communication of the gospel*. Vernon, British Columbia: Laurel Publications.

Kilham, Christine. 1977. *Thematic organization of Wik-Munkan discourse*. *Pacific Linguistics*, Series B, 52. Canberra: Australian National Univ.

Kinsbourne, Marcel. 1980. "Cognition and the brain." In *The brain and psychology*, ed. by M. C. Wittrock, pp. 325-43. New York: Academic Press.

Kintsch, Walter and Edith Greene. 1978. "The role of culture-specific schemata in the comprehension and recall of stories." *Discourse Processes* 1:1-13.

Kline, Morris. 1980. *Mathematics: the loss of certainty*. New York: Oxford University Press.

Kottak, Conrad Phillip. 1979. *Cultural anthropology*. New York: Random House.

Krashen, Stephen. 1977. "The left hemisphere." In *The human brain*, ed. by M. C. Wittrock, pp. 107-30. Englewood Cliffs, N.J.: Prentice-Hall.

Kuhn, Thomas. 1962. *The structure of scientific revolutions*. Chicago: The Univ. of Chicago Press.

Kummer, Werner. 1972. "Aspects of a theory of argumentation." In *Textsorten: Differenzierungskriterien aus linguisticher sicht*, ed. by Elisabeth Gulich and Wolfgang Raible, pp. 25-49. Frankfurt and Main: Athenaum.

Kupperman, Joel J. 1982. "Value judgments." *Philosophy and Phenomenological Research* 42:4:506-18.

Labov, William. 1972. *Sociolinguistic patterns*. Philadelphia: Univ. of Pennsylvania.

Lacey, A. R. 1976. *A dictionary of philosophy*. New York: Charles Scribner's Sons.

Lamb, Sydney. 1966. *Outline of stratificational grammar*. Washington, D.C.: Georgetown University Press.

Langsdorf, Lenore. 1980. "Meaning and reference: an intentional approach." *The Southwestern Journal of Philosophy* 11:1:105-13.

_____. 1981. "The relevance of the Popper-Kuhn debate to the understanding of language use." Paper given at the University of Texas at Arlington Conference in Linguistics and the Humanities.

_____ and Harry P. Reeder. 1983. "The whole business of seeing: nature, world, and paradigm in Kuhn's account of science." Ms. Univ. of Texas at Arlington.

Larson, Mildred. 1978. *The functions of reported speech in discourse.* SIL Publications in Linguistics 59. Dallas: SIL and Univ. of Texas at Arlington.

Lee, Dorothy. 1980. "Codifications of reality: lineal and nonlineal." In *Conformity and conflict,* ed. by James Spradley and David McCurdy, pp. 75-90. Boston: Little, Brown.

Lehmann, Winfred P. 1981. "Literature and linguistics: text linguistics." Ms. Univ. of Texas.

Lehnert, W. G. 1980. "The role of scripts in understanding." In *Research in Text Theory 5,* ed. by Dieter Metzing, pp. 79-95. Berlin: Walter de Gruyter.

Levin, Michael E. 1979. "The universalizability of moral judgments revisited." *Mind* 88:115-19.

Levy, Jerre. 1979. "Strategies of linguistic processing in human split-brain patients." In *Individual differences in language ability and language behavior,* ed. by Charles Fillmore, Daniel Kempler, and William S-Y. Wang, pp. 289-300. New York: Academic Press.

_____. 1980. "Cerebral asymmetry and the psychology of man." In *The brain and psychology,* ed. by M. C. Wittrock, pp. 245-323. New York: Academic Press.

Ley, Robert G. and M. P. Bryden. 1979. "Hemispheric differences in processing emotions and faces." *Brain and Language* 7:127-38.

Lishman, W. A. 1971. "Emotion, consciousness and will after brain bisection in man." *Cortex* 7:181-92.

Longacre, Robert E. 1964. *Grammar discovery procedures.* The Hague: Mouton.

_____, ed. 1968. *Philippine languages: discourse, paragraph, and sentence structure.* Glendale, Calif.: SIL.

_____. 1976. *An anatomy of speech notions.* Lisse: Peter de Ridder Press.

_____. 1979a. "The discourse structure of the flood narrative." *Journal of the American Academy of Religion* 47:1:89-133.

_____. 1979b. "The paragraph as a grammatical unit." In *Syntax and Semantics 12,* ed. by Talmy Givón, pp. 115-34. New York: Academic Press.

_____. 1979c. "Text and text linguistics." In *Text vs. sentence,* ed. by János Petöfi, pp. 258-71. Papers in Textlinguistics 20, Part 1. Hamburg: Buske.

_____. 1979d. "Why we need a vertical revolution in linguistics." In *The Fifth LACUS Forum 1978*, ed. by Wolfgang Wölck and Paul Garvin, pp. 247-70. Columbia, South Carolina: Hornbeam Press.

_____. 1982. "Verb ranking and the constituent structure of discourse." *The Journal of the Linguistic Association of the Southwest* 5:177-202.

_____. 1983a. *The grammar of discourse*. New York: Plenum Press.

_____. 1983b. *Exhortation and mitigation in First John*. Selected Technical Articles Related to Translation 9. Dallas: SIL.

_____, ed. 1984. *Theory and application in processing texts in non-Indoeuropean languages*. [Papiere zur Textlinguistik/Papers in Textlinguistics 43] Hamburg: Helmut Buske.

_____. 1985. "Discourse peak as zone of turbulence." In *Beyond the sentence: discourse and sequential form*, ed. by Jessica Wirth, pp. 81-98. Ann Arbor, Michigan: Karoma.

_____ and Stephen Levinsohn. 1976. "Field analysis of discourse." In *Current trends in textlinguistics*, ed. by Wolfgang U. Dressler, pp. 103-22. Berlin: de Gruyter.

_____ and Frances Woods, eds. 1976, 1977. *Discourse grammar: studies in indigenous languages of Colombia, Panama, and Ecuador*. 3 vols. SIL Publications in Linguistics 52. Dallas: SIL and Univ. of Texas at Arlington.

Loos, Victor. 1978. "Philosophical aspects of semantics." In *Research papers of the SIL 2*, pp. 1-40. Dallas: SIL.

Lottis, William. 1974. "Communication, Indian style." Ms.

Makkai, Adam and David Lockwood, eds. 1973. *Readings in stratificational linguistics*. University, Alabama: Univ. of Alabama Press.

Maranda, P. and E. Kongas Maranda. 1979. "Myth as a cognitive map: a sketch of the Okanogan myth automaton." In *Research in Text Theory 3*, ed. by Wolfgang Burghardt and Klaus Holker, pp. 253-75. Berlin: Walter de Gruyter.

Marsella, Anthony J. Michael Murray; and Charles Golden. 1976. "Ethnic variations in the phenomenology of emotions." In *Intercultural communication: a reader*, ed. by Larry Samovar and Richard Porter, pp. 134-43. Belmont, California: Wadsworth.

Martin, Harold; Richard Ohmann; and James Wheatley. 1969. *The logic and rhetoric of exposition*. New York: Holt, Rinehart and Winston.

Martin, Howard and William Colburn. 1972. *Communication and consensus: an introduction to rhetorical discourse*. New York: Harcourt Brace Jovanovich.

Martindale, Colin. 1976. "More on split-brain research and anthropology." *Current Anthropology* 17:4:738-42.

Mayfield, Roy. 1983. "Some features of hortatory discourse in Central Cagayan Agta." *Studies in Philippine Linguistics* 4:2:88-124.

McCrimmon, James M. 1976. *Writing with a purpose.* Boston: Houghton Mifflin Co.

McGee-Cooper, Ann. 1982. *Building brain power.* Dallas: McGee-Cooper.

McLuhan, Marshall. 1962. *The Gutenberg galaxy.* New York: New American Library.

_____. 1964. *Understanding media.* New York: New American Library.

_____. 1967. *McLuhan: hot and cool.* New York: New American Library.

Mercado, Leonardo N. 1977. *Applied Filipino philosophy.* Tacloban City, Philippines: Divine Word University.

Metzing, Dieter, ed. 1980. *Frame conceptions and text understanding.* Research in Text Theory 5. Berlin: Walter de Gruyter.

Meynell, Hugo. 1975. "Science, the truth, and Thomas Kuhn." *Mind* 84:79-93.

Miller, George A. and Elizabeth Lenneberg, eds. 1978. *Psychology and biology of language and thought: essays in honor of Eric Lenneberg.* New York: Academic Press.

Minsky, M. 1980. "A framework for representing knowledge." In *Research in Text Theory 5,* ed. by Dieter Metzing, pp. 1-25. Berlin: Walter de Gruyter.

Nader, Laura. 1967. "An analysis of Zapotec law cases." In *Law and warfare: studies in the anthropology of conflict,* ed. by Paul Bohannan, pp. 117-38. Austin: Univ. of Texas Press.

_____ and Duane Metzger. 1973. "Conflict resolution in two Mexican communities." In *The social organization of law,* ed. by Donald Black and Maureen Mileski, pp. 95-105. New York: Seminar Press.

Nathanson, Stephen. 1982. "Nonevidential reasons for belief: a Jamesian view." *Philosophy and Phenomenological Research* 42:4:572-80.

Nebes, Robert. 1977. "Man's so-called minor hemisphere." In *The human brain,* ed. by M. C. Wittrock, pp. 97-106. Englewood Cliffs, N.J.: Prentice-Hall.

Neisser, Ulric. 1976. *Cognition and reality.* San Francisco: W.H. Freeman.

Nicholas, J. Karl and James Nicholl. 1978. *Rhetorical models for effective writing.* Cambridge: Winthrop.

Noble, Lowell L. 1975. *Naked and not ashamed: an anthropological, biblical, and psychological study of shame.* Jackson, Michigan: Jackson Printing.

Norris, Christopher. 1982. *Deconstruction: theory and practice.* New York: Methuen.

Nowakowska, M. 1979. "Towards a formal theory of dialogues." In *Research in Text Theory 3,* ed. by Wolfgang Burghardt and Klaus Holker, pp. 191-212. Berlin: Walter de Gruyter.

Oliver, Robert. 1950. *Persuasive speaking.* New York: Longmans, Green and Co.

_____. 1962. *Culture and communication.* Springfield, Ill.: Charles C. Thomas Publisher.

_____. 1968. *The psychology of persuasive speech.* New York: David McKay Co.

Olson, David R. 1977. "From utterance to text: the bias of language in speech and writing." *Harvard Educational Review* 47:3:257-81.

Ong, Walter. 1982. *Orality and literacy.* New York: Methuen.

Packard, Vance. 1957. *The hidden persuaders.* Montreal: Pocket Books of Canada.

Paredes, Anthony and Marcus J. Hepburn. 1976. "The split brain and the culture-and-cognition paradox." *Current Anthropology* 17:1:121-27.

Parkinson, G. H. R. 1968. *The theory of meaning.* London: Oxford Press.

Pawley, Andrew. 1987. "Encoding events in Kalam and English: different logics for reporting experience." In *Coherence and grounding in discourse,* ed. by Russell S. Tomlin, pp. 329-60. Amsterdam and Philadelphia: John Benjamins.

Penfield, Wilder. 1968. *The cerebral cortex of man.* New York: Hafner Publishing.

Perelman, Chaim. 1979. *The new rhetoric and the humanities.* London: Reidel.

Pike, Kenneth L. 1964. "Beyond the sentence." *College Composition and Communication* 15:129-35.

_____. 1967. *Language in relation to a unified theory of the structure of human behavior.* The Hague: Mouton.

_____. 1978. "Social interaction as the break-in point for the analysis of verbal behavior." In *Proceedings of the 12th International Congress of Linguists, Vienna, August 28-September 2, 1977,* ed. by W. U. Dressler and W. Meid, pp. 739-41. Innsbruck: Innsbrucker Beiträge zur Sprachwissenschaft.

_____ and Evelyn Pike. 1977. *Grammatical analysis.* SIL Publications in Linguistics 53. Dallas: SIL and Univ. of Texas at Arlington.

Polanyi, Michael. 1959. *The study of man.* Chicago: Univ. of Chicago Press.

Postow, B. C. 1978. "Ethical relativism and the ideal observer." *Philosophy and Phenomenological Research* 39:1:120-123.

Quine, W. V. 1969. "Linguistics and philosophy." In *Language and philosophy,* ed. by Sidney Hook. New York: NYU Press.

Raz, J. 1975. "Reasons for action, decisions and norms." *Mind* 84:481-99.

Reagan, Charles E. and David Stewart, eds. 1978. *The philosophy of Paul Ricoeur: an anthology of his work.* Boston: Beacon Press.

Redfield, Robert. 1967. "Primitive law." In *Law and warfare: studies in the anthropology of conflict,* ed. by Paul Bohannan, pp. 3-24. Austin: Univ. of Texas Press.

Reeder, Harry P. 1983. "Practical phenomenology: introductory lectures in the theory and method of Husserl's phenomenology." Ms. Univ. of Texas at Arlington.

Reid, Aileen; Ruth Bishop; Ella Button; and R. E. Longacre. 1968. *Totonac: from clause to discourse.* SIL Publications in Linguistics 17. Norman, Oklahoma: SIL of the Univ. of Oklahoma.

Reid, Lawrence. 1970. *Central Bontoc: sentence, paragraph and discourse.* SIL Publications in Linguistics 27. Norman, Oklahoma: SIL and the Univ. of Oklahoma.

_____. 1971. *Philippine minor languages: word lists and phonologies. Oceanic Linguistics,* Special Publication 8.

Ricoeur, Paul. 1977. *The rule of metaphor.* Translated by Robert Czerny. Toronto: Univ. of Toronto Press.

_____. 1976. *Interpretation theory: discourse and the surplus of meaning.* Fort Worth: Texas Christian University.

_____. 1978. "Structure, word, event." In *The philosophy of Paul Ricoeur,* ed. by Charles E. Reagan and David Stewart, pp. 109-33. Boston: Beacon Press.

Rosaldo, Michelle Zimbalist. 1975. "It's all uphill: the creative metaphors of Ilongot magical spells." In *Sociocultural dimensions of language use,* ed. by Mary Sanches and Ben G. Blount, pp. 177-203. New York: Academic Press.

_____. 1980. *Knowledge and passion: Ilongot notions of self and social life.* Cambridge: Cambridge Univ. Press.

Rose, Mary Carman. 1979. "The investigative interrelatedness between the study of the human mind and the present-day philosophy." *Philosophy East and West* 29:2:189-200.

Rosen, Steven and Walter Jones. 1974. *The logic of international relations.* Cambridge: Winthrop.

Ross, Elliot D. and Marek-Marsel Mesulam. 1979. "Dominant language functions of the right hemisphere? prosody and emotional gesturing." *Archives of Neurology* 36:144-48.

Ross, Raymond. 1970. *Speech communication: fundamentals and practice.* Englewood Cliffs, N.J.: Prentice-Hall.

Rubinstein, Robert A. and Charles D. Laughlin, Jr. 1977. "Bridging levels of systemic organization." *Current Anthropology* 18:3:459-81.

Rusher, William. 1981. *How to win arguments.* New York: Doubleday.

Ryan, Cheyney C. 1980. "The normative concept of coercion." *Mind* 89:481-98.

Sackeim, Harold; Ruben Gur; and Marcel Saucy. 1978. "Emotions are expressed more intensely on the left side of the face." *Science* 202:434-35.

Samovar, Larry and Jack Mills. 1972. *Oral communication: message and response.* Dubuque, Iowa: Wm. C. Brown Co.

_____; Richard Porter; and Nemi Jain. 1981. *Understanding intercultural communication.* Belmont, Calif.: Wadsworth.

Sanches, Mary and Ben G. Blount. 1975. *Sociocultural dimensions of language use.* New York: Academic Press.

Sayers, Barbara J. 1980. "Christianity confronts aboriginal culture." *Alata* 5:1:7-22 [supplement]

_____. 1981. "Australian aboriginal argumentation: an exercise in comprehension." Ms. Melbourne: SIL.

Schaeffer, Francis. 1968. *Escape from reason.* Downers Grove, Ill.: Inter-Varsity Press.

Schank, Roger and Robert Abelson. 1977. *Scripts, plans, goals and understanding: an inquiry into human knowledge structures.* Hillsdale, N.J.: Lawrence Erlbaum Associates.

Scharbach, Alexander and Ralph Singleton. 1968. *The lively rhetoric.* New York: Holt, Rinehart and Winston.

Schein, Edgar; Inge Schneier; and Curtis Barker. 1961. *Coercive persuasion.* New York: W.W. Norton and Co.

Schumacher, John A. and Robert M. Anderson. 1979. "In defense of mystical science." *Philosophy East and West* 29:1:74-90.

Schwartz, Gary; Richard Davidson; and Foster Maer. 1975. "Right hemisphere lateralization for emotion in the human brain: interactions with cognition." *Science* 190:286-88.

Schwartz, Richard D. 1973. "Social control in two Israeli settlements." In *The social organization of law,* ed. by Donald Black and Maureen Mileski, pp. 107-29. New York: Seminar Press.

Scott, Robert L. 1975. "A synoptic view of systems of western rhetoric." *Quarterly Journal of Speech* 61:439-47.

Scribner, Sylvia. 1978. "Modes of thinking and ways of speaking: culture and logic reconsidered." In *Thinking: readings in cognitive science,* ed. by P. N. Johnson-Laird and P. C. Wason, pp. 483-99. Cambridge: Cambridge Univ. Press.

Searle, John R., ed. 1971. *The philosophy of language.* Oxford: Oxford Press.

_____. 1981. *Metaphor.* Minneapolis: Univ. of Minnesota Press.

Segal, D. 1979. "Approaches to the analysis of ethnopoetic texts." In *Research in Text Theory 3,* ed. by Wolfgang Burghardt and Klaus Holker, pp. 217-20. Berlin: Walter de Gruyter.

Seidel, Gerd. 1981. "Cross-cultural training procedures: their theoretical framework and evaluation." In *The mediating person: bridges between cultures,* ed. by Stephen Bochner, pp. 184-213. Cambridge: Schenkman.

Shetler, Joanne and Michael Walrod. 1983. "Semantic and thematic structure of discourse in Balangao." *Studies in Philippine Linguistics* 4:2:10-87.

Silverberg, R.; S. Bentin; T. Gaziel; L. K. Obler; and M. L. Albert. 1979. "Shift of visual field preference for English words in native Hebrew speakers." *Brain and Language* 8:184-90.

_____; H. W. Gordon; S. Pollack; and S. Bentin. 1980. "Shift of visual field preference for Hebrew words in native speakers learning to read." *Brain and Language* 11:99-105.

Simons, Gary F. 1984. *Powerful ideas for text processing: an introduction to computer programming with the PTP language.* Dallas: SIL.

Sitelman, Robert. 1977. "Morality and value." *Mind* 86:591-94.

Siverns, Lloyd E. 1979. "Parable interpretation from Julicher to Ricoeur: a critique and alternative proposal." Ph.D. dissertation. Montreal: McGill Univ.

Skinner, B. F. 1957. *A functional analysis of verbal behavior.* New York: Appleton-Century-Crofts.

Smith, Aaron. 1978. "Lenneberg, Locke, Zangwill, and the neuropsychology of language and language disorders." In *Psychology and biology of language and thought: essays in honor of Eric Lenneberg,* ed. by George A. Miller and Elizabeth Lenneberg, pp. 133-48. New York: Academic Press.

Smith, Alfred G. 1966. *Communication and culture.* New York: Holt, Rinehart and Winston.

Snow, Craig Bradford. 1980. *A guide to the Norton reader.* New York: W.W. Norton and Co.

Somerville, John and Ronald Santoni. 1963. *Social and political philosophy.* New York: Doubleday.

Sperry, R. W.; E. Zaidel; and D. Zaidel. 1979. "Self recognition and social awareness in the deconnected minor hemisphere." *Neuropsychologia* 17:153-66.

Spradley, Barbara and Carolyn McCurdy. 1980. *Conformity and conflict.* Boston: Little, Brown and Co.

Spradley, James. 1972. *Culture and cognition: rules, maps, and plans.* New York: Chandler.

Sprague, Elmer. 1961. *What is philosophy?* New York: Oxford Univ. Press.

Steinberg, Danny and Leon Jakobovits, eds. 1971. *Semantics: an interdisciplinary reader in philosophy, linguistics, and psychology.* Cambridge: Cambridge Univ. Press.

Stillinger, Jack. 1965. *Selected poems and prefaces by William Wordsworth.* Boston: Houghton Mifflin.

Stolzenberg, Gabriel. 1978. "Can an inquiry in the foundations of mathematics tell us anything interesting about mind?" In *Psychology and biology of language and thought: essays in honor of Eric Lenneberg,* ed. by George A. Miller and Elizabeth Lenneberg, pp. 221-69. New York: Academic Press.

Tannen, Deborah. 1982. "Oral and literate strategies in spoken and written narratives." *Language* 58:1-21.

Taylor, Gabriele. 1975. "Justifying the emotions." *Mind* 84:390-402.

Taylor, Paul. 1976. *Normative discourse.* Westport, Conn.: Greenwood Press.

TenHouten, Warren; S. I. Korolev; and Jo Scheder. 1976. "More on split-brain research, culture, and cognition." *Current Anthropology* 17:3:503-11.

Teyler, Timothy. 1977. "An introduction to the neurosciences." In *The human brain,* ed. by M. C. Wittrock, pp. 3-38. Englewood Cliffs, N.J.: Prentice-Hall.

Thompson, Richard F. 1975. *Introduction to physiological psychology.* New York: Harper and Row.

Thompson, Wayne. 1975. *The process of persuasion.* New York: Harper and Row.

Thorndyke, Perry W. 1977. "Cognitive structures in comprehension and memory of narrative discourse." *Cognitive Psychology* 9:77-110.

Thornton, M. T. 1982. "Aristotelian practical reason." *Mind* 91:57-76.

Tomlin, Russell S., ed. 1987. *Coherence and grounding in discourse.* Amsterdam and Philadelphia: John Benjamins.

Toulmin, Stephen. 1970. *Reason in ethics.* 8th ed. Cambridge: Cambridge Univ. Press.

_____. 1981. "The emergence of post-modern science." In *The great ideas today,* pp. 68-115. Chicago and London: Encyclopaedia Britannica.

Townsend, Dabney. 1980. "Demythologizing metaphor." *Kodikas/Code, an International Journal of Semiotics* 3:285-96.

Trudgill, Peter. 1974. *Sociolinguistics.* New York: Penguin.

Tyler, Stephen A. 1978. *The said and the unsaid: mind, meaning, and culture.* New York: Academic Press.

Uyehara, June M. and William A. Cooper, Jr. 1980. "Hemispheric differences for verbal and nonverbal stimuli in Japanese- and English-speaking subjects assessed by Tsunoda's method." *Brain and Language* 10:405-17.

van Dijk, Teun A. 1972. *Some aspects of text grammars.* The Hague: Mouton.

_____. 1977. *Text and context: explorations in the semantics and pragmatics of discourse.* New York: Longman.

_____. 1979. "Recalling and summarizing complex discourse." In *Research in Text Theory 3,* ed. by Wolfgang Burghardt and Klaus Holker, pp. 49-118. Berlin: Walter de Gruyter.

_____ and Janos Petofi, eds. 1977. *Grammars and descriptions: studies in text theory and text analysis. Research in Text Theory 1.* Berlin: Walter de Gruyter.

Van Doren, Charles. 1981. "Morris Kline: mathematics—the loss of certainty (a review)." In *The great ideas today*, pp. 204-18. Chicago and London: Encyclopaedia Britannica.

Van de Pitte, Frederick P. 1980. "Descartes' role in the faith-reason controversy." *Philosophy and Phenomenological Research* 40:3:344-53.

Via, Dan O., Jr. 1975. *Kerygma and comedy in the New Testament: a structuralist-literary approach to New Testament hermeneutic.* Philadelphia: Fortress Press.

Vygotsky, L. S . 1962. *Thought and language.* Translated by Eugenia Hanfmann and Gertrude Vakar. Cambridge: MIT Press.

Wallace, Karl R. 1963. "The substance of rhetoric: good reasons." *Quarterly Journal of Speech* 49:239-48.

Walker, Mary Margaret. 1983. "Argumentation in Romans 1-11." M.A. thesis. Grand Forks: Univ. of North Dakota.

Walrod, Michael R. 1976. "Case in Ga'dang verbal clauses." *Pacific Linguistics,* Series A, 46:21-44.

[_____]. 1977. "Meaning in language: a study in semantics." In *Research papers of the SIL* 1, pp. 71-110. Dallas: SIL.

_____. 1979. *Discourse grammar in Ga'dang.* SIL Publications in Linguistics 63. Dallas: SIL and Univ. of Texas at Arlington.

_____. 1981. "Social and cognitive structures of the Ga'dang people." Ms.

_____. 1983. "Introduction to discourse in northern Philippine langauges." *Studies in Philippine Linguistics* 4:2:1-9.

_____. 1984. "Grammatical features of peak in Ga'dang narrative." *Papers in Textlinguistics* 43:93-112. Hamburg: Helmut Buske.

Watson, Richard. 1984. "Scheme and point in Pacoh expository discourse." *Papers in Textlinguistics* 43:113-52. Hamburg: Helmut Buske.

Wheelwright, Philip. 1962. *Metaphor and reality.* Bloomington: Indiana Univ. Press.

Whorf, Benjamin Lee. 1956. *Language, thought, and reality.* Cambridge: MIT Press.

Wilks, Y. 1980. "Frames, semantics, and novelty." In *Research in Text Theory* 5, ed. by Dieter Metzing, pp. 134-63. Berlin: Walter de Gruyter.

Wittgenstein, Ludwig. 1953. *Philosophical Investigations 1.* Translated by G.E.M. Anscombe. New York: McMillan.

Wittrock, M. C. 1977. *The human brain.* Englewood Cliffs, N.J.: Prentice-Hall.

_____, ed. 1980. *The brain and psychology.* New York: Academic Press.

Woods, Frances M. 1980. "The interrelationship of cultural information, linguistic structure and symbolic representations in a Halbi myth." Ph.D. dissertation. Univ. of Texas at Arlington.

Yoder, Perry B. 1978. *Toward understanding the Bible.* Newton, Kansas: Faith and Life Press.

Young, J. Z. 1951. *Doubt and certainty in science.* New York: Oxford Univ. Press.

Young, Richard E.; Alton L. Becker; and Kenneth L. Pike. 1970. *Rhetoric: discovery and change.* New York: Harcourt, Brace and World.

Zangwill, O. L. 1978. "Aphasia and the concept of brain centers." In *Psychology and biology of language and thought: essays in honor of Eric Lenneberg,* ed. by George A. Miller and Elizabeth Lenneberg, pp. 119-31. New York: Academic Press.